Seventh Named Entity Workshop (NEWS 2018)

Held at ACL 2018

Melbourne, Australia
20 July 2018

Editors:

Nancy Chen
Rafael E. Banchs
Xiangyu Duan

Min Zhang
Haizhou Li

ISBN: 978-1-5108-6711-6

ACL 2018

Named Entities
Proceedings of the Seventh Workshop

Nancy Chen, Rafael E. Banchs, Xiangyu Duan, Min Zhang, Haizhou Li

July 20, 2018
Melbourne, Australia

Introduction

The workshop series, Named Entities WorkShop (NEWS), focus on research on all aspects of the Named Entities, such as, identifying and analyzing named entities, mining, translating and transliterating named entities, etc. The first of the NEWS workshops (NEWS 2009) was held as a part of ACL-IJCNLP 2009 conference in Singapore; the second one, NEWS 2010, was held as an ACL 2010 workshop in Uppsala, Sweden; the third one, NEWS 2011, was held as an IJCNLP 2011 workshop in Chiang Mai, Thailand; and the fourth one, NEWS 2012, was held as an ACL 2012 workshop in Jeju, Korea. The fifth one, NEWS 2015, was held as an ACL-IJCNLP 2015 workshop in Beijing, China. The sixth one, NEWS2016, was held as an ACL 2016 workshop in Berlin, Germany. The current edition, NEWS2018, was held as an ACL 2018 workshop in Melbourne, Australia.

The purpose of the NEWS workshop series is to bring together researchers across the world interested in identification, analysis, extraction, mining and transformation of named entities in monolingual or multilingual natural language text corpora. The workshop scope includes many interesting specific research areas pertaining to the named entities, such as, orthographic and phonetic characteristics, corpus analysis, unsupervised and supervised named entities extraction in monolingual or multilingual corpus, transliteration modeling, and evaluation methodologies, to name a few. For this year edition, 7 research papers were submitted, each paper was reviewed by at least 2 reviewers from the program committee. The 7 papers were all chosen for publication, covering named entity recognition and machine transliteration, which applied various new trend methods such as deep neural networks and graph-based semi-supervised learning.

Following the tradition of the NEWS workshop series, NEWS 2018 continued the machine transliteration shared task this year as well. The shared task was first introduced in NEWS 2009 and continued in NEWS 2010, NEWS 2011, NEWS 2012, NEWS 2015, and NEWS 2016. In NEWS 2018, by leveraging on the previous success of NEWS workshop series, the Shared Task featured 19 tasks on proper name transliteration, including 13 different languages and two different Japanese scripts. A total of 6 teams from 8 different institutions participated in the evaluation, submitting 424 runs, involving different transliteration methodologies.

We hope that NEWS 2018 would provide an exciting and productive forum for researchers working in this research area, and the NEWS-released data continues to serve as a standard dataset for machine transliteration generation and mining. We wish to thank all the researchers for their research submission and the enthusiastic participation in the transliteration shared tasks. We wish to express our gratitude to CJK Institute (Japan), Institute for Infocomm Research (Singapore), National University of Singapore (NUS), Artificial Intelligence Laboratory at the Ho Chi Minh City University of Science (AILab, VNU-HCMUS, Vietnam), Microsoft Research India, the Computer Science & Engineering Department of Jadavpur University (India), the National Electronics and Computer Technology Center (NECTEC, Thailand) and Sarvnaz Karim (RMIT, Australia) for providing the corpora and technical support for the shared task. Without those, the Shared Task would not be possible. In addition, we want to thank Grandee Lee and Snigdha Singhania for their help and support with CodaLab and the baseline systems, respectively. Finally, we thank all the program committee members for reviewing the submissions in spite of the tight schedule.

Organizers:

Nancy Chen, Singapore University of Technology and Design
Rafael E. Banchs, Nanyang Technological University, Singapore
Xiangyu Duan, Soochow University
Min Zhang, Soochow University, China
Haizhou Li, Institute for Infocomm Research, Singapore

Program Committee:

Rafael E. Banchs, Nanyang Technological University
Sivaji Bandyopadhyay, Jadavpur University
Marta R. Costa-jussà, Instituto Politécnico Nacional
Xiangyu Duan, Soochow University
Guohong Fu, Heilongjiang University
Sarvnaz Karimi, CSIRO
Mitesh M. Khapra, IBM Research India
Grzegorz Kondrak, University of Alberta
Jong-Hoon Oh, NICT
Richard Sproat, Google
Keh-Yih Su, Institute of Information Science, Academia Sinica
Raghavendra Udupa, Microsoft Research India
Chai Wutiwiwatchai, Intelligent Informatics Research Unit, National Electronics and Computer
Technology Center
Deyi Xiong, Soochow University
Muyun Yang, Harbin Institute of Technology
Min Zhang, Soochow University

Table of Contents

Conference Program

Friday, 20 July, 2018

8:30–8:40   **Opening Remarks**

8:40–9:00   *Automatic Extraction of Entities and Relation from Legal Documents*
Judith Jeyafreeda Andrew

9:00–9:20   *Connecting Distant Entities with Induction through Conditional Random Fields for Named Entity Recognition: Precursor-Induced CRF*
Wangjin Lee and Jinwook Choi

9:20–9:40   *A Sequence Learning Method for Domain-Specific Entity Linking*
Emrah Inan and Oguz Dikenelli

9:40–10:00   *Attention-based Semantic Priming for Slot-filling*
Jiewen Wu, Rafael E. Banchs, Luis Fernando D'Haro, Pavitra Krishnaswamy and Nancy Chen

10:00–10:20   *Named Entity Recognition for Hindi-English Code-Mixed Social Media Text*
Vinay Singh, Deepanshu Vijay, Syed Sarfaraz Akhtar and Manish Shrivastava

10:30–11:00   *Coffee Break*

11:00–11:20   *Forms of Anaphoric Reference to Organisational Named Entities: Hoping to widen appeal, they diversified*
Christian Hardmeier, Luca Bevacqua, Sharid Loáiciga and Hannah Rohde

11:20–11:40   *Named-Entity Tagging and Domain adaptation for Better Customized Translation*
Zhongwei Li, Xuancong Wang, AiTi Aw, Eng Siong Chng and Haizhou Li

12:00–14:00   *Lunch*

14:10–14:20   *NEWS 2018 Whitepaper*
Nancy Chen, Xiangyu Duan, Min Zhang, Rafael E. Banchs and Haizhou Li

14:20–14:40   *Report of NEWS 2018 Named Entity Transliteration Shared Task*
Nancy Chen, Rafael E. Banchs, Min Zhang, Xiangyu Duan and Haizhou Li

14:40–15:00   *Statistical Machine Transliteration Baselines for NEWS 2018*
Snigdha Singhania, Minh Nguyen, Gia H Ngo and Nancy Chen

15:00–15:20   *A Deep Learning Based Approach to Transliteration*
Soumyadeep Kundu, Sayantan Paul and Santanu Pal

15:30–16:00   Coffee Break

16:00–16:20   *Comparison of Assorted Models for Transliteration*
Saeed Najafi, Bradley Hauer, Rashed Rubby Riyadh, Leyuan Yu and Grzegorz Kondrak

16:20–16:40   *Neural Machine Translation Techniques for Named Entity Transliteration*
Roman Grundkiewicz and Kenneth Heafield

16:40–17:00   *Low-Resource Machine Transliteration Using Recurrent Neural Networks of Asian Languages*
Ngoc Tan Le and Fatiha Sadat

Automatic Extraction of Entities and Relation from Legal Documents

Judith Jeyafreeda Andrew[1]
GREYC , Campus 2 UniCaen,
Bâtiment F
6 Boulevard Maréchal Juin , 14000 Caen
judithjeyafreeda@gmail.com

Xavier Tannier[1]
Sorbonne Université,
Inserm, LIMICS, Paris, France
xavier.tannier@
sorbonne-universite.fr

Abstract

In recent years, the journalists and computer sciences speak to each other to identify useful technologies which would help them in extracting useful information. This is called "computational Journalism". In this paper, we present a method that will enable the journalists to automatically identifies and annotates entities such as names of people, organizations, role and functions of people in legal documents; the relationship between these entities are also explored. The system uses a combination of both statistical and rule based technique. The statistical method used is Conditional Random Fields and for the rule based technique, document and language specific regular expressions are used.

1 Introduction

Everyday there are a number of legal documents that are being recorded and made available as text documents. In this paper, we present a system that automatically identifies named entities and the relationships between various entities within a dataset of certain type of legal documents which contains information about people investing in property. This helps journalists to identify some useful information - information like the name of the person investing and company invested in. We propose a hybrid method to automatically detect different types of relationship after identifying the entities within the corpus. We follow a combination of statistical and rule based techniques to achieve the goal.

The objective of this project therefore are:

- To identify and classify the entities within each of the text documents

- To identify the relationships between the entities

To achieve the objectives, we present a hybrid system which explores a combination of two techniques for Named Entity recognition (a statistical approach using Conditional Random Fields (CRF) and rule based techniques) and produces a graph with all entities and their relationships, in the perspective of a investigative journalism use.

2 Data

The data used in this project is a corpus taken from the so-called "Luxembourg" corpus. This publicly available legal register contains information about people and companies who are investing money or property in the state of Luxembourg. Most of the documents are written in French, and we only worked on this language.

Some of the data set has been annotated manually with the help of the brat tool (Stenetorp et al., 2012) for the different classes and the relationship between the classes by our journalist partners. The annotations have been done manually for 35 documents which can be used as a training set to develop a model.

2.1 Entities

The classes used for classification of the entities are as follows:

- PERSONNE represents the name of the person

- NOM represents the first name of the person

- ADDRESS represents the address of the organization

---

[1]The work was done while the authors were affiliated with LIMSI, CNRS and Univ. Paris-Sud.

Proceedings of the Seventh Named Entities Workshop, pages 1–8
Melbourne, Australia, July 20, 2018. ©2018 Association for Computational Linguistics

- SOCIETE_PRINCIPALE represents the name of the main company participating in the transaction

- SOCIETE_SECONDAIRE represents the name of the secondary companies participating in the transaction

- ROLE represents the role of the identified person or company in the transaction

- FONCTION is the function or position held by the identified person in the transaction

- TYPE_SOCIÉTÉ is the type of the companies identified

2.2 Relations

The relationships between the entities are classified as follows:

- 'PERSONNE_FONCTION" is the relationship between the class "PERSONNE" and the class "FONCTION"

- "PERSONNE_ROLE" is the relationship between the class "PERSONNE" and the class "ROLE"

- "SOCIÉTÉ_ROLE" is the relationship between the class "SOCIÉTÉ" and the class "ROLE"

- "SOCIÉTÉ_TYPE" is the relationship between the class "SOCIÉTÉ" and the class "TYPE_SOCIÉTÉ"

2.3 Structure of the corpus

The structure and language of legal documents are more rigid than free text. When the persons and companies are identified, then the other classes appear in the same sentence and can be identified by only a few specific expressions. Below are few examples, the translation in English are given in the "[]".

- "Ensuite les souscripteurs prédésignés, représentés par Me Catherine Dessoy, prénommée, en vertu des procurations susvantées" ["Then the underwriters, represented by Catherine Dessoy, prenamed, under the aforementioned powers of attorney"], where "représentés par" is the ROLE and "Me Catherine Dessoy" is the PERSONNE.

- "Par-devant Maître Blanche Moutrier, notaire de résidence à Esch-sur-Alzette."["Before Maître Blanche Moutrier, notary of residence in Esch-sur-Alzette."], where "Maître Blanche Moutrier" is the PERSONNE and "notaire" is the FONCTION.

- "CUBE INVEST S.A.-SPF, une société de gestion de patrimoine familial, en abrégé SPF, sous forme d'une société anonyme" ["CUBE INVEST S.A.-SPF, a family wealth management company, in abbreviated SPF, in the form of anonymous company"], where "CUBE INVEST S.A.-SPF" is the SOCIÉTÉ and "société de gestion de patrimoine familial" is the TYPE_SOCIÉTÉ.

Because of this rigid structure of the legal documents, rule-based techniques will be able to identify some of the entities. However, the basic classes PERSONNE and SOCIÉTÉ have to be identified first in order to take advantage of this rigid structure. Figure 1 shows an example of an annotated document as seen by the BRAT visualization tool emphasizing on the structure of the legal documents.

2.4 Training and Test data sets

The data is divided into training and test set. The training set is a set of corpus consisting of 35 text files and test set is a collection of 21 text documents. The method has been trained and tested on this small corpus, however it is developed with the scope of being able to build a graph with all the documents available in the Luxembourg register. This mounts up to data between the years 2002 to 2016, containing about 2,041,111 text documents. For this reason, the training documents have been taken randomly from the entire collection.

3 Related Work

3.1 Conditional Random Fields

Conditional Random Field (CRF (Lafferty, 2001)) is a sequence modeling technique belonging to the class of statistical modeling methods. It is often used in labeling and parsing sequential data. A CRF has a single exponential model for the joint probability of the entire sequence of labels given the observation sequence. (Sutton and McCallum, 2012) gives a detailed tutorial on Condition Random fields. Since the CRF model is conditional, dependencies among the input variables x

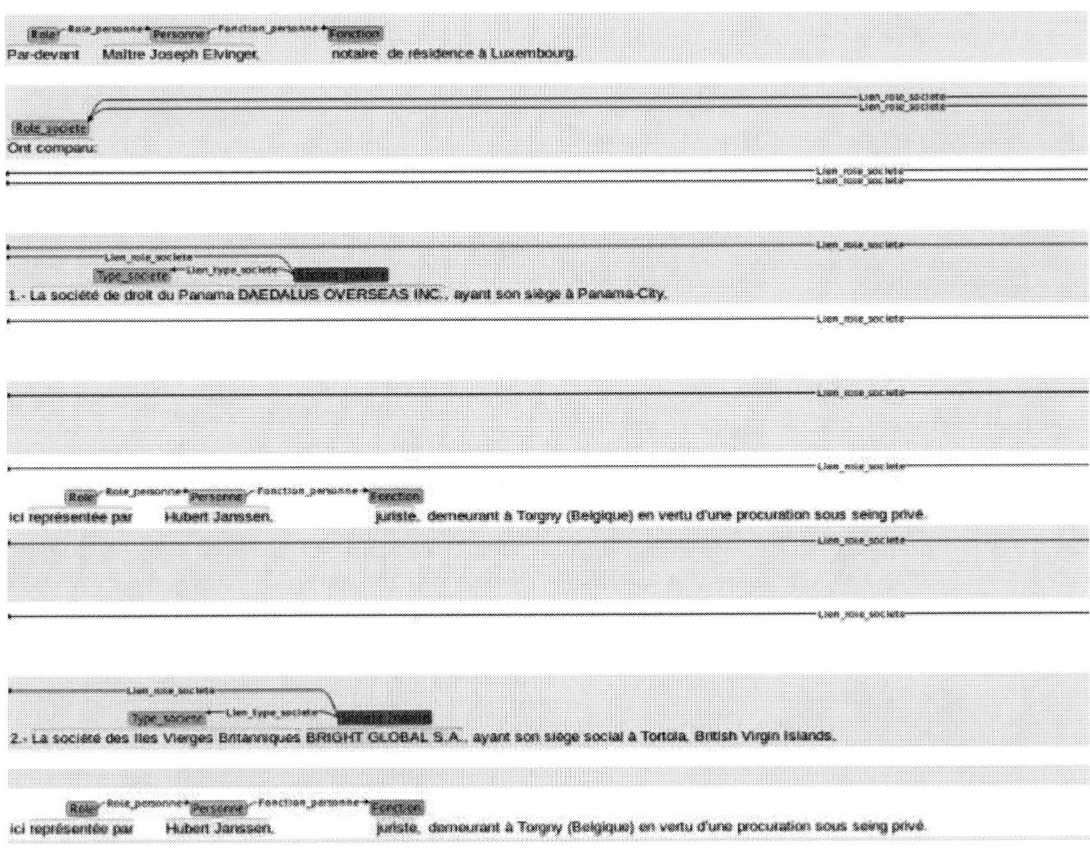

Figure 1: Annotated document presented with the BRAT visualization tool

do not need to be explicitly represented. This allows CRF to be used widely in Natural Language Processing. (Sutton and McCallum, 2012) also suggests that some of the useful features that could be used in Natural Language Processing are capitalization, word bigrams, neighboring words etc. In this work, word bigrams and capitalization have been used extensively.

3.1.1 Conditional Random Fields for Entity Recognition

There have been quite a lot of work done with respect to entity recognition and classification using CRF.

(N.V et al., 2010) describes the use conditional Random Fields for Entity Recognition in geological text. (McCallum and Li, 2003) presents a named entity recognition technique with conditional random fields, where web enhanced lexicons are used for feature induction. (Ghamrawi and McCallum, 2005) present the multi-label classification of corpora using classification. Multi-label classification is a task of assigning an object simultaneously to one or multiple classes. (Ghamrawi and McCallum, 2005) present two graphical models for multi-label classification, namely the Collective Multi-Label classifier and the Collective Multi-Label with Features classifier. CRFs have better performances than many other techniques. (Li et al., 2008) compares SVM with CRF for named entity recognition with clinical data and concludes that CRF outperforms SVM.

4 Approach

The approach used is a combination of statistical approach (CRF) and the rule based technique.

4.1 Process

In order to annotate the corpus with the entities and the relationship, the work uses two techniques which are conditional random fields and rules based on regular expressions. Conditional Random Fields (CRF) is used to annotate the document only for the classes "PERSONNE", "SOCIÉTÉ", "NOM","ADDRESS". These classes are the basic classes and therefore they have to be identified first. Moreover, we only expect the other classes to appear in the same sentence as a "PERSONNE" or a SOCIÉTÉ or a "NOM" or a "ADDRESS". Therefore, identifying these classes will be the first and basic step. For the other classes, a rule based technique are used. 2 shows the process flow used for the annotation of text. The rules are written in such a way that they identify the other classes and their relation with the main classes ("PERSONNE" and "SOCIÉTÉ").

5 Implementation

5.1 Conditional Random Fields (CRF)

In order to annotate the document for the base classes ("PERSONNE", "SOCIÉTÉ", "ADDRESS", "NOM"), Conditional Random Fields are used. The system uses the wapiti toolkit (Lavergne et al., 2010) to train the CRF.

In order to use wapiti, the training set and the test set are converted into the BIO format. Figure 3 shows how the wapiti tool works in order to train and test using CRF.

In order to use conditional random fields, one has to create a pattern file with which CRF can be trained. A pattern file defines some features that are going to be used by the wapiti.

5.2 Regular Expressions for entity recognition and relationship

In order to identify the other classes (ROLE, FONCTION, TYPE_SOCIÉTÉ), regular expressions are used. The rules are written such that once the entities are identified the relationship can be established with the same rule. This is done by writing the rules using the relationship itself. For example, if there is a "PERSONNE" in a sentence, then the sentence should have a "ROLE" and a "FONCTION" for the identified person. This suggests that there exist a relationship between the person and his/her "ROLE" and "FONCTION". Therefore, the entities "ROLE" and "FONCTION" should occur somewhere close to the entity "PERSONNE". This rule-based system is established with the help of the GATE tool (Cunningham et al., 2011) and the rules are written as JAPE grammar(Thakker et al., 2009)

5.2.1 Formation of JAPE rules for the various classes

Class "FONCTION" The class "FONCTION" is the job of the person in question. The GATE gazetteer is used to annotate the function of a person. GATE gazetteer does not have a dictionary for the function of a person. Therefore, a dictionary is created with all the words that could be the function of a person. This dictionary has been cre-

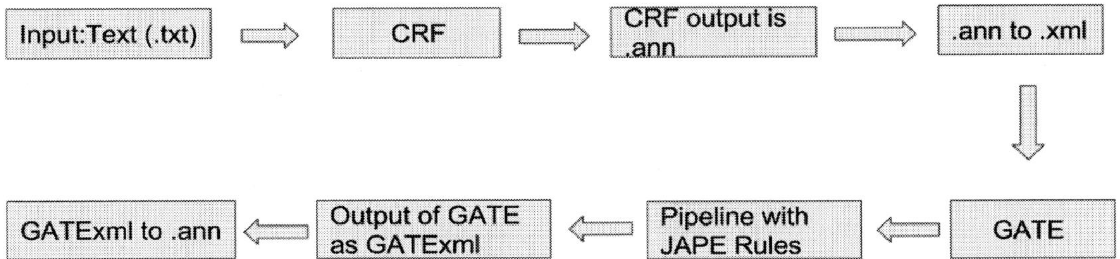

Figure 2: Process Flow for identifying entities and relationships

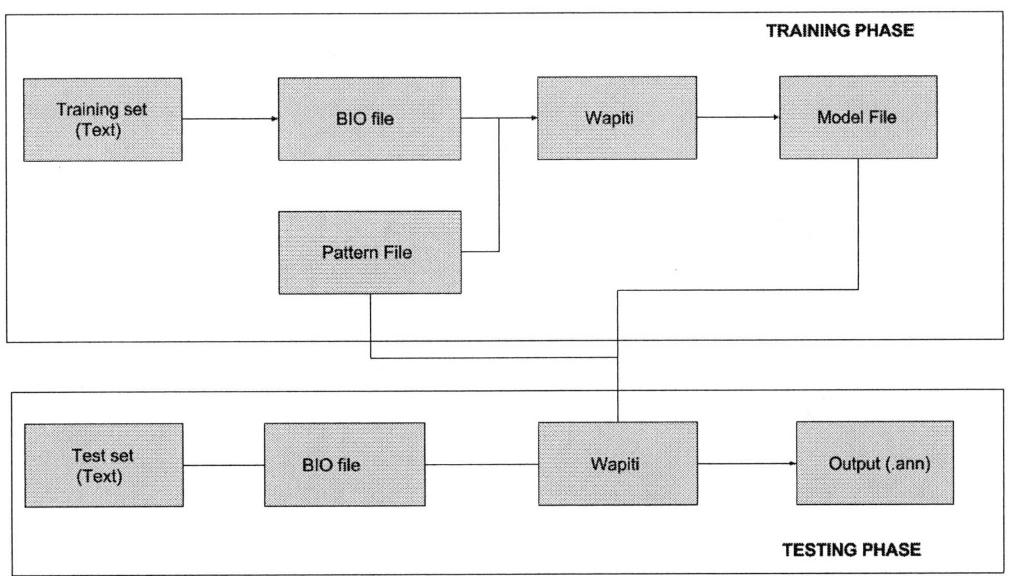

Figure 3: The process flow as followed by wapiti

ated with about 500 words and added to the GATE gazetteer. The rule for the class "FONCTION" was developed as per the structure of all the documents in the training set, where it was identified that the class "FONCTION" appears with the same sentence as the class "PERSONNE". Thus using the gazetteer and the class "PERSONNE", the class "FONCTION" can be annotated and the relation 'PERSONNE_FONCTION" is drawn. For example, "Par-devant Maître Blanche Moutrier, notaire de résidence à Esch-sur-Alzette." ["Before Maître Blanche Moutrier, notary of residence in Esch-sur-Alzette."]. In this sentence, "Maître Blanche Moutrier" is the class "PERSONNE" and this is followed by the "notaire" which is the "FONCTION" of "Maître Blanche Moutrier".

class "ROLE" The "ROLE" of a "PERSONNE" almost always occur in the same sentence as the class "PERSONNE". It could occur after or before "PERSONNE" "ROLE" could also be associated with the class "SOCIÉTÉ" as well. In this case, the class "ROLE" occurs in the same sentence as the "SOCIÉTÉ". This leads to the "PERSONNE_ROLE" and "SOCIÉTÉ_ROLE" relation.

For example: "Pardevant Maître Henri Hellinckx, notaire de résidence à Luxembourg." ["Late Maître Henri Hellinckx, notary residing in Luxembourg."] In the above sentence, "Pardevant" is the "ROLE" played by "Maître Henri Hellinckx" and the "FONCTION" is "notaire". Therefore the rule is to identify the sequence "PERSONNE" "FONCTION" and identify the word before the sequence as "ROLE".

Another example: "Ont comparu: 1.- La sociètè de droit du Panama DAEDALUS OVERSEAS INC., ayant son siège à Panama-City" ["Appeared: 1.- The company of law of Panama DAEDALUS OVERSEAS INC., Having its headquarters in Panama-City"], where "Ont comparu" is the "ROLE" and "DAEDALUS OVERSEAS INC." is the "SOCIÉTÉ" . Here the "ROLE" is followed by tokens like punctuations and numbers before the "SOCIÉTÉ" which also have to be incorporated with the rules.

Another example: "Les parts sociales ont ètè souscrites par LUXEMBOURG CORPORATION COMPANY S.A., prèqualifièe, qui est l'associèe unique de la sociè té " ["The shares have been subscribed by LUXEMBOURG CORPORATION COMPANY S.A., prequalified, which is the sole partner of the company."], where " parts sociales ont été souscrites" and "l'associèe unique de la société ." are both "ROLE" of the "SOCIÉTÉ" "LUXEMBOURG CORPORATION COMPANY S.A." This state of having two roles is handled with a different rule as well.

Therefore, in order to help handle all these different situations, multiple different rules are used. A total of 20 different JAPE rules has been written to annotate all the roles in all the different situations. This count includes identifying the roles of the société as well.

class "TYPE_SOCIÉTÉ" The class "TYPE_SOCIÉTÉ" tells about the type of the "SOCIÉTÉ". Therefore the type has to be occurring in the same sentence as the "SOCIÉTÉ". It is also identified that all the texts in the training set had the type of the société in the same sentence as the SOCIÉTÉ. Also, the type of the société always starts with the word "société" followed by a type. This then leads to the relationship of "SOCIÉTÉ_TYPE". Example: "S'est réunie l'Assemblée Générale Extraordinaire des associé s de la société à responsabilité limité e thermo haus, S.à r.l., ayant son siè ge social à L-6940 Niederanven, 141, route de Trèves, inscrite au Registre du Commerce et des Socié tés à Luxembourg, section B sous le numéro 74.172, constituée suivant acte reçu par Maître Alex Weber, notaire de résidence à Bascharage, en date du 2 février 2000, publié au Mémorial C de 2000, page 16652." ["The Extraordinary General Assembly of the associates of the limited liability company, S.à rl, having its if it is located at L-6940 Niederanven, 141, route de Trvesves, entered in the Register of Commerce and Companies in Luxembourg, section B under number 74.172, incorporated according to the deed of the Court, given to Alex Weber, notary residing at Bascharage, on February 2, 2000, published in the Mémorial C of 2000, page 16652."]. In the above sentence, "thermo haus, S.à r.l." is the SOCIÉTÉ and "la société à responsabilité limitée" is the TYPE_SOCIÉTÉ.

5.2.2 The GATE pipeline

The JAPE rules are incorporated with the other inbuilt modules of the GATE tool to create a pipeline. A GATE pipeline with modules for tokenization , POS tagging along with the JAPE rules is used to annotate the document for the other classes.

Mode	True Positive	False Positive	False Negative	Precision	Recall
Exact	318	61	0	83.91%	100%
Partial	348	30	0	92.08%	100%

Table 1: Results of brat evaluation tool on the training set.

Mode	True Positive	False Positive	False Negative	Precision	Recall
Exact	81	4	88	95.29%	47.93%
Partial	191	9	12	95.50%	94.09%

Table 2: Results of brat evaluation tool on the test set.

6 Evaluation

For the evaluation of annotations, the brat evaluation tool is used (Stenetorp et al., 2012). The comparisons can be done in two ways: either by comparing the file for exact matches or by partial matches. By exact matches we mean that the offset have to be exactly matched between the two files. By partial matches, we mean that even if the offsets do not match perfectly, partial annotations are also considered to be correct.

7 Results

The results are shown in Tables 1 and 2. Table 1 corresponds to the results from the training set and the table 2 corresponds to the results from the test test. The results depend on both the processes - the CRF and the rule based technique. The performance of the CRF is with an error rate of 3.12%.

The low recall value for the exact matches of the test set as compared with the training set is due the tailoring of the rules. While training, the data set has been referred to at many times to come up with expressions that will help in retrieving all the possible instances of every annotations. However, while the same rules have been run on test data which has not been seen before hand, it is noted that there requires many more rules that need to added to the already existing rules to improve the recall value.

However it has to be noted that the recall value is quite high with the partial matches. For example: instead of annotating "ici représenté par", it annotates "représenté par". This is not totally wrong. Considering the knowledge base, this annotation is still useful. Though it is not the exact same annotation as in the manual annotation, it is still considered valid.

Thus considering the results of partial annotations only, this method proves to be quite efficient in annotating the files from the "Luxembourg" register.

As indicated above, the process has been developed over a small set of data, but the process can be run over huge volumes of data. The total amount of documents tested are 2,041,111. The number of relations found in these documents are 3,026,560. However, since these data have no manual annotations, no evaluation was performed on this set of data.

References

Hamish Cunningham, Diana Maynard, Kalina Bontcheva, Valentin Tablan, Niraj Aswani, Ian Roberts, Genevieve Gorrell, Adam Funk, Angus Roberts, Danica Damljanovic, Thomas Heitz, Mark A. Greenwood, Horacio Saggion, Johann Petrak, Yaoyong Li, and Wim Peters. 2011. Text Processing with GATE (Version 6).

Nadia Ghamrawi and Andrew McCallum. 2005. Collective multi-label classification. In *Proceedings of the 14th ACM International Conference on Information and Knowledge Management*, CIKM '05, pages 195–200, New York, NY, USA. ACM.

John Lafferty. 2001. Conditional random fields: Probabilistic models for segmenting and labeling sequence data. pages 282–289. Morgan Kaufmann.

Thomas Lavergne, Olivier Cappé, and François Yvon. 2010. Practical Very Large Scale CRFs. In *Proceedings the 48th Annual Meeting of the Association for Computational Linguistics (ACL)*, pages 504–513, Uppsala, Sweden. Association for Computational Linguistics.

Dingcheng Li, Karin Kipper-Schuler, and Guergana Savova. 2008. Conditional random fields and support vector machines for disorder named entity recognition in clinical texts. In *Proceedings of the Workshop on Current Trends in Biomedical Natural Language Processing*, BioNLP '08, pages 94–95, Stroudsburg, PA, USA. Association for Computational Linguistics.

Andrew McCallum and Wei Li. 2003. Early results for named entity recognition with conditional random fields, feature induction and web-enhanced lexicons. In *Proceedings of the Seventh Conference on Natural Language Learning, CoNLL 2003, Held in cooperation with HLT-NAACL 2003, Edmonton, Canada, May 31 - June 1, 2003*, pages 188–191.

Sobhana N.V, Pabitra Mitra, and S.K. Ghosh. 2010. Article: Conditional random field based named entity recognition in geological text. *International Journal of Computer Applications*, 1(3):119–125. Published By Foundation of Computer Science.

Pontus Stenetorp, Sampo Pyysalo, Goran Topić, Tomoko Ohta, Sophia Ananiadou, and Jun'ichi Tsujii. 2012. BRAT: A Web-based Tool for NLP-assisted Text Annotation. In *Proceedings of the Demonstrations at the 13th Conference of the European Chapter of the Association for Computational Linguistics (EACL'12)*, pages 102–107, Avignon, France. Association for Computational Linguistics.

Charles Sutton and Andrew McCallum. 2012. An introduction to conditional random fields. *Found. Trends Mach. Learn.*, 4(4):267–373.

Dhaval Thakker, Taha Osman, and Phil Lakin. 2009. GATE JAPE grammar tutorial.

Connecting Distant Entities with Induction through Conditional Random Fields for Named Entity Recognition: Precursor-Induced CRF

Wangjin Lee[1] and **Jinwook Choi**[1,2,3]*

[1] Interdisciplinary Program for Bioengineering, Seoul National University, South Korea
[2] Department of Biomedical Engineering, College of Medicine, Seoul National University, South Korea
[3] Institute of Medical and Biological Engineering, Medical Research Center, Seoul National University, South Korea

`{jinsamdol,jinchoi}@snu.ac.kr`

Abstract

This paper presents a method of designing specific high-order dependency factor on the linear chain conditional random fields (CRFs) for named entity recognition (NER). Named entities tend to be separated from each other by multiple outside tokens in a text, and thus the first-order CRF, as well as the second-order CRF, may innately lose transition information between distant named entities. The proposed design uses outside label in NER as a transmission medium of precedent entity information on the CRF. Then, empirical results apparently demonstrate that it is possible to exploit long-distance label dependency in the original first-order linear chain CRF structure upon NER while reducing computational loss rather than in the second-order CRF.

1 Introduction

The concept of conditional random fields (CRFs) (John Lafferty, Andrew McCallum, & Fernando Pereira, 2001) has been successfully adapted in many sequence labeling problems (Andrew McCallum & Wei Li, 2003; Fei Sha & Fernando Pereira, 2003; John Lafferty et al., 2001; McDonald & Pereira, 2005). Even in deep-learning architecture, CRF has been used as a fundamental element in named entity recognition (Lample, Ballesteros, Subramanian, Kawakami, & Dyer, 2016; Liu, Tang, Wang, & Chen, 2017).

One of the primary advantages of applying the CRF to language processing is that it learns transition factors between hidden variables corresponding to the label of single word. The fundamental assumption of the model is that the current hidden state is conditioned on present observation as well as the previous state. For example, a part-of-speech (POS) tag depends on the word itself, as well as the POS tag transitions from the previous word. In the problem, the POS tags are adjacent to each other in a text forming a tag sequence; therefore, the sequence labeling model can fully capture dependencies between labels.

In contrast, a CRF in named entity recognition (NER) cannot fully capture dependencies between named entity (NE) labels. According to Ratinov & Roth (2009), named entities in a text are separated by successive "outside tokens" (i.e., words that are non-named entities syntactically linking two NEs) and considerable number of NEs have a tendency to exist at a distance from each other. Therefore, high-order interdependencies of named entities between successive *outside* tokens are not captured by first-order or second-order transition factors.

One major issue in previous studies was concerned with the way in which to explore long-distance dependencies in NER. Only dependencies between neighbor labels are generally used in practice because conventional high-order CRFs are known to be intractable in NER (Ye, Lee, Chieu, & Wu, 2009). Previous studies have demonstrated that implementation of the higher-order CRF exploiting pre-defined label patterns leads to slight performance improvement in the conventional CRF in NER (Cuong, Ye, Lee, & Chieu, 2014; Fersini, Messina, Felici, & Roth, 2014; Sarawagi & Cohen, 2005; Ye et al., 2009). However, there are certain drawbacks associated with handling named entity transitions within arbitrary length outside tokens.

In an attempt to utilize long-distance transition information of NEs through non-named entity to-

9

Proceedings of the Seventh Named Entities Workshop, pages 9–13
Melbourne, Australia, July 20, 2018. ©2018 Association for Computational Linguistics

kens, this study explores the method which modifies the first-order linear-chain CRF by using the induction method.

2 Precursor-induced CRF

Prior to introducing the new model formulation, the following information presents the general concept of CRF. As a sequence labeling model, the conventional CRF models the conditional distribution $P(y|x)$ in which x is the input (e.g., token, word) sequence and y is the label sequence of x. A hidden state value set consists of target entity labels and a single *outside* label. By way of illustration, presume a set $\{A, B, O\}$ as the hidden state value set; assign A or B to NEs, likewise, assign O to outside words. From the hidden state set, a label sequence is formed in a linear chain in NER; for example, a sequence $\langle A, O, \cdots O, B \rangle$ in which successive outside words are between the two NE words. Because the first-order model assumes that state transition dependencies exist only between proximate two labels to prevent an increase in computational complexity, the first-order CRF learns bigram label transitions from the subsequence; $\{(A, O), (O, O), (O, B)\}$ that is, label transition data learnt from the example sequence. In the example, dependency (A, B) is not captured in the model.

The main purpose of the precursor-induced CRF model, introduced in this study, is to capture specific high-order named entity dependency that is an outside word sequence between two NEs. The main idea can be explained in the following manner:

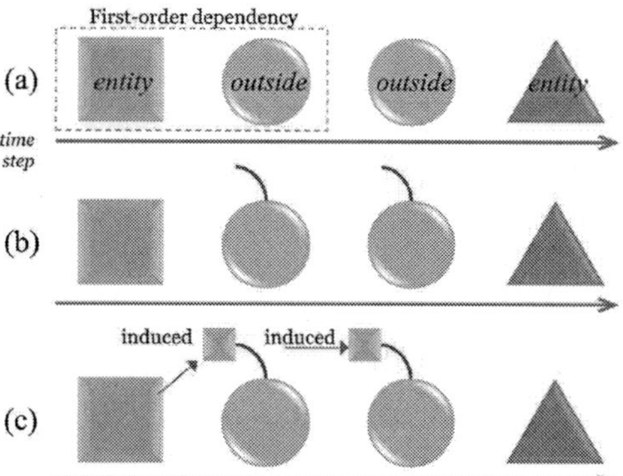

Figure 1: Transformation from conventional CRF to precursor-induced CRF; two entities (polygons) are separated and the only dependency between states are within first-order.

- It mainly focuses on beneficial use of *outside* label as a medium delivering dependency between separated NEs.

- Focuses on label subsequence having $\langle entity, outside^+, entity \rangle$ pattern. (Figure 1 (a))

- Adds memory element to the hidden variables for the *outside* states (Figure 1(b)).

- The first *outside* label in an outside subsequence explicitly has a first-order dependency with its adjacent *entity*. If the first *outside* label tosses the information to the next, the information possibly flows forward.

- By induction process, the information of the first *entity* can flow through multiple *outside* labels to the second *entity* state (Figure 1(c)).

In the pre-induced CRF, the *outside* state with a memory element behaves as if an information transmission medium is delivering information about the presence or absence of the preceding entity forward. It is required to expand state set. States are collected and only entity states are selected. Multiplied *outside* state set is derived by multiplication of entity states and *outside* state. Expanded state set is consequently derived as a union of entity states and multiplied *outside* states.

Turning to the formulation, the conditional probability distribution of a label sequence y, given an observation x in the CRF has a form as Eq.(1),

$$p(y|x) = \frac{1}{Z(x)} \cdot$$
$$\prod_{t=1}^{T} exp\{\sum_{k=1}^{K} \theta_k f_k(y_t, y_{t-1}, x_t)\} \qquad (1)$$

where f_k is an arbitrary feature function having corresponding weight θ_k, the $Z(x)$ is a partition function, and t is time step (Sutton & McCallum, 2011). The feature function f_k is generally indicator function that has value 1 only if the function is matched to a certain condition, otherwise 0. Transition factor in CRF has a form of function $f_{ij}(y, y', x) = \mathbf{1}_{\{y=i\}} \mathbf{1}_{\{y'=j\}}$, and observation factor has a form of a function $f_{io}(y, y', x) = \mathbf{1}_{\{y=i\}} \mathbf{1}_{\{x=o\}}$. Derived from Eq.(1), conditional probability distribution of the precursor-induced CRF takes a form as Eq.(2),

$$p(y|x, a) = \frac{1}{Z(x,a)} \cdot$$
$$\prod_{t=1}^{T} exp\{\sum_{k=1}^{K} \theta_k f_k(y_t, y_{t-1}, x_t, a_t, a_{t-1})\} \qquad (2)$$

where the variable a is to store the induced state

information, and the value of "a_t" is activated by the value of "a_{t-1}" and "y_t." Once the "a_t" is activated, the "a_t" eventually transmutes the value of "y_t."

This induction process eventually expands the original label value set. It produces newly induced *outside* states instead of the single *outside* state; for example, the process modifies an original label sequence $\langle A, O, \cdots O, B \rangle$ to $\langle A, A[O]^+, \cdots A[O]^+, B \rangle$. This transformation helps the CRF learn long-distance named entity transitions, even in the first-order form; from the modified example sequence, the model can learn label transition data $\{(A[O]^+, B)\}$ where entity B depends on entity A preceding itself. In terms of the number of newly produced states, when $N=|States|$ in the original first-order CRF (a state set consists of NE states and one outside state), this procedure introduces N new states. (if the IOB2 tagging scheme (Tjong & Sang, 1995) is applied, $(N-1)/2 + 1$ new states are introduced).

To train the precursor-induced CRF, L-BFGS optimization method (Fei Sha & Fernando Pereira, 2003) and *l2*-regularization (Ng, 2004) are used as conventional first-order CRF exploits (Sutton & McCallum, 2011). Furthermore, the Viterbi algorithm is used for inference.

During training and inference, it is also required to treat the fragmented *outside* states as a single *outside* label in practice. First, a weight of an observation feature f_{io} depends on the frequency of an observation as well as co-occurrence label data. Fragmenting a single *outside* state into multiple states may cause data-sparseness problems especially for observation features occurring within the fine-grained *outside* states in training time. To prevent the data sparseness problem derived by the precursor-induced CRF, observation factor $f_{io}(y, y', x)$ is customized as $(\mathbf{1}_{\{i \in \neg \text{Outside}, \ y=i\}} + \mathbf{1}_{\{i \in \text{Outside}\}}) \mathbf{1}_{\{x=o\}} \mathbf{1}_{\{y'=1\}}$. Second, the expected label alphabets in inference time are required to be matched to the label alphabets of given annotation. Therefore, the fragmented *outside* state reverts to the original *outside* label.

3 Experiments

All the experiments were performed by implementing both the original and precursor-induced CRF[1]. The activity refers to CRF implemented in MALLET (Andrew Kachites McCallum, 2002). To compare precursor-induced CRF with the original CRF in NER on the real-world clinical documents and biomedical literatures, three annotated NER corpus were used; i2b2 2012 NLP shared task data

(Sun, Rumshisky, & Uzuner, 2013), discharge summaries of rheumatism patients at Seoul National University Hospital (SNUH), and JNLPBA 2004 Bio-Entity Recognition shared task data (Kim, Ohta, Tsuruoka, Tateisi, & Collier, 2004). The discharge summary of rheumatism patient corpus is built for this evaluation. This corpus consists of 200 electronic clinical documents where English and Korean words are jointly used for recording patient history. We used the division of training and test set provided by the i2b2 2012 and JNLPBA corpus in this evaluation. For the SNUH corpus, 10-fold cross validation was used.

Annotated named entities involved in the clinical NER evaluation are related to mentions describing the patient's history. In the i2b2 2012 corpus, *problem*, *test*, and *treatment* named entity classes are used. In the SNUH corpus, *symptom*, *test*, *diagnosis*, *medication*, and *procedure-operation* classes are used. The named entity classes in the biomedical NER evaluation are *DNA*, *RNA*, *protein*, *cell line*, and *cell type*.

In the i2b2 2012 training data, 9,942 entities have *outside* state precedence, and approximately 63.8% cases of them take a pattern $\langle entity, outside^+, entity \rangle$. Likewise, in SNUH corpus, 58.9% cases of NEs having *outside* precedence have a preceding named entity. Median value of the distance between consecutive entities tend to be within 3-4 in the datasets. The long distance dependency is restricted within a single instance (i.e., a sentence).

To perform NER evaluation, two types of feature families are used: (a) token itself and neighbor tokens in window size 3. In addition, morphologically normalized tokens are used together. (b) morphology features such as character prefix and suffix of length 2–4. Our *feature setting 1* uses the single feature family (a) and *feature setting 2* simultaneously uses both of the feature family (a) and (b). The reason for setting these simple feature configurations is for the purpose of reducing bias that the feature will affect the performance comparison of the models.

In order to compare the proposed model with the conventional CRF, both the first-order and the second-order CRF are used as baseline models.

---

[1] https://github.com/jinsamdol/precursor-induced_CRF

Fea-ture set	Model	i2b2 2012			JNLPBA 2004			SNUH		
		P	R	F	P	R	F	P	R	F
Set 1 (a)	first-order CRF	**77.04**	63.88	69.84	66.27	62.61	64.39	82.42	73.81	77.85
	second-order CRF	74.72	63.35	68.56	68.03	**63.53**	65.70	83.27	75.45	79.14
	pre-induced CRF	76.25	**65.13**	**70.25**	**69.23**	62.54	**65.71**	**83.73**	**75.83**	**79.57**
Set 2 (a)+(b)	first-order CRF	**75.73**	67.09	**71.15**	67.38	69.43	68.39	84.83	80.30	82.49
	Second-order CRF	74.32	65.01	69.35	67.12	67.26	67.19	84.88	79.15	81.90
	pre-induced CRF	75.41	**67.14**	71.04	**68.86**	**69.50**	**69.18**	**84.95**	**80.45**	**82.63**

Table 1: Overall performance comparison. Shaded cells: baseline models. Bolded values: best performance within the comparison group (P: precision, R: recall, F: F_1-score).

The performance comparison result is shown in the Table 1. The result shows a tendency that precursor-induced (pre-induced) CRF leads to a slight performance improvement compared to both the first-order and second-order CRFs in most cases. However, the overall improvement is small.

Table 2 compares the elapsed time per iteration in parameter training for each model. The result shows that the second-order CRF takes quite more time than the first-order CRF to compute one training iteration. The pre-induced CRF takes 1.7 times more computation time than the first-order CRF in average. The pre-induced CRF takes significantly less time than the second-order CRF while the pre-induced CRF exploits longer label transition dependency than the second-order CRF.

These results indicate that the precursor-induced CRF, where long-distance dependency is introduced in CRF by label induction, slightly improves the effectiveness in clinical and biomedical NER while also significantly reducing computational cost rather than building second- or higher-order CRFs.

Model	i2b2	JNLPBA	SNUH
first-order	3.97	39.39	5.44
second-order	30.34	497.15	87.49
pre-induced	6.55	69.78	9.08

Table 2: Elapsed training time (s/iteration)

4   Conclusion

The requirement utilizing high-order dependencies often holds in sequence labeling problems; however, second-order or higher-order models are considered computationally infeasible. Therefore, this study focuses on beneficial use of single *outside* label as a medium delivering long-distance dependency. The design of the precursor-induced CRF apparently allows precedent named entity information to pass through *outside* labels by induction, even when the model maintains a first-order template. Although the performance improvement is small in both the clinical and biomedical NER evaluations, this study has shown that the proposed design enables reduced computational cost in utilizing long-distance label dependency compared to the second-order CRF.

Evidence from this study suggests that the utilization of *outside* labels as precedent NE information transmission medium presumably can enhance the expressiveness of the CRF while keeping the first-order template. Considerable work is required to validate the model. For example, the validation of the precursor-induced CRF in deep neural architecture for NER, such as the LSTM-CRF neural architecture (Lample et al., 2016), will be worth performing in the future. In addition, validation of the model in various problems, such as NER in general domain (Tjong, Sang, & Meulder, 2003) and de-identification problem of personal health information in clinical natural language processing (Stubbs, Filannino, & Uzuner, 2017; Stubbs, Kotfila, & Uzuner, 2015), will be performed in the future study.

Acknowledgements

This work was supported by the Basic Science Research Program through the National Research Foundation of Korea (NRF) funded by the Ministry of Education (No. NRF-2015R1D1A1A01058075), and also supported by a grant of the Korea Health Technology R&D Project through the Korea Health Industry Development Institute (KHIDI), funded by the Ministry of Health & Welfare, Republic of Korea (grant number : HI14C1277). Deidentified English clinical records used in this research were provided by the i2b2 National Center for Biomedical Computing funded by U54LM008748 and were originally prepared for the Shared Tasks for Challenges in NLP for Clinical Data organized by Dr. Ozlem Uzuner, i2b2 and SUNY.

References

Andrew Kachites McCallum. (2002). MALLET: A Machine Learning for Language Toolkit. Retrieved March 27, 2013, from http://mallet.cs.umass.edu

Andrew McCallum, & Wei Li. (2003). Early Results for Named Entity Recognition with Conditional Random Fields , Feature Induction and Web-Enhanced Lexicons. In *Proceeding of CoNLL 2003* (pp. 188–191).

Cuong, N. V., Ye, N., Lee, W. S., & Chieu, H. L. (2014). Conditional Random Field with High-order Dependencies for Sequence Labeling and Segmentation. *ACM JMLR, 15*, 981–1009.

Fei Sha, & Fernando Pereira. (2003). Shallow Parsing with Conditional Random Fields. In *Proceedings of the 2003 Conference of the North American Chapter of the Association for Computational Linguistics on Human Language Technology* (pp. 134–141).

Fersini, E., Messina, E., Felici, G., & Roth, D. (2014). Soft-constrained inference for Named Entity Recognition. *Information Processing and Management, 50*(5), 807–819.

John Lafferty, Andrew McCallum, & Fernando Pereira. (2001). Conditional Random Fields : Probabilistic Models for Segmenting and Labeling Sequence Data. In *Proceedings of the 18th International Conference on Machine Learning 2001* (pp. 282–289).

Kim, J.-D., Ohta, T., Tsuruoka, Y., Tateisi, Y., & Collier, N. (2004). Introduction to the bio-entity recognition task at JNLPBA. *Proceedings of the International Joint Workshop on Natural Language Processing in Biomedicine and Its Applications - JNLPBA '04*, 70.

Lample, G., Ballesteros, M., Subramanian, S., Kawakami, K., & Dyer, C. (2016). Neural Architectures for Named Entity Recognition. In *Proceedings of NAACL-HLT 2016* (pp. 260–270).

Liu, Z., Tang, B., Wang, X., & Chen, Q. (2017). De-identification of clinical notes via recurrent neural network and conditional random field. *Journal of Biomedical Informatics*.

McDonald, R., & Pereira, F. (2005). Identifying gene and protein mentions in text using conditional random fields. *BMC Bioinformatics, 6 Suppl 1*, S6. https://doi.org/10.1186/1471-2105-6-S1-S6

Ng, A. Y. (2004). Feature selection, L1 vs. L2 regularization, and rotational invariance. In *ICML 2004*.

Ratinov, L., & Roth, D. (2009). Design challenges and misconceptions in named entity recognition. In *Proceedings of the Thirteenth Conference on Computational Natural Language Learning* (pp. 147–155).

Sarawagi, S., & Cohen, W. W. (2005). Semi-Markov Conditional Random Fields for Information Extraction. In *Advances in neural information processing systems* (pp. 1185–1192).

Stubbs, A., Filannino, M., & Uzuner, Ö. (2017). De-identification of psychiatric intake records: Overview of 2016 CEGS N-GRID shared tasks Track 1. *Journal of Biomedical Informatics, 75*, S4–S18.

Stubbs, A., Kotfila, C., & Uzuner, Ö. (2015). Automated systems for the de-identification of longitudinal clinical narratives: Overview of 2014 i2b2/UTHealth shared task Track 1. *Journal of Biomedical Informatics, 58*, S11–S19.

Sun, W., Rumshisky, A., & Uzuner, O. (2013). Evaluating temporal relations in clinical text: 2012 i2b2 Challenge. *Journal of the American Medical Informatics Association : JAMIA*, 1–8.

Sutton, C., & McCallum, A. (2011). An Introduction to Conditional Random Fields. *Foundations and Trends in Machine Learning, 4*(4), 267–373. https://doi.org/10.1561/2200000013

Tjong, E. F., & Sang, K. (1995). Representing Text Chunks, 173–179.

Tjong, E. F., Sang, K., & Meulder, F. De. (2003). Introduction to the CoNLL-2003 Shared Task : Language-Independent Named Entity Recognition. In *Proceedings of the seventh conference on Natural language learning at HLT-NAACL 2003* (pp. 142–147).

Ye, N., Lee, W. S., Chieu, H. L., & Wu, D. (2009). Conditional Random Fields with High-Order Features for Sequence Labeling. In *Advances in Neural Information Processing Systems* (pp. 2196–2204).

A Sequence Learning Method for Domain-Specific Entity Linking

Emrah Inan
Department of Computer Engineering
Ege University
emrah.inan@ege.edu.tr

Oguz Dikenelli
Department of Computer Engineering
Ege University
oguz.dikenelli@ege.edu.tr

Abstract

Recent collective Entity Linking studies usually promote global coherence of all the mapped entities in the same document by using semantic embeddings and graph-based approaches. Although graph-based approaches are shown to achieve remarkable results, they are computationally expensive for general datasets. Also, semantic embeddings only indicate relatedness between entity pairs without considering sequences. In this paper, we address these problems by introducing a two-fold neural model. First, we match easy mention-entity pairs and using the domain information of this pair to filter candidate entities of closer mentions. Second, we resolve more ambiguous pairs using bidirectional Long Short-Term Memory and CRF models for the entity disambiguation. Our proposed system outperforms state-of-the-art systems on the generated domain-specific evaluation dataset.

1 Introduction

Entity Linking is the task of matching ambiguous mentions in a text to the corresponding entities in the given knowledge base. The output of the entity linking is a crucial step for many tasks, including relation extraction (Weston et al., 2013), link prediction (Nickel et al., 2015) and knowledge graph completion (Minervini et al., 2016). The main challenge is to disambiguate candidate entities for the given mentions. For instance, it requires to resolve the mention *Wicker Park* in the following text *"Wicker Park is a 2004 American psychological drama mystery film directed by Paul McGuigan and starring Josh Hartnett..."* to the referent entity *Wicker_Park_(film)*[1] in DBpedia. But the mention *Wicker Park* has three different candidate entities as indicated in the Wikipedia disambiguation page of this mention.

The key step for entity disambiguation is the similarity computation between mention-entity and entity-entity pairs. Early studies focused on modeling the similarity between local context that computes the similarity between mention context and relevant candidate entities (Bunescu and Paşca, 2006; Mihalcea and Csomai, 2007). Recent state-of-the-art methods consider global coherence that is the relatedness between all candidate entities in the same document (Milne and Witten, 2008; Kulkarni et al., 2009; Ratinov et al., 2011). These methods depend on well-defined link structures as seen in Wikipedia to compute global coherence. After the emergence of word embeddings (Mikolov et al., 2013), it facilitates to produce more generalized coherence computations without using hand-crafted features. Hence, the dependency of well-defined knowledge bases has decreased and knowledge base agnostic approaches become revealed (Zwicklbauer et al., 2016). Most recent deep learning approaches have been presented as a way to support better generalization for the similarity measurement of context, mention and entity (Sun et al., 2015). Also, mentions and entities are combined into the same continuous vector space for the entity disambiguation (Yamada et al., 2016). From a different perspective, the entity disambiguation should be transformed into as a sequence learning task to capture more generalized semantics between candidate entities and also mentions.

In this paper, we generate RDF embeddings (Ristoski and Paulheim, 2016) as the input of a sequence learning model using bidirectional

---

[1] http://dbpedia.org/resource/Wicker_Park_(film)

Proceedings of the Seventh Named Entities Workshop, pages 14–21
Melbourne, Australia, July 20, 2018. ©2018 Association for Computational Linguistics

Long Short-Term Memory (LSTM) (Graves and Schmidhuber, 2005). Then, we perform Conditional Random Field (CRF) to match the best mention-entity pairs. LSTM networks are not suitable for large entity vocabularies since English DBpedia contains more than 5M entities. To reduce the size of these vocabularies, our study employs the two-fold method. First, we match easy mention-entity pairs in which each mention contains only one candidate entity. Similar to AIDA-light study (Hoffart et al., 2013) we identify the domain of the given text and the size of candidate entities are reduced to reasonable dimensions for the detected domain. The contributions of our study can be summarized as below:

- Our study proposes a novel algorithm that first disambiguates easy mention-entity pairs for a specific domain. Thereafter, it applies CRF model to link more ambiguous entities.

- Our study provides a sequence learning model like a translation task in which a sequence of mentions will be translated into a sequence of referent entities in the domain-specific knowledge base.

Our method employs one of prominent Named Entity Recognition approaches (Lample et al., 2016) to perform a domain-specific Entity Linking. We aim to model the topical coherence of the mention-entity pairs in terms of a sequence labeling task. We conduct the experimental setup using the well-known evaluation framework called GERBIL (Usbeck et al., 2015) to compare our study with the state-of-the-art Entity Linking systems. The rest of this paper is organized as follows: In Section 2, it gives an overview of related work. In Section 3, the sequence learning method is proposed for a specific domain. Section 4 presents the experiments are for the selected approaches on the prepared evaluation dataset. We conclude our study and highlight the research questions in Section 5.

2   Related Work

Common trends in Entity Linking employs the global coherence to identify entities. Traditional studies mainly depend on Wikipedia link structure to disambiguate entities (Milne and Witten, 2008; Cucerzan, 2007). Also, TAGME (Ferragina and Scaiella, 2010) exploits Wikipedia anchor link texts for the mention detection and aims on-the-fly annotation of short texts using agreement approach based on Wikipedia link structure. Moreover, these approaches focus on global coherence approaches that emphasize the consistency of all mention-entity pairs in the given text. AIDA-light (Nguyen et al., 2014) considers global coherence to disambiguate the entities and exploits YAGO2 (Hoffart et al., 2013) and Wikipedia domain hierarchy. DBpedia Spotlight (Mendes et al., 2011), Babelfy (Moro et al., 2014) and WAT (Piccinno and Ferragina, 2014) have achieved remarkable results while using open domain knowledge bases. However, these type of systems tends to work inherently worse in domain intensive environment. These studies generally exploit hand-crafted features to represent mentions and entities. Methods based on word embeddings (Mikolov et al., 2013) are recently popular including continuous word vectors representations from large unstructured texts. Doser (Zwicklbauer et al., 2016) leverages word embeddings as the input of Personalized-PageRank algorithm to disambiguate candidate entities.

Most recently, neural models have been presented as a way to promote better generalization without hand-crafted features. Sun et al. (2015) presents a neural network approach using mention, entity and context embeddings in a unified way. They leverage a Convolutional Neural Network model for context representation and consider positions of context words around mentions. They identify entity disambiguation as a ranking task that computes the similarity between mention-context inputs and candidate entities. Yamada et al. (2016) present a joint learning method combining word and entity embeddings into the same continuous vector space to disambiguate entities. Similar to these two studies, Gupta et al. (2017) extends the joint encoding of context, mention, and entities with a fine-grained type information defined for candidate entities. Similarly, we use this entity type information as a domain indicator to filter the candidate entities.

NeuPL (Phan et al., 2017) employs LSTM and attention mechanism to disambiguate entities. Also, it provides a fast Pair-Linking algorithm which matches mention entity pairs starting from the easiest pair. NeuPL considers positional information and word orderings. Therefore, two LSTM networks are used to model the context of left and right sides of each mention. Our study is similar to NeuPL in terms of resolving closer mention-entity pairs rather than all pairs. Our disambiguation method of closer mention-entity pairs is different from the pair linking method of NeuPL. Our method leverages CRFs to disambiguate closer neighbors as a named entity recognition task for a specific domain.

3 Method

Our study implies Entity Linking as a sequence learning task. For a given sequence mapping between mentions and entities, it consists a set of mentions $M = \{m_1, m_2, ..., m_N\}$ and a set of referent entities $E = \{e_1, e_2, ..., e_N\}$ in the Entity Linking task. In our work, the input size of mentions are equal to the output size of entities for each sequence mapping and N indicates the size of sequence elements rather than defining the size of the entire dictionary. The mention dictionary may contain variations of a proper noun. For instance, founder of the Republic of Turkey is "Mustafa Kemal Ataturk" and M may include "Ataturk", "Mustafa Kemal". Therefore, the size of the entity dictionary is much less than the mention dictionary. Also, sequence mappings contain duplicates and the entity dictionary includes a limited number of unique entities for a specific domain.

In this study, we aim to map each mention to a corresponding entity $(M_i \rightarrow E_i)$ in the given knowledge base for specific domains. Similar to recent studies (Zwicklbauer et al., 2016; Usbeck et al., 2014) we assume that documents with already detected mentions are the inputs of our method. Also, we have another assumption in which every mention contains one or more referent entities in the given knowledge base.

Figure 1 illustrates the general architecture of our method including 3 layers

1. **RDF2Vec Layer:** RDF2Vec (Ristoski and Paulheim, 2016) layer transforms each mention into a numerical d-dimensional vectors. We focus on entities and mentions, relations are not taken into considerations in this study.

2. **Bi-LSTM Layer:** Bidirectional LSTM layer will output hidden vector h_t per time step t and h_t is computed for the given sequence $S = \{r_1, r_2, ..., r_N\}$ where $\overrightarrow{r_t}$ and $\overleftarrow{r_t}$ are

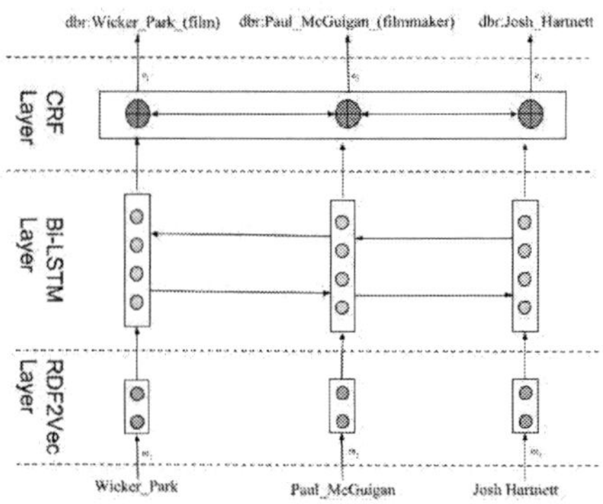

Figure 1: General structure of our method.

forward and backward pass vectors of RDF elements.

3. **CRF Layer:** This layer is composed of full-connected CRFs for ambiguous candidate entities and maps the best mention-entity pairs as a joint disambiguation task for specific domains.

We obtain training data by extracting mentions from Wikipedia and corresponding entities from DBpedia for the movie domain. In the previous sample text about the mention *Wicker Park*, three mentions are detected and these are inputs of RDF2Vec layer. On the other hand, three referent entities of these mentions are given as the output of CRF layer.

To increase ambiguity of training data, we extract Wikipedia disambiguation pages for this type of mentions. For instance, the mention *Wicker Park* has three candidate entities such as *Wicker_Park_(film)*[2], *Wicker_Park_(Chicago_park)*[3] and *Wicker_Park_(soundtrack)*[4]. Also, another mention *Paul_McGuigan* includes two different candidate entities. In the sample text, the last mention *Josh_Hartnett* has only one candidate entity and it can be recognized as an easy tag and is an indicator that this text might be related to the movie domain.

3.1 Candidate Entity Generation

To generate candidate entities we select DBpedia as the base knowledge base. We gather texts with

---

[2]http://dbpedia.org/resource/Wicker_Park_(film)
[3]http://dbpedia.org/resource/Wicker_Park_(Chicago_park)
[4]http://dbpedia.org/resource/Wicker_Park_(soundtrack)

already detected mentions for these entities from Wikipedia pages. For each mention, we query candidate entities and their domain information from DBpedia. To do it, we check "dct:subject" and "rdf:type" properties of entities. Then, mentions and candidate entities with their domain information are recorded in a key-value store.

Wikipedia articles are separated into paragraphs and each paragraph is retrieved in the key-value store whether the paragraph includes any annotated entity. If there is one or more entity in the given paragraph and this paragraph does not exist in the annotated text list, the given paragraph is loaded into a document store. At the same time, Wikipedia disambiguation pages are searched for each mention found in the paragraph. If there exists any disambiguation page for any mention, annotated texts with ambiguous entities are also stored.

3.2 RDF2Vec

RDF2Vec model (Ristoski and Paulheim, 2016) transforms word representations of Word2Vec model into representations of RDF elements such as classes, relations and instances. Instead of using words, dense RDF vectors are generated by entities and relations from the given RDF model. The overall structure of RDF2Vec model is listed as follows:

1. Entity-relation sequences are constructed from one of the strategies (Weistfeiler-Lehman Subtree RDF Graph Kernels, graph walks, etc.)

2. Neural language model is built by either Skip-gram or CBOW algorithm from entity-relation sequences

3. Entity relatedness is computed with Softmax function from the neural language model

Before the neural language model is trained, RDF model is transformed into the form of RDF embeddings. Consequently, each embedding can be represented as a numerical vector in Latent Feature Space. In this study, we do not use graph walks to transform RDF model into entity-relation sequences. Instead, we generate sequences of mentions and their entities considering their positions in the Wikipedia pages. Then, we obtain two different sequence documents for mention and entity sequences like a neural translation model as

denoted in Figure 1. As sketched in this figure, mentions of the sample text of *Wicker Park* and corresponding entity sequences without relations are the input of RDFVec model.

3.3 Bi-LSTM Layer

Recurrent Neural Networks (RNNs) employ sequential information to make predictions. It differs from classical neural networks by considering dependency between sequences of inputs and outputs. RNNs operate recurrent tasks for every element of the sequence and memorizes information what has been computed so far. Bengio et al. (Bengio et al., 1994) emphasizes that RNNs can operate on long sequences in theory but in practice, they fail because they remember their most recent inputs in the sequence. Long Short-term Memory Networks(LSTMs) have been proposed to overcome this problem by producing a memory-cell to operate on long sequences (Hochreiter and Schmidhuber, 1997).

To disambiguate entities, we first operate an LSTM over input and output sequences. It will output the hidden state h_t at timestep t. Then the entity disambiguation rule for e_i^*

$$e_i^* = argmax_j(log\sigma(Ohi + b))_j \qquad (1)$$

where $log\sigma$ is the log softmax function of the hidden state, and e_i^* is the annotated entity which has the highest score in this vector. The output space of O is $|E|x|E|$ dimensions in which E is the length of candidate entities.

For the given input sequences of mentions, this LSTM model computes a representation $\overrightarrow{h_t}$ from beginning to end in this sequence at every mention t. But it may ignore the critical information from the reverse order. To achieve it, a second LSTM operates over the same sequence from end to beginning. Then, this forward and backward LSTM pair denotes as a bidirectional LSTM (Graves and Schmidhuber, 2005). Bi-LSTM represents mentions with its left and right context and it is useful to gather more comprehensive information from the sequences.

3.4 Entity Disambiguation with CRFs

We model the entity disambiguation jointly using a Conditional Random Field (CRF) (Lafferty et al., 2001). In this situation, we use CRF as a sequence model where Bi-LSTM provides features.

Hence, CRF computes a conditional probability as a log-linear formulation

$$p(e|m) = \frac{exp(lp(m,e))}{\sum_{e'} exp(lp(m,e'))} \qquad (2)$$

where m is the input sequence of mentions, e is the output sequence of entities. Then, lp indicates the log potential score of mention and entity sequences. To generate a tractable function, the potentials should be only included at local features. Then we define Emission and Transition as two types of potential scores in the Bi-LSTM CRF. Then, the score is determined for these log potentials such that

$$lp(e,m) = \sum_i log\theta_E(e_i \rightarrow m_i) + log\theta_T(e_{i-1} \rightarrow e_i)$$
$$(3)$$

where $(log\theta_E)$ is the emission potential score for the mention at index i comes from the hidden state of the Bi-LSTM at timestep i. The transition potential scores $(log\theta_T)$ are stored in a $|E|x|E|$ matrix P, where E is the entity dictionary and consists of unique entities from short texts.

We use PyTorch[5] to compute LSTM, Bi-LSTM and CRF models. PyTorch is a dynamic neural network tool in which we can define a computation graph for each instance and can be executed on-the-fly.

4 Experimental Setup

4.1 Dataset Generation

Manually annotated texts tend to be biased because people usually select familiar terms for the entity annotation. Also, this annotation process is sometimes noisy for unpopular terms. Therefore, Wikipedia should be chosen because it is curated by crowdsourcing and involves structured annotation process. MSNBC (Cucerzan, 2007), IITB (Kulkarni et al., 2009) and Wikilinks (Singh et al., 2012) proposes experimental datasets for general entity annotation tasks. Wikilinks provides a large-scale labeled corpus automatically constructed via links to Wikipedia. Wikilinks presents an automated method to identify a collection of massive amounts of entity mentions and is based on crawling anchor links in Wikipedia pages and exploiting anchor text as mentions. However, Wikipedia can also be employed for the level of

ambiguity adjustments in order to use disambiguation pages and this is not directly indicated in Wikilinks.

Ambiguity is the ratio between ambiguous and unique entities and provides more realistic environment to entity annotators (Li et al., 2012). To adjust ambiguity and generate annotated texts for specific domains, we use a recent study (Inan and Dikenelli, 2017) which extracts the latest Wikipedia dump in English[6] for specific domains. To do it, they use Wikipedia category pages and DBpedia "dct:subject"[7] property. Also, they provide an ambiguous environment in which, Wikipedia disambiguation pages are used for the selected domains. As an example, the mention *Wicker Park* has a Wikipedia disambiguation page[8] and it can be used to increase ambiguity in the movie domain.

The movie evaluation dataset involves 123 annotated texts in English. For each text, the average number of entities is 4.99 and there are 614 entities in total. Entities such as movies, directors, and starring are extracted from infoboxes of Wikipedia articles and mapped with referent entities by DBpedia. Disambiguation pages of these entities are extracted in other domains such as music and location to increase the ratio of ambiguity in the evaluation dataset for the movie domain. The ambiguity ratio of the evaluation dataset is 48.79% computed as the division of all ambiguous entities to the total number of unique entities extracted for the movie domain. Therefore, a more realistic ambiguous dataset can be generated to evaluate Entity Linking systems.

4.2 Results

We evaluate our method with several Entity Linking approaches from GERBIL benchmarking framework (Usbeck et al., 2015). We select Disambiguate to Knowledge Base (D2KB) task which focuses on the disambiguation of detected mentions to the related entities in the knowledge base. In this task, a given mention is guaranteed to map to the corresponding entity.

AGDISTIS (Usbeck et al., 2014) chooses candidate entities for the detected mentions from surface forms and generates a disambiguation graph for these candidates. The generated disambiguation graph is used in graph-based HITS algorithm

---

[5]http://pytorch.org/tutorials/index.html

[6]https://dumps.wikimedia.org/enwiki/20170420/
[7]http://purl.org/dc/terms/subject
[8]https://en.wikipedia.org/wiki/Wicker_Park

EL System	Micro-F1	Micro-P	Micro-R	Macro-F1	Macro-P	Macro-R
AGDISTIS	0.2063	0.2097	0.2031	0.3093	0.3098	0.309
AIDA	0.1485	0.1559	0.1417	0.1975	0.2035	0.1932
Babelfy	0.2101	0.2273	0.1953	0.284	0.2887	0.2812
Dbpedia Spotlight	0.1515	0.1515	0.1515	0.2044	0.2044	0.2044
Kea	0.1478	0.149	0.1466	0.1942	0.1976	0.1922
PBOH	0.2193	0.25	0.1953	0.282	0.282	0.282
WAT	0.2174	0.2451	0.1953	0.3124	0.3439	0.2967
LSTM	0.336	0.342	0.33	0.436	0.45	0.422
Bi-LSTM+CRF	0.446	0.488	0.41	0.546	0.564	0.53

Table 1: Evaluation scores of Entity Linking (EL) systems in GERBIL.

to match the best mention-entity pairs in the disambiguation step.

AIDA (Hoffart et al., 2011b) relies on a computation of global coherence between candidate entities and dense subgraph algorithms executing on the YAGO (Hoffart et al., 2011a) knowledge base.

Babelfy uses a graph-based disambiguation algorithm and finds the densest subgraph surrounded by candidate entities for the given mention. Then, Babelfy leverages the densest subgraph to match the best mention and entity pair.

DBpedia Spotlight (Mendes et al., 2011) uses a Vector Space Model (VSM) including DBpedia entity occurrences where a multidimensional word space has a representation per entity. Disambiguation task of DBpedia spotlight transforms Inverse Term Frequency (ITF) into an Inverse Candidate Frequency (ICF) which depends on candidate entities rather than terms and is an inverse proportion of candidate entities associated with words in VSM.

KEA (Waitelonis and Sack, 2016) proposes a combination of dictionary and knowledge based approaches. They analyze word co-occurrences of Wikipedia pages and merge these co-occurences with a graph analysis on the Wikipedia link structure and DBpedia.

PBOH (Ganea et al., 2016) is a collective entity linking system that is based on lightweight Wikipedia statistics. PBOH computes co-occurrence of words and entities for a probabilistic graphical model.

WAT (Piccinno and Ferragina, 2014) system is a complex version of TagMe (Ferragina and Scaiella, 2010). WAT depends on graph-based algorithm and selection of the best mention-entity pair from a vote-based algorithm.

Cornolti et al. (2013) expands general F1 measures to the Macro- and Micro- measures. While Macro- measures are the average of the corresponding measure over each document in all annotated documents, the Micro- measures consider all tags together thus giving more importance to documents having more tags. Table 1 illustrates the overall scores for Entity Linking task is measured in the generated evaluation set with respect to precision, recall, and F1-score. All scores are low because of high ambiguity of the generated evaluation dataset. F1 scores show that our study outperforms state-of-the-art studies using Bi-LSTM+CRF model on the generated evaluation dataset in the movie domain.

5 Conclusion

This study mainly presents a sequence learning method for domain-specific entity linking using sequence learning as a neural machine translation task. We filter candidate entities leveraging domain information and eliminating easy matches of mention-entity pairs. We employ a domain-specific dataset to compare our work with existing studies in GERBIL. Our method outperforms the state-of-the-art methods in the domain-specific configuration.

In the future, we apply other decoder models using the attention mechanism to the current model as a different joint disambiguation method of candidate entities. Also, we will examine many domain-specific datasets on this method.

References

Yoshua Bengio, Patrice Simard, and Paolo Frasconi. 1994. Learning long-term dependencies with gradient descent is difficult. *IEEE transactions on neural networks*, 5(2):157–166.

Razvan Bunescu and Marius Paşca. 2006. Using encyclopedic knowledge for named entity disambiguation. In *11th conference of the European Chapter of the Association for Computational Linguistics*.

Marco Cornolti, Paolo Ferragina, and Massimiliano Ciaramita. 2013. A framework for benchmarking entity-annotation systems. In *Proceedings of the 22nd international conference on World Wide Web*, pages 249–260. ACM.

Silviu Cucerzan. 2007. Large-scale named entity disambiguation based on wikipedia data. In *Proceedings of the 2007 Joint Conference on Empirical Methods in Natural Language Processing and Computational Natural Language Learning (EMNLP-CoNLL)*.

Paolo Ferragina and Ugo Scaiella. 2010. Tagme: On-the-fly annotation of short text fragments (by wikipedia entities). In *Proceedings of the 19th ACM International Conference on Information and Knowledge Management*, CIKM '10, pages 1625–1628, New York, NY, USA. ACM.

Octavian-Eugen Ganea, Marina Ganea, Aurelien Lucchi, Carsten Eickhoff, and Thomas Hofmann. 2016. Probabilistic bag-of-hyperlinks model for entity linking. In *Proceedings of the 25th International Conference on World Wide Web*, pages 927–938. International World Wide Web Conferences Steering Committee.

Alex Graves and Jürgen Schmidhuber. 2005. Framewise phoneme classification with bidirectional lstm and other neural network architectures. *Neural Networks*, 18(5-6):602–610.

Nitish Gupta, Sameer Singh, and Dan Roth. 2017. Entity linking via joint encoding of types, descriptions, and context. In *Proceedings of the 2017 Conference on Empirical Methods in Natural Language Processing*, pages 2681–2690.

Sepp Hochreiter and Jürgen Schmidhuber. 1997. Long short-term memory. *Neural computation*, 9(8):1735–1780.

Johannes Hoffart, Fabian M Suchanek, Klaus Berberich, Edwin Lewis-Kelham, Gerard De Melo, and Gerhard Weikum. 2011a. Yago2: exploring and querying world knowledge in time, space, context, and many languages. In *Proceedings of the 20th international conference companion on World wide web*, pages 229–232. ACM.

Johannes Hoffart, Fabian M. Suchanek, Klaus Berberich, and Gerhard Weikum. 2013. Yago2: A spatially and temporally enhanced knowledge base from wikipedia. *Artif. Intell.*, 194:28–61.

Johannes Hoffart, Mohamed Amir Yosef, Ilaria Bordino, Hagen Fürstenau, Manfred Pinkal, Marc Spaniol, Bilyana Taneva, Stefan Thater, and Gerhard Weikum. 2011b. Robust disambiguation of named entities in text. In *Proceedings of the Conference on Empirical Methods in Natural Language Processing*, pages 782–792. Association for Computational Linguistics.

Emrah Inan and Oguz Dikenelli. 2017. Wedgem: A domain-specific evaluation dataset generator for multilingual entity linking systems. In *International Conference on Web Information Systems Engineering*, pages 221–228. Springer.

Sayali Kulkarni, Amit Singh, Ganesh Ramakrishnan, and Soumen Chakrabarti. 2009. Collective annotation of wikipedia entities in web text. In *Proceedings of the 15th ACM SIGKDD international conference on Knowledge discovery and data mining*, pages 457–466. ACM.

John Lafferty, Andrew McCallum, and Fernando CN Pereira. 2001. Conditional random fields: Probabilistic models for segmenting and labeling sequence data.

Guillaume Lample, Miguel Ballesteros, Sandeep Subramanian, Kazuya Kawakami, and Chris Dyer. 2016. Neural architectures for named entity recognition. *arXiv preprint arXiv:1603.01360*.

Xuansong Li, Stephanie M Strassel, Heng Ji, Kira Griffitt, and Joe Ellis. 2012. Linguistic resources for entity linking evaluation: from monolingual to cross-lingual. *Annotation*, 1:1.

Pablo N. Mendes, Max Jakob, Andrés García-Silva, and Christian Bizer. 2011. Dbpedia spotlight: Shedding light on the web of documents. In *Proceedings of the 7th International Conference on Semantic Systems*, I-Semantics '11, pages 1–8, New York, NY, USA. ACM.

Rada Mihalcea and Andras Csomai. 2007. Wikify!: linking documents to encyclopedic knowledge. In *Proceedings of the sixteenth ACM conference on Conference on information and knowledge management*, pages 233–242. ACM.

Tomas Mikolov, Kai Chen, Greg Corrado, and Jeffrey Dean. 2013. Efficient estimation of word representations in vector space. *arXiv preprint arXiv:1301.3781*.

David Milne and Ian H. Witten. 2008. Learning to link with wikipedia. In *Proceedings of the 17th ACM Conference on Information and Knowledge Management*, CIKM '08, pages 509–518, New York, NY, USA. ACM.

Pasquale Minervini, Claudia d'Amato, Nicola Fanizzi, and Floriana Esposito. 2016. Leveraging the schema in latent factor models for knowledge graph completion. In *Proceedings of the 31st Annual ACM Symposium on Applied Computing, Pisa, Italy, April 4-8, 2016*, pages 327–332.

Andrea Moro, Alessandro Raganato, and Roberto Navigli. 2014. Entity Linking meets Word Sense Disambiguation: a Unified Approach. *Transactions of the*

Association for Computational Linguistics (TACL), 2:231–244.

Dat Ba Nguyen, Johannes Hoffart, Martin Theobald, and Gerhard Weikum. 2014. Aida-light: High-throughput named-entity disambiguation. In *LDOW*, volume 1184 of *CEUR Workshop Proceedings*. CEUR-WS.org.

Maximilian Nickel, Kevin Murphy, Volker Tresp, and Evgeniy Gabrilovich. 2015. A review of relational machine learning for knowledge graphs: From multi-relational link prediction to automated knowledge graph construction. *CoRR*, abs/1503.00759.

Minh C Phan, Aixin Sun, Yi Tay, Jialong Han, and Chenliang Li. 2017. Neupl: Attention-based semantic matching and pair-linking for entity disambiguation. In *Proceedings of the 2017 ACM on Conference on Information and Knowledge Management*, pages 1667–1676. ACM.

Francesco Piccinno and Paolo Ferragina. 2014. From tagme to WAT: a new entity annotator. In *ERD'14, Proceedings of the First ACM International Workshop on Entity Recognition & Disambiguation, July 11, 2014, Gold Coast, Queensland, Australia*, pages 55 62.

Lev Ratinov, Dan Roth, Doug Downey, and Mike Anderson. 2011. Local and global algorithms for disambiguation to wikipedia. In *Proceedings of the 49th Annual Meeting of the Association for Computational Linguistics: Human Language Technologies-Volume 1*, pages 1375–1384. Association for Computational Linguistics.

Petar Ristoski and Heiko Paulheim. 2016. Rdf2vec: RDF graph embeddings for data mining. In *The Semantic Web - ISWC 2016 - 15th International Semantic Web Conference, Kobe, Japan, October 17-21, 2016, Proceedings, Part I*, pages 498–514.

Sameer Singh, Amarnag Subramanya, Fernando Pereira, and Andrew McCallum. 2012. Wikilinks: A large-scale cross-document coreference corpus labeled via links to wikipedia. *University of Massachusetts, Amherst, Tech. Rep. UM-CS-2012-015*.

Yaming Sun, Lei Lin, Duyu Tang, Nan Yang, Zhenzhou Ji, and Xiaolong Wang. 2015. Modeling mention, context and entity with neural networks for entity disambiguation. In *IJCAI*, pages 1333–1339.

Ricardo Usbeck, Axel-Cyrille Ngonga Ngomo, Michael Röder, Daniel Gerber, SandroAthaide Coelho, Sören Auer, and Andreas Both. 2014. AGDISTIS - Graph-Based Disambiguation of Named Entities Using Linked Data. In Peter Mika, Tania Tudorache, Abraham Bernstein, Chris Welty, Craig Knoblock, Denny Vrandečić, Paul Groth, Natasha Noy, Krzysztof Janowicz, and Carole Goble, editors, *The Semantic Web – ISWC 2014*, volume 8796 of *Lecture Notes in Computer Science*, pages 457–471. Springer International Publishing.

Ricardo Usbeck, Michael Röder, Axel-Cyrille Ngonga Ngomo, Ciro Baron, Andreas Both, Martin Brümmer, Diego Ceccarelli, Marco Cornolti, Didier Cherix, Bernd Eickmann, Paolo Ferragina, Christiane Lemke, Andrea Moro, Roberto Navigli, Francesco Piccinno, Giuseppe Rizzo, Harald Sack, René Speck, Raphaël Troncy, Jörg Waitelonis, and Lars Wesemann. 2015. GERBIL – general entity annotation benchmark framework. In *24th WWW conference*.

Jörg Waitelonis and Harald Sack. 2016. Named entity linking in# tweets with kea. In *# Microposts*, pages 61–63.

Jason Weston, Antoine Bordes, Oksana Yakhnenko, and Nicolas Usunier. 2013. Connecting language and knowledge bases with embedding models for relation extraction. In *Proceedings of the 2013 Conference on Empirical Methods in Natural Language Processing, EMNLP 2013, 18-21 October 2013, Grand Hyatt Seattle, Seattle, Washington, USA, A meeting of SIGDAT, a Special Interest Group of the ACL*, pages 1366–1371.

Ikuya Yamada, Hiroyuki Shindo, Hideaki Takeda, and Yoshiyasu Takefuji. 2016. Joint learning of the embedding of words and entities for named entity disambiguation. *arXiv preprint arXiv:1601.01343*.

Stefan Zwicklbauer, Christin Seifert, and Michael Granitzer. 2016. *DoSeR - A Knowledge-Base-Agnostic Framework for Entity Disambiguation Using Semantic Embeddings*. Springer International Publishing, Cham.

Attention-based Semantic Priming for Slot-filling

**Jiewen Wu[1,2], Rafael E. Banchs[2], Luis Fernando D'Haro[2],
Pavitra Krishnaswamy[2], and Nancy Chen[2]**

[1]A*STAR AI Initiative, Singapore
[2]Institute for Infocomm Research, A*STAR, Singapore
{wujw, rembanchs, luisdhe, pavitrak, nfychen}@i2r.a-star.edu.sg

Abstract

The problem of sequence labelling in language understanding would benefit from approaches inspired by semantic priming phenomena. We propose that an attention-based RNN architecture can be used to simulate semantic priming for sequence labelling. Specifically, we employ pre-trained word embeddings to characterize the semantic relationship between utterances and labels. We validate the approach using varying sizes of the ATIS and MEDIA datasets, and show up to 1.4-1.9% improvement in F1 score. The developed framework can enable more explainable and generalizable spoken language understanding systems.

1 Introduction

Priming (Waltz and Pollack, 1985) is a cognitive mechanism in which a primary stimulus (i.e. the prime) influences the response to a subsequent stimulus (i.e. the target) in an implicit and intuitive manner. In the case of *semantic priming*, both the prime and the target typically belong to the same semantic category. Semantic priming can be explained in terms of induced activation in associative neural networks (McClelland and Rogers, 2003). Further, there is empirical evidence to suggest that the processing of words in natural language is influenced by preceding words that are semantically related (Foss, 1982). Therefore, semantic priming approaches would enable improvements in sequence labelling.

Previous studies have leveraged contextual information in utterance sequences (Mesnil et al., 2015) and dependencies between labels (Ma and Hovy, 2016) to improve performance in sequence labelling tasks. However, there is limited work to use contextual information in utterances to inform inference of the subsequent labels through semantic priming. For instance, *"I'd like to book ..."* not only suggests the next word(s), e.g., flight, but also the label of the next word(s), e.g., *services.* We posit that systems employing this mode of cross-linked semantic priming could enhance performance in a variety of sequence labelling tasks.

In this work, we hypothesize that semantic priming in human cognition can be simulated by means of an attention mechanism that uses word context to enhance the discriminating power of sequence labelling models. We propose and explore the use of attention (Bahdanau et al., 2014) in a deep learning architecture to simulate the semantic priming mechanism. We apply this concept to slot filling, an example of sequence labelling in spoken language understanding, which aims to label the utterance sequences with a set of begin/in/out (BIO) tags. Specifically, we use pre-trained word embeddings to characterise not only the context of words, but also the semantic relationship between words in utterances and words in labels.

Overall, we develop a semantic priming based approach for the task of slot-filling to associate utterances and label sequences. Our contributions are as follows: (1) We propose an approach that applies semantic priming to sequence labelling. To capture semantic associations between utterance words and label words, we use three different strategies for deriving label embeddings from pre-trained embeddings. (2) We implemented the approach in an LSTM-based architecture and validate the efficacy of the approach.

In Section 2 we review related work. Section 3 elaborates the proposed approach. An empirical evaluation is provided in Section 4. Finally, Section 5 concludes the paper.

2 Related Work

Our proposed method draws on the attention mechanism, which has shown to be effective for

Proceedings of the Seventh Named Entities Workshop, pages 22–26
Melbourne, Australia, July 20, 2018. ©2018 Association for Computational Linguistics

sequence-based NLP tasks, particularly, machine translation (Bahdanau et al., 2014; Luong et al., 2015). Since attention allows the neural networks to dynamically attend to important features in the inputs, it is a suitable mechanism to achieve the objective of semantic priming between utterances and labels. Conditional random field (CRF) has been used together with RNNs, sometimes also including CNNs, to improve accuracy (Mesnil et al., 2013, 2015; Ma and Hovy, 2016; Reimers and Gurevych, 2017b). Dinarelli et al. (2017) proposes to learn label embedding for improving tagging accuracy, while our label embedding is computed directly from pre-trained word embeddings. Furthermore, our approach does not require shifted label sequences as input.

To use external knowledge, previous studies consider graph or entity embedding (Huang et al., 2017; Chen et al., 2016; Yang and Mitchell, 2017), together with other contextual information, such as dependency graph (Huang et al., 2017) or sentence structures (Chen et al., 2016). Specifically, Yang and Mitchell (2017) extends LSTM with graph embedding to learn concepts from knowledge bases and integrate the concept embedding into the state vectors of words. In contrast, our approach does not learn or parse sentences to get extra contextual information, which is suitable for languages lacking well trained parsers. Moreover, context integration is achieved without fine-tuning the underlying RNN structure yet rather through the attention mechanism.

3　Semantic Priming

Figure 1 depicts an LSTM-based neural network architecture for semantic priming. Given an utterance, a priming matrix is computed to connect the labels to input features generated by a bi-directional LSTM. The priming effects are then used for prediction.

3.1　Computing Priming Matrix

This section considers three different strategies of the proposed attention-based semantic priming mechanism. In all the three cases the input words are compared to proxies of the semantic categories over word vectors.

Let m denote the number of labels. An utterance of length n is represented by the matrix $X : n \times k$, where k is the dimension of pre-trained word vectors. Given a word vector x_j, semantic priming is achieved by comparing x_j with a label embedding matrix $L : m' \times k$, with m' unique con-

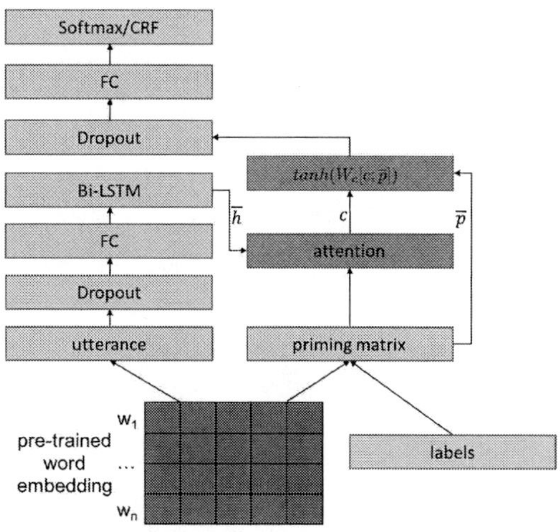

Figure 1: Proposed topology for priming. FC denotes a fully connected layer.

cepts, each encoded in k dimensions. In addition, let $E_{l_i, 1 \leq i \leq m'}$ denote the set of embedded words tagged with the label l_i in the dataset. Note that the corresponding embedding of l_i is L_i. Below are the definitions of three different strategies to compute the label embeddings L.

- Priming using Instance Centroid (**PIC**): L is defined to be $m \times k$ and $L_i = mean(E_{l_i})$. Intuitively, the proxy of the concept, L_i, is the centroid (mean vector) of the cluster of all known instance words in the concept.

- Priming using Instance Neighbor (**PIN**): L is defined to be $m \times k$ and

$$L_i = \underset{\forall e \in E_{l_i}}{\operatorname{argmin}}(1 - cos(x_j, e))$$

In this case, the proxy of the concept is the nearest instance having the same label as x_j.

- Priming using Concepts (**PC**): L is defined to be $m' \times k$, m' is pre-specified, and $L_i = \mathbf{c}_i$, where c_i is a manually selected concept from l_i. The embedding representation, $\mathbf{c}_i$, is of dimension k as it is either the word vector per se of a single concept label or the mean vector of a set of such word vectors.

While **PIN** is a straightforward simulation of the semantic priming mechanism between a prime and its potential targets in different classes, **PIC** and **PC** are variants of a categorization mechanism referred to as the Basic Level (Rosch et al., 1976), in which the targets are intermediate, dominant concepts that represent the category.

	ATIS	MEDIA
# utterances in train	3982	12908
# utterances in dev	995	1259
# utterances in test	893	3005
# labels	127	138
vocab. size[†]	572	1671
max utterance length	46	192

Table 1: Statistics of datasets. [†]The vocabulary is a mix of words and entities.

Once L is computed, the priming matrix is computed by the cosine similarity, or the induced distance, between the word embedding of the utterance and L, i.e., $\overline{p} = cos(X, L)$.

3.2 Attention to Semantic Priming

In Figure 1, the hidden states, $\overline{h}$, of the bi-directional LSTM are considered to be the source, while the priming matrix $\overline{p}$ is analogous to the target. Following (Luong et al., 2015), we define the alignment scoring function to be $s(\overline{p}, h) = \overline{p}W_a h$ and compute the final output as follows:

$$\alpha = \frac{exp(s(\overline{p}, h))}{\sum_{i=1}^{n} exp(s(\overline{p}, h_i))}$$
$$c = \sum_{h} \alpha h$$
$$t = tanh(W_c[c; \overline{p}])$$

4 Experiments

To validate the efficacy of the architecture in Figure 1, an empirical evaluation was performed and implemented in Keras[1]. This section elaborates the experimental setup and presents our results.

4.1 Datasets

Two datasets on spoken dialogues were used in the experiments, namely, the Air Travel Information System (ATIS) task (Dahl et al., 1994) and MEDIA, French dialogues collected by ELDA (Bonneau-Maynard et al., 2005). The statistics of the two datasets is given in Table 1. For MEDIA, using entities significantly impacts the performance. Thus entities are used together with words in utterances, as implied by the size of vocabulary in Table 1. Since bi-directional LSTM is used in the architecture in Figure 1, no context word windows (Mesnil et al., 2015) were used as additional inputs in the datasets. The pre-trained

word embedding sources for the two datasets are GloVe (English) (Pennington et al., 2014) and fast-Text (French) (Bojanowski et al., 2016), respectively. In particular, we found that there are about 100 words missing in the fastText French word embedding. Some of the words, however, are due to original tokenization in MEDIA.

4.2 Setup and Hyperparameters

To facilitate mini-batching for training, the utterances were padded to the maximum utterance length. For all experiments, we use one set of fixed hyperparameters to enable meaingful comparison. The dimension of word embedding is 300 for both GloVe and fastText. Following the recommendations in (Reimers and Gurevych, 2017a), all dropout layers have a rate of 0.5, and LSTM has an additional recurrent dropout of 0.5 between recurrent units. During learning phase, a mini-batch size of 18 and an initial learning rate of 0.004 was used with the Adam optimizer to minimize the cross-entropy loss. The learning rate was reduced by 50% after no improvement in three epochs.

As semantic priming provides connections between words and labels through the use of the same pre-training embedding, it will enable more robust performance even when the datasets are small. To validate this, we investigated the effects of semantic priming in cases where the datasets are reduced. Note that both ATIS and MEDIA have many short utterances; in particular, MEDIA has over 4000 utterances consisting of a single word. For reduction, we rank vocabulary by word frequency in the training and development sets and choose utterances containing the words until 100% of vocabulary is covered.

4.3 Results

In this section the conlleval-F1[2] scores are reported. The experiments were run on a NVIDIA DGX1 station (Tesla V100 and 16GB memory), and the F1 scores are the average of that in the first 30 epochs in three independent runs.

The results shown are for baseline with trainable embedding (**BE**), baseline with pre-trained embedding (**BP**), and the strategies defined in Section 3.1, i.e., **PIC**, **PIN** and **PC**. For **PC**, the concepts are the keywords that have occurred in the labels. Example concepts include *airline* in ATIS and *chambre* in MEDIA. A total of 30 and 53 concepts are extracted for **PC** in ATIS and MEDIA, respectively.

---

[1] https://keras.io/

[2] http://www.cnts.ua.ac.be/conll2000/chunking/output.html

Although **BE** yields much higher F1, we compare the proposed approach with the baseline approach, **BP**, where F1 is computed using pre-trained embedding. This is because all strategies, except for **BE**, are based on pre-trained word embedding. We also compare the results in the MEDIA dataset with and without CRF. Since CRF in ATIS was shown to lead to no improvement (Dinarelli et al., 2017), so, no CRF layer was applied to ATIS in the experiments.

	ATIS	MEDIA	
BP	94.22	**72.66**	79.46†
PIC	94.23	69.37	80.49†
PIN	94.41	69.79	**80.56**†
PC	**94.51**	72.55	78.35†
BE	94.75	82.16	86.38†

Table 2: F1 of the two datasets. †CRF used.

Table 2 shows the F1 computed over the full datasets. In ATIS, although no significant conclusions can be drawn, all strategies, in particular, **PC**, outperform the baseline **BP**. Note that, when CRF, instead of SOFTMAX, is used in MEDIA, there is an increase of 4% for **BE**, 7% for **BP**, and 10% for **PIC/PIN**. For MEDIA, F1 has a considerable drop when pre-trained word embedding is used instead of trainable embedding. When SOFTMAX is used, none of the strategies outperformed the baselines **BP** or **BE**. In contrast, once CRF is used both **PIC** and **PIN** gained over 1% increase compared with **BP**.

	ATIS$_{100}$	MEDIA$_{100}$	
BP	85.39	67.64	76.95†
PIC	**87.25**	66.84	76.81†
PIN	86.31	**68.25**	**78.34**†
PC	87.01	67.37	77.95†
BE	86.04	78.81	83.77†

Table 3: F1 of the reduced datasets. †CRF used. 100% of the vocabulary in datasets are retained.

Table 3 describes the results over reduced datasets that cover the full (100%) vocabulary in the datasets. ATIS$_{100}$ has a total of 583 utterances for training/development, while MEDIA$_{100}$ has 1717 for training/development. Note that reduction was *not* performed to test datasets, i.e., full test sets were used. For both ATIS and MEDIA,

PIN shows consistent performance gain (+1%) over the pre-trained baseline approach (**BP**).

	ATIS$_{70}$	MEDIA$_{70}$	
BP	83.21	65.37	76.34†
PIC	83.23	**66.44**	75.2†
PIN	82.65	66.09	**77.12**†
PC	**83.4**	65.75	75.4†
BE	81.62	76.3	80.3†

Table 4: F1 of the reduced datasets. †CRF used. 70% of the vocabulary in datasets are retained.

Table 4 describes the results over further reduced datasets, i.e., these two reduced datasets covers only 70%[3] of the whole vocabulary, containing 348 and 1216 utterances (train/dev) for ATIS and MEDIA, respectively. As shown in Table 4, **PC** was the best strategy for ATIS while **PIN** consistently outperformed the baseline **BP** in MEDIA.

Overall, we have seen performance gains when priming is used over the original and reduced datasets, compared to the pre-trained baseline approach **BP**. In particular, we recommend **PIN** over the other strategies as it is less computational expensive compared with **PIC** while it seems to provide more consistent improvement over **BP** than other strategies.

5 Conclusions and Future Work

We have demonstrated an approach to leverage semantic priming for natural language understanding tasks. The approach employs pre-trained embeddings to prime label concepts based on utterance words. Our experimental results suggest improvements over baselines are feasible. However, we note that the coverage of the dataset vocabulary in the pre-trained word embedding may limit performance improvements. For example, the missing words in the pre-trained French word embedding adversely affected the F1 scores for MEDIA. The approach can be easily adapted to a variety of different network architectures (e.g., (Dinarelli et al., 2017)) and word embeddings (e.g., (Reimers and Gurevych, 2017a)). Future studies will focus on how to choose a good set of concepts for the PC priming strategy. It will also be fruitful to understand how to explain the sequence labelling outputs using attention mechanisms.

---

[3]70% allows for a considerable reduction of the full vocabulary yet not resulting in too small datasets.

References

Dzmitry Bahdanau, Kyunghyun Cho, and Yoshua Bengio. 2014. Neural machine translation by jointly learning to align and translate. *CoRR*, abs/1409.0473.

Piotr Bojanowski, Edouard Grave, Armand Joulin, and Tomas Mikolov. 2016. Enriching word vectors with subword information. *arXiv preprint arXiv:1607.04606*.

Helene Bonneau-Maynard, Sophie Rosset, Christelle Ayache, A Kuhn, and Djamel Mostefa. 2005. Semantic annotation of the french media dialog corpus.

Yun-Nung Chen, Dilek Z. Hakkani-Tür, Gökhan Tür, Asli Çelikyilmaz, Jianfeng Gao, and Li Deng. 2016. Knowledge as a teacher: Knowledge-guided structural attention networks. *CoRR*, abs/1609.03286.

Deborah A. Dahl, Madeleine Bates, Michael Brown, William Fisher, Kate Hunicke-Smith, David Pallett, Christine Pao, Alexander Rudnicky, and Elizabeth Shriberg. 1994. Expanding the scope of the atis task: The atis-3 corpus. In *Proceedings of the Workshop on Human Language Technology*, HLT '94, pages 43–48, Stroudsburg, PA, USA. Association for Computational Linguistics.

Marco Dinarelli, Vedran Vukotic, and Christian Raymond. 2017. Label-dependency coding in simple recurrent networks for spoken language understanding. In *INTERSPEECH*.

Donald Foss. 1982. A discourse on semantic priming. *Cognitive Psychology*, 14:590?607.

Lifu Huang, Avirup Sil, Heng Ji, and Radu Florian. 2017. Improving slot filling performance with attentive neural networks on dependency structures. In *EMNLP*.

Thang Luong, Hieu Pham, and Christopher D. Manning. 2015. Effective approaches to attention-based neural machine translation. In *EMNLP*.

Xuezhe Ma and Eduard Hovy. 2016. End-to-end sequence labeling via bi-directional lstm-cnns-crf. In *Proceedings of the 54th Annual Meeting of the Association for Computational Linguistics (Volume 1: Long Papers)*, pages 1064–1074, Berlin, Germany. Association for Computational Linguistics.

James L. McClelland and Timothy T. Rogers. 2003. The parallel distributed processing approach to semantic cognition. *Nature Reviews Neuroscience*, 4:310–322.

Grégoire Mesnil, Yann Dauphin, Kaisheng Yao, Yoshua Bengio, Li Deng, Dilek Hakkani-Tur, Xiaodong He, Larry Heck, Gokhan Tur, Dong Yu, and Geoffrey Zweig. 2015. Using recurrent neural networks for slot filling in spoken language understanding. *Trans. Audio, Speech and Lang. Proc.*, 23(3):530–539.

Grégoire Mesnil, Xiaodong He, Li Deng, and Yoshua Bengio. 2013. Investigation of recurrent-neural-network architectures and learning methods for spoken language understanding. In *INTERSPEECH*.

Jeffrey Pennington, Richard Socher, and Christopher D. Manning. 2014. Glove: Global vectors for word representation. In *Empirical Methods in Natural Language Processing (EMNLP)*, pages 1532–1543.

Nils Reimers and Iryna Gurevych. 2017a. Optimal hyperparameters for deep lstm-networks for sequence labeling tasks. *CoRR*, abs/1707.06799.

Nils Reimers and Iryna Gurevych. 2017b. Reporting Score Distributions Makes a Difference: Performance Study of LSTM-networks for Sequence Tagging. In *Proceedings of the 2017 Conference on Empirical Methods in Natural Language Processing (EMNLP)*, pages 338–348, Copenhagen, Denmark.

Eleanor Rosch, Carolyn B Mervis, Wayne D Gray, David M Johnson, and Penny Boyes-Braem. 1976. Basic objects in natural categories. *Cognitive Psychology*, 8(3):382 – 439.

David L. Waltz and Jordan B. Pollack. 1985. Massively parallel parsing: A strongly interactive model of natural language interpretation. *Cognitive Science*, 9(1):51 – 74.

Bishan Yang and Tom M. Mitchell. 2017. Leveraging knowledge bases in lstms for improving machine reading. In *ACL*.

Named Entity Recognition for Hindi-English Code-Mixed Social Media Text

Vinay Singh, Deepanshu Vijay, Syed S. Akhtar, Manish Shrivastava
Language Technologies Research Centre (LTRC)
International Institute of Information Technology Hyderabad, Telangana, India
{vinay.singh, deepanshu.vijay, syed.akhtar}@research.iiit.ac.in
m.shrivastava@iiit.ac.in

Abstract

Named Entity Recognition (NER) is a major task in the field of Natural Language Processing (NLP), and also is a sub-task of Information Extraction. The challenge of NER for tweets lies in the insufficient information available in a tweet. There has been a significant amount of work done related to entity extraction, but only for resource rich languages and domains such as the newswire. Entity extraction is, in general, a challenging task for such an informal text, and code-mixed text further complicates the process with it's unstructured and incomplete information. We propose experiments with different machine learning classification algorithms with word, character and lexical features. The algorithms we experimented with are Decision tree, Long Short-Term Memory (LSTM), and Conditional Random Field (CRF). In this paper, we present a corpus for NER in Hindi-English Code-Mixed along with extensive experiments on our machine learning models which achieved the best f1-score of 0.95 with both CRF and LSTM.

1 Introduction

Multilingual speakers often switch back and forth between languages when speaking or writing, mostly in informal settings. This language interchange involves complex grammar, and the terms "code-switching" and "code-mixing" are used to describe it Lipski. Code-mixing refers to the use of linguistic units from different languages in a single utterance or sentence, whereas code-switching refers to the co-occurrence of speech extracts belonging to two different grammatical systems Gumperz. As both phenomena are frequently observed on social media platforms in similar contexts, we use only the code-mixing scenario in this work.

Following are some instances from a Twitter corpus of Hindi-English code-mixed texts also transliterated in English.

T1 : *"Finally India away series jeetne mein successful ho hi gayi :D"*

Translation: *"Finally India got success in winning the away series :D"*

T2 : *"This is a big surprise that Rahul Gandhi congress ke naye president hain."*

Translation: *"This is a big surprise that Rahul Gandhi is the new president of Congress."*

However, before delving further into code-mixed data, it is important to first address the complications in social media data itself. First, the shortness of micro-blogs makes them hard to interpret. Consequently, ambiguity is a major problem since semantic annotation methods cannot easily make use of co-reference information. Second, micro-texts exhibit much more language variation, tend to be less grammatical than longer posts, contain unorthodox capitalization, and make frequent use of emoticons, abbreviations and hashtags, which can form an important part of the meaning. Most of the research has, however, been focused on resource rich languages, such as English Sarkar, GermanTjong Kim Sang and De Meulder, French Azpeitia et al. and Spanish Zea et al.. However entity extraction and recognition from social media text for Indian languages Saha et al.; Ekbal and Bandyopadhyay; Malarkodi et al. and Code-Mixed text Gupta et al. have been

Proceedings of the Seventh Named Entities Workshop, pages 27–35
Melbourne, Australia, July 20, 2018. ©2018 Association for Computational Linguistics

introduced a bit late. Chieu and Ng A shared task in FIRE-15 workshop[1] and explicitly NER task on Code-Mixed in FIRE 2016[2].

The structure of the paper is as follows. In Section 2, we review related research in the area of Named Entity Extraction on code-mixed social media texts. In Section 3, we describe the corpus creation and annotation scheme. In Section 4, we discuss the data statistics. In Section 5, we summarize our classification systems which includes the pre-processing steps and construction of feature vector. In Section 6, we present the results of experiments conducted using various character, word level and lexical features using different machine learning models. In the last section, we conclude our paper, followed by future work and the references.

2 Background and Related work

Bali et al. performed analysis of data from Facebook posts generated by English-Hindi bilingual users. Analysis depicted that significant amount of code-mixing was present in the posts. Vyas et al. formalized the problem, created a POS tag annotated Hindi-English code-mixed corpus and reported the challenges and problems in the Hindi-English code-mixed text. They also performed experiments on language identification, transliteration, normalization and POS tagging of the Dataset. Sharma et al. addressed the problem of shallow parsing of Hindi-English code-mixed social media text and developed a system for Hindi-English code-mixed text that can identify the language of the words, normalize them to their standard forms, assign them their POS tag and segment into chunks. Barman et al. addressed the problem of language identification on Bengali-Hindi-English Facebook comments.

In Named Entity Recognition there has been significant research done so far in English and other resource rich languages Morwal et al.; Srihari et al., but same cannot be said for code-mixed text due to lack of structured resources in this domain. Bhargava et al. proposed a hybrid model for NER on Hindi-English and Tamil-English code-mixed Dataset. Bhat et al. proposed a neural network architecture for NER on Hindi-English code-mixed Dataset. Code-mixing got attention in FIRE-2016 with the introduction of tasks on Code-

Mixed resources. Now code-mixing has found its application in different areas such as Query Labeling Bhargava et al., Sentiment Analysis Bhargava et al., Question Classification etc.

3 Corpus and Annotation

The corpus that we created for Hindi-English code-mixed tweets contains tweets from last 8 years on topics like politics, social events, sports, etc. from the Indian subcontinent perspective. The tweets were scrapped from Twitter using the Twitter Python API[3] which uses the advanced search option of twitter. The mining of the tweets are done using some specific hash-tags and are mined in a json format which consist all the information regarding the tweets like time-stamps, URL, text, user, replies, etc. Extensive pre-processing (Section 5.4) was carried out to remove the noisy and non-useful tweets. Noisy tweets are the ones which comprise only of hashtags or urls. Also, tweets in which languages other than Hindi or English are used were also considered as noisy and hence removed from the corpus . Furthermore, all the tweets which were either in only English or used Devanagari script text are removed too, keeping only the code-mixed tweets. Further cleaning of data is done in the annotation phase.

3.1 Annotation: Named Entity Tagging

We label the tags with the present three Named Entity tags 'Person', 'Organization', 'Location', which using the BIO standard become six NE tags (B-Tag referring to beginning of a named entity and I-Tag refers to the intermediate of the entity) along with the 'Other' tag to all those which don't lie in any of the six NE tags.

'Per' tag refers to the 'Person' entity which is the name of a Person, twitter handles and common nick names of people. The 'B-Per' states the beginning and 'I-Per' for the name of the Person, if the Person name or reference is split into multiple continuous. In the example **T3** we show the instance of 'Per' tag in a tweet chosen from our corpus.

T3: *"modi/B-Per ji/I-Per na/Other kya/Other de/Other rakha/Other hai/Other media/B-Org ko/Other ?/Other"*

Translation: "What has modi ji given to media?"

[1]http://fire.irsi.res.in/fire/2015/home
[2]http://www.au-kbc.org/nlp/CMEE-FIRE2016/
[3]https://pypi.python.org/pypi/twitterscraper/0.2.7

Tag	Count of Tokens
B-Loc	762
B-Org	1,432
B-Per	2,138
I-Loc	31
I-Org	90
I-Per	554
Total NE tokens	5,007

Table 1: Tags and their Count in Corpus

	Cohen Kappa
B-Loc	0.98
B-Org	0.96
B-Per	0.94
I-Loc	0.98
I-Org	0.91
I-Per	0.93

Table 2: Inter Annotator Agreement.

'Loc' tag refers to the location named entity which is assigned to the names of places for eg. 'Kashmir', '#Delhi', 'Hindustan', etc. The 'B-Loc' states the beginning and 'I-Loc' intermediate of name of the location, if the location name is split into multiple tokens. Example **T4** shows the instance of 'Loc' tag.

T4 : *"jis/Other ki/Other asar/Other saudi/B-Loc arab/I-Loc mein/Other bhi/Other dikhai/Other de/Other raha/Other hai/Other corruption/Other ke/Other khilaf/Other"*
Translation: "The effect of which is visible in saudi arab against corruption"

'Org' tag refers to social, political groups like Dalit, Bhartiya, Bhartiya Jnata Party (BJP), Hindus, Muslims, social media organizations like facebook, twitter, whatsapp, etc. and also govt. institutions like Reserve bank of India (RBI), banks, Swiss banks, etc. 'B-Org' states the beginning and 'I-Org' intermediate of name of the organization, if the organizations' name is split into multiple tokens. Example **T5** shows instance of 'Org' tag in the tweet.

T5: *"saare/Other black/Other money/Other to/Other swiss/B-Org bank/I-Org mein/Other the/Other"*
Translation: "all of the black money was in the swiss bank"

With these six NE tags and the seventh 7th tag as "Other" we annotated 3,638 tweets which meant tagging 68,506 tokens. The annotated Dataset with the classification system is made available online.[4] The distribution of the tags in the Dataset is shown in Table 1.

---

[4]https://github.com/SilentFlame/Named-Entity-Recognition

3.2   Inter Annotator Agreement

Annotation of the Dataset for NE tags in the tweets was carried out by two human annotators having linguistic background and proficiency in both Hindi and English. In order to validate the quality of annotation, we calculated the inter annotator agreement (IAA) between the two annotation sets of 3,638 code-mixed tweets having 68,506 tokens using Cohen's Kappa coefficient Hallgren. Table 2 shows the results of agreement analysis. We find that the agreement is significantly high. Furthermore, the agreement of 'I-Per' and 'I-Org' annotation is relatively lower than that of 'I-Loc', this is because, the presence of uncommon/confusing names of Organization as well as Person with unclear context.

4   Data statistics

Using the twitter API we retrieved 1,10,231 tweets. After manually filtering as described in Section 3, we are left with 3,638 code-mixed tweets. This number is close to the size of Dataset provided by FIRE 2016 which introduced the NER task for code-mixed text in 2015 with it's one shared task on Entity recognition on code-mixed data. Table 1 shows the distribution of different tags in the corpus. We use the standard CONLL tags (Loc, Org, Per, Other) for tagging in the annotation stage. The Named Entity (NE) Tag Person ("Per"), Organization ("Org") and Location ("Loc") are the ones we used to tag our corpus tokens. The 'Person' tag comprises names of famous people, politicians, actresses, sports personalities, news reporters and social media celebrities and their twitter handles and nick names if used frequently as known to the annotator (like "Pappu for Mr. Rahul Gandhi"). 'Organizations' comprises names of social or political organizations as well as major groups present in India, eg. Bhartiya Janta Party (BJP), Hindu, Muslim, twit-

Tag	Precision	Recall	F1-score
B-Loc	0.47	0.50	0.49
B-Org	0.54	0.59	0.56
B-Per	0.65	0.60	0.63
Other	0.97	0.97	0.97
I-Loc	0.27	0.30	0.29
I-Org	0.23	0.22	0.22
I-Per	0.43	0.38	0.40
avg / total	0.94	0.94	0.94

Table 3: Decision Tree Model with 'max-depth=32'

ter, etc. The Tag 'Location' comprises names of cities, towns, states and countries of the world. Major of the location entities are present for Indian subcontinent places in the corpus. The ones which does not lie in any of the mentioned tags are assigned 'Other' tag.

5 System Architecture

In this section we'll explain working of different machine learning algorithms we used for experiments on our annotated dataset.

5.1 Decision Tree

Decision Tree algorithm belongs to the family of supervised learning algorithms. Unlike other supervised learning algorithms, decision tree algorithm can be used for solving regression and classification problems too. Szarvas et al. takes a multilingual named entity recognition system using boosting and C4.5 decision tree learning algorithm. The decision tree algorithm tries to solve the problem, by using tree representation. Each internal node of the tree corresponds to an attribute, and each leaf node corresponds to a class label. In decision trees, for predicting a class label for a record we start from the root of the tree. We compare the values of the root attribute with record's attribute. On the basis of comparison, we follow the branch corresponding to that value and jump to the next node. The primary challenge in the decision tree implementation is to identify which attributes do we need to consider as the root node and each level. Handling this is know the attributes selection. We have different attributes selection measure to identify the attribute which can be considered as the root note at each level. The popular attribute selection measures:

- Information gain

- Gini index

Information gain: Using information gain as a criterion, we try to estimate the information contained by each attribute. By calculating entropy measure of each attribute we can calculate their information gain. Information Gain calculates the expected reduction in entropy due to sorting on the attribute. Information gain can be calculated as:

$$H(X) = E_X[I(X)] = - \sum_{x \in X} p(x) log(p(x))$$

Where $p(x)$ is the probability of a class for the feature we are calculating information gain. The node/feature with lowest entropy is chosen as root and process is repeated for other level feature selection.

Gini index: It refers to a metric to measure how often a randomly chosen element would be incorrectly identified. It means an attribute with lower gini index should be preferred. It is calculated as:

$$Gini - index = 1 - \sum_{j} p_j^2$$

Where p_j is the probability of a class for a given feature we are calculating gini index for.

5.2 Conditional Random Field (CRF)

For sequence labeling (or general structured prediction) tasks, it is beneficial to consider the correlations between labels in neighborhoods and jointly decode the best chain of labels for a given input sentence. For example, in POS tagging an adjective is more likely to be followed by a noun than a verb, and in NER with standard BIO2 annotation (Tjong Kim Sang and Veenstra, 1999) I-ORG cannot follow I-PER. Therefore, we model label sequence jointly using a conditional random field (CRF) (Lafferty et al., 2001), instead of decoding each label independently. Since here we are focusing on sentence level and not individual positions hence it is generally known that CRF can produce higher tagging accuracy.

Say we are given a sequence of inputs we denote by X where $X = (x_1, x_2, x_3, \ldots, x_m)$ which are nothing but the words of the sentence and $S = (s_1, s_2, s_3, \ldots, s_m)$ as the sequence of output states, i.e the named entity tags. In conditional random field we model the conditional probability as

$$p(s_1, s_2, \ldots, s_m | x_1, x_2, \ldots, x_m)$$

Tag	Precision	Recall	F1-score
B-Loc	0.76	0.57	0.65
B-Org	0.67	0.33	0.44
B-Per	0.82	0.56	0.67
I-Loc	0.70	0.23	0.34
I-Org	0.68	0.27	0.39
I-Per	0.75	0.43	0.55
Other	0.96	0.99	0.98
avg / total	0.95	0.95	0.95

Table 4: CRF Model with 'c1=0.1' and 'c2=0.1' and 'L-BFGS' algorithm

We do this by defining a feature map

$$\Phi(x_1, x_2, \ldots, x_m, s_1, s_2, \ldots, s_m) \in \Re^d$$

that maps the entire input sequence X paired with an entire state sequence S to some d-dimensional feature vector. Then we can model the probability as a log-linear model with parameter vector $w \subset \Re^d$

$$p(s|x; w) = \frac{exp(w.\Phi(x, s))}{\sum_{s'} exp(w.\Phi(x, s'))}$$

where s' ranges over all possible input sequences.

For the estimation of w, we assume that we have a set of n labelled examples $(x^i, s^i)_{i=1}^n$. Now we define regularized log likelihood function L as

$$L(w) = \sum_{i=1}^{n} log(p(s^i|x^i; w)) - \frac{\lambda_2}{2}||w||_2^2 - \lambda_1||w||_1$$

The terms $\frac{\lambda_2}{2}||w||_2^2$ and $\lambda_1||w||_1$ force the parameter vector to be small in the respective norm. This penalizes the model complexity and is known as regularization. The parameters λ_2 and λ_1 allows to enforce more or less regularization. The parameter vector w^* is then estimated as

$$w^* = argmax_{w \in \Re^d} L(w)$$

If we estimated the vector w^*, we can find the most likely tag for a sentence s^* for a given sentence sequence x by

$$s^* = argmax_s p(s|x; w^*)$$

5.3 LSTMs

Recurrent neural networks (RNN) are a family of neural networks that operate on sequential data. They take an input sequence of vectors $(x_1, x_2, \ldots, x_n)$ ad return another sequence $(h_1, h_2, \ldots, h_n)$ that represents some information about the sequence at every step of the input. In theory RNNs can learn long dependencies but in practice they fail to do so and tend to be biased towards the most recent input in the sequence.Bengio et al. Long Short Term Memory networks usually just called "LSTMs" are a special kind of RNN, capable of learning long-term dependencies. Here with our data where tweets are not very long in the size LSTMs can provide us a better result as keeping previous contexts is one of the specialty of LSTM networks. LSTM networks were first introduced by Hochreiter and Schmidhuber and then were refined and popularized by many other authors. They work well with large variety of problems specially the one consisting of sequence and are now widely used. They do so using several gates that control the proportion of the input to give to the memory cell, and the proportion from the previous state to forget.

5.4 Pre-processing

This step is done to make the data uniform which will be beneficial for our system. The preprocessing step consist of

- Removing noisy tweets

- Removing links from tweets

- Tokenization

- Separating words which appear continuous (i.e Modi.ji.Ke.Liye as 'Modi ji Ke Liye')

- Converting to lowercase

- Token encoding (mapping of tokens to their Tags)

5.5 Features

The feature set consists of word, character and lexical level information like char N-Grams of Gram size 2 and 3 for suffixes, patterns for punctuation, emoticons, numbers, numbers inside strings, social media specific characters like '#', '@' and also previous tag information, and the same all

Tag	Precision	Recall	F1-score
B-Loc	0.71	0.59	0.64
B-Org	0.62	0.37	0.47
B-Per	0.78	0.57	0.66
I-Loc	0.57	0.26	0.36
I-Org	0.60	0.26	0.36
I-Per	0.70	0.42	0.52
Other	0.97	0.99	0.98
avg / total	0.95	0.95	0.95

Table 5: CRF Model with 'Avg. Perceptron' Algorithm

features of the previous and next tokens are used as context features.

in this paper we have used the following feature vectors for training of our supervised model.

1. **Character N-Grams:** Character N-Grams are language independent Majumder et al. and have proven to be very efficient for classifying text. These are also useful in situations when the text suffers from errors such as misspellings Cavnar et al.; Huffman; Lodhi et al.. Group of characters can help in capturing semantic meaning, especially in the code-mixed language where there is an informal use of words, which vary significantly from the standard Hindi and English words. We use character N-Grams as one of the features, where n is 2 and 3.

2. **Word N-Grams:** Bag of word features have been widely used for NER tasks in languages other than English Jahangir et al.. Thus we use word N-Grams, where we used the previous and the next word as a feature vector to train our model. These are also called contextual features.

3. **Capitalization:** It is a very general trend of writing any language in Roman script that people write the names of person, place or a things starting with capital letter von Däniken and Cieliebak or for aggression on someone/something use the capitalization of the entire entity name. This will make for two binary feature vectors one for starting with capital and other for the entire word capitalized.

4. **Mentions and Hashtags:** It is observed that in twitter users generally tend to address other people or organization with their user names which starts with '@' and to emphasize on something or to make something notable they use '#' before that word. Hence presence of these two gives a good probability for the word being a named entity.

5. **Numbers in String:** In social media content, users often express legitimate vocabulary words in alphanumeric form for saving typing effort, to shorten message length, or to express their style. Examples include abbreviated words like gr8' ('great'), 'b4' ('before'), etc. We observed by analyzing the corpus that alphanumeric words generally are not NEs. Therefore, this feature serves as a good indicator to recognize negative examples.

6. **Previous Word Tag:** As mentioned in word N-Gram feature the context helps in deciding the tag for the current word, hence the previous tag will help in learning the tag of current word and all the I-Tags always come after the B-Tags.

7. **Common Symbols:** It is observed that currency symbols as well as brackets like '(', '[', etc. symbols in general are followed by numbers or some mention not of importance. Hence are a good indicator for the words following or before to not being an NE.

6 Experiments

This section present the experiments we performed with different combinations of features and systems.

6.1 Feature and parameter experiments

In order to determine the effect of each feature and parameter of different models we performed several experiments with some set of feature vectors at a time and all at a time simultaneously changing the values of the parameters of our models like criterion ('Information gain', 'gini'), maximum depth of the tree for Decision tree model, optimization algorithms, loss functions in LSTM, regularization parameters and algorithms of optimization for CRF like 'L-BFGS' [5], 'L2 regularization' [6], 'Avg. Perceptron', etc. In all the models

---

[5]https://en.wikipedia.org/wiki/Limited-memory_BFGS
[6]https://towardsdatascience.com/l1-and-l2-regularization-methods-ce25e7fc831c

we mentioned above we validated our classification models with 5-fold cross-validation.

Tables 3 shows the experiment result on Decision tree model with maximum depth = 32 which we arrived at after fine empirical tuning. Tables 4 and 5 provides the experiments on CRF model. The c1 and c2 parameters for CRF model refers to L1 regularization and L2 regularization. These two regularization parameters are used to restrict our estimation of w^* as mentioned in Section 5.1. When experimented with algorithm of optimization as 'L2 regularization' or 'Average Perceptron' there is not any significant change in the results of our observation both in the per class statistics as well as the overall. We arrived at these values of $c1$ and $c2$ after fine empirical tuning. Table 4 and 5 refers to this observation.

Next we move to our experiments with **LSTM** model. Here we experimented with the optimizer, activation function along with the number of units as well as number of epochs. The best result that we came through was with using 'softmax' as activation function, 'adam' as optimizer and 'sparse categorical cross-entropy' for our loss function. Table 7 shows the statistics of running LSTM on our Dataset with 5-fold cross-validation having validation-split of 0.2 with our char, word and lexical feature set of our tokens. Table 6 shows one prediction instance of our **LSTM** model.

6.2 Results and Discussion

From the above results we can say that our system learns from the structure of the text the specific NE types like from Table 6 we can see that our system is understanding well as it tagged most tokens correctly.

We also observe that our system is getting confused in the 'Org' names that resemble to name of locations like 'America' is tagged as 'B-Org' this is because our system has seen many 'American' tokens tagged as 'B-Org' hence this confusion.

From the example in the Table 11 we can see that our system learns to tag tokens that starts with '#' as beginning of a NE but majority of the time tags it as 'B-Per' which is a problem. Our model needs to learn more generic details about these specific characters.

For 'Loc' and 'Other' tags our system works good, giving accurate predictions. The presence of confusing names of 'Location', 'Organization' and that of 'Person' in our corpus makes it diffi-

Word	Truth	Predicted
#ModiMeetTrump	Other	Other
kya	Other	Other
#Modi	B-Per	B-Per
gi	I-Per	Other
#America	B-Loc	B-Per
main	Other	Other
#Trump	B-Per	B-Per
ke	Other	Other
shaath	Other	Other
mil	Other	Other
kar	Other	Other
#Pakistan	B-Loc	B-Org
ka	Other	Other
koi	Other	Other
rasta	Other	Other
nikalenge	Other	Other
kya	Other	Other
hoga	Other	Other
#EidMubarak	Other	Other
#India	B-Loc	B-Per
#India	B-Loc	B-Org

Table 6: An Example Prediction of our LSTM Model

Tag	Precision	Recall	F1-score
B-Loc	0.91	0.89	0.86
B-Org	0.80	0.57	0.63
B-Per	0.88	0.82	0.87
I-Loc	0.93	0.47	0.60
I-Org	0.91	0.89	0.89
I-Per	0.82	0.76	0.78
Other	0.87	0.83	0.84
avg / total	0.96	0.93	0.95

Table 7: LSTM model with "optimizer='adam'"

cult for our machine learning models to learn the proper tags of these names. For eg. 'Hindustan' is labeled as 'B-Loc' in our annotation and 'Hindustani' is as 'B-Org' as the former is one of the 5 names of the country India and the later represent the citizens which makes it a group representation which we used for Organization during our annotation. Hence lexically similar words with different tags makes the learning phase of our model difficult and hence some incorrect tagging of the tokens as we can see in Table 6.

7   Conclusion and future work

In this paper, we present a freely available corpus of Hindi-English code-mixed text, consisting of tweet ids and the corresponding annotations. We also present NER systems on this Dataset with experimental analysis and results. This paper first explains about the reason of selection of some features specific to this task at the same time experimenting our results on different machine learning classification models. Decsion Tree, CRF and LSTM models worked with a best individual f1-score of 0.94, 0.95 and 0.95 which is good looking at the fact that there haven't been much research in this domain.

To make the predictions and models' result more significant the size of the corpus needed to be expanded. Our corpus has just 3,638 tweets, but due to unavailability of Hindi-English Code-Mixed Dataset it is difficult to get large corpus for our system.

Our contribution in this paper includes the following points:

1. Annotated corpus for Hindi-English Code-Mixed, kind of which are not available anywhere on the internet.

2. Introduction an addressing of Hindi-English Code-Mixed data as a research problem.

3. Proposal of suitable features targeted towards this task.

4. Different models which deals with sequential tagging and multi-class classification.

5. Developing machine learning models on our annotated corpus for the NE task.

As a part of future work, the corpus can be annotated with part-of-speech tags at word level which may yield better results. Moreover, the Dataset contains very limited tweets having NE tokens. Thus it can be extended to include more tweets more of these specific NE tokens as well as introducing a more number of tags on the existing corpus. The annotations and experiments described in this paper can also be carried out for code-mixed texts containing more than two languages from multilingual societies in future.

References

Andoni Azpeitia, Montse Cuadros, Seán Gaines, and German Rigau. 2014. Nerc-fr: supervised named entity recognition for french. In *International Conference on Text, Speech, and Dialogue*, pages 158–165. Springer.

Kalika Bali, Jatin Sharma, Monojit Choudhury, and Yogarshi Vyas. 2014. " i am borrowing ya mixing?" an analysis of english-hindi code mixing in facebook. In *Proceedings of the First Workshop on Computational Approaches to Code Switching*, pages 116–126.

Utsab Barman, Amitava Das, Joachim Wagner, and Jennifer Foster. 2014. Code mixing: A challenge for language identification in the language of social media. In *Proceedings of the first workshop on computational approaches to code switching*, pages 13–23.

Yoshua Bengio, Patrice Simard, and Paolo Frasconi. 1994. Learning long-term dependencies with gradient descent is difficult. *IEEE transactions on neural networks*, 5(2):157–166.

Rupal Bhargava, Yashvardhan Sharma, and Shubham Sharma. 2016a. Sentiment analysis for mixed script indic sentences. In *Advances in Computing, Communications and Informatics (ICACCI), 2016 International Conference on*, pages 524–529. IEEE.

Rupal Bhargava, Yashvardhan Sharma, Shubham Sharma, and Abhinav Baid. 2015. Query labelling for indic languages using a hybrid approach. In *FIRE Workshops*, pages 40–42.

Rupal Bhargava, Bapiraju Vamsi, and Yashvardhan Sharma. 2016b. Named entity recognition for code mixing in indian languages using hybrid approach. *Facilities*, 23:10.

Irshad Ahmad Bhat, Manish Shrivastava, and Riyaz Ahmad Bhat. 2016. Code mixed entity extraction in indian languages using neural networks. In *FIRE (Working Notes)*, pages 296–297.

William B Cavnar, John M Trenkle, et al. 1994. N-gram-based text categorization. *Ann arbor mi*, 48113(2):161–175.

Hai Leong Chieu and Hwee Tou Ng. 2002. Named entity recognition: a maximum entropy approach using global information. In *Proceedings of the 19th international conference on Computational linguistics-Volume 1*, pages 1–7. Association for Computational Linguistics.

Pius von Däniken and Mark Cieliebak. 2017. Transfer learning and sentence level features for named entity recognition on tweets. In *Proceedings of the 3rd Workshop on Noisy User-generated Text*, pages 166–171.

Asif Ekbal and Sivaji Bandyopadhyay. 2008. Bengali named entity recognition using support vector machine. In *Proceedings of the IJCNLP-08 Workshop on Named Entity Recognition for South and South East Asian Languages.*

John J Gumperz. 1982. *Discourse strategies*, volume 1. Cambridge University Press.

Deepak Gupta, Shubham Tripathi, Asif Ekbal, and Pushpak Bhattacharyya. 2016. A hybrid approach for entity extraction in code-mixed social media data. *MONEY*, 25:66.

Kevin A Hallgren. 2012. Computing inter-rater reliability for observational data: an overview and tutorial. *Tutorials in quantitative methods for psychology*, 8(1):23.

Sepp Hochreiter and Jürgen Schmidhuber. 1997. Long short-term memory. *Neural computation*, 9(8):1735–1780.

Stephen Huffman. 1995. Acquaintance: Language-independent document categorization by n-grams. Technical report, DEPARTMENT OF DEFENSE FORT GEORGE G MEADE MD.

Faryal Jahangir, Waqas Anwar, Usama Ijaz Bajwa, and Xuan Wang. 2012. N-gram and gazetteer list based named entity recognition for urdu: A scarce resourced language. In *24th International Conference on Computational Linguistics*, page 95.

John Lipski. 1978. Code-switching and the problem of bilingual competence. *Aspects of bilingualism*, 250:264.

Huma Lodhi, Craig Saunders, John Shawe-Taylor, Nello Cristianini, and Chris Watkins. 2002. Text classification using string kernels. *Journal of Machine Learning Research*, 2(Feb):419–444.

P Majumder, M Mitra, and BB Chaudhuri. 2002. N-gram: a language independent approach to ir and nlp. In *International conference on universal knowledge and language.*

CS Malarkodi, RK Pattabhi, and Lalitha Devi Sobha. 2012. Tamil ner–coping with real time challenges. In *24th International Conference on Computational Linguistics*, page 23.

Sudha Morwal, Nusrat Jahan, and Deepti Chopra. 2012. Named entity recognition using hidden markov model (hmm). *International Journal on Natural Language Computing (IJNLC)*, 1(4):15–23.

Sujan Kumar Saha, Sanjay Chatterji, Sandipan Dandapat, Sudeshna Sarkar, and Pabitra Mitra. 2008. A hybrid approach for named entity recognition in indian languages. In *Proceedings of the IJCNLP-08 Workshop on NER for South and South East Asian languages*, pages 17–24.

Kamal Sarkar. 2015. A hidden markov model based system for entity extraction from social media english text at fire 2015. *arXiv preprint arXiv:1512.03950.*

Arnav Sharma, Sakshi Gupta, Raveesh Motlani, Piyush Bansal, Manish Srivastava, Radhika Mamidi, and Dipti M Sharma. 2016. Shallow parsing pipeline for hindi-english code-mixed social media text. *arXiv preprint arXiv:1604.03136.*

Rohini Srihari, Cheng Niu, and Wei Li. 2000. A hybrid approach for named entity and sub-type tagging. In *Proceedings of the sixth conference on Applied natural language processing*, pages 247–254. Association for Computational Linguistics.

György Szarvas, Richárd Farkas, and András Kocsor. 2006. A multilingual named entity recognition system using boosting and c4. 5 decision tree learning algorithms. In *International Conference on Discovery Science*, pages 267–278. Springer.

Erik F Tjong Kim Sang and Fien De Meulder. 2003. Introduction to the conll-2003 shared task: Language-independent named entity recognition. In *Proceedings of the seventh conference on Natural language learning at HLT-NAACL 2003-Volume 4*, pages 142–147. Association for Computational Linguistics.

Yogarshi Vyas, Spandana Gella, Jatin Sharma, Kalika Bali, and Monojit Choudhury. 2014. Pos tagging of english-hindi code-mixed social media content. In *Proceedings of the 2014 Conference on Empirical Methods in Natural Language Processing (EMNLP)*, pages 974–979.

Jenny Linet Copara Zea, Jose Eduardo Ochoa Luna, Camilo Thorne, and Goran Glavaš. 2016. Spanish ner with word representations and conditional random fields. In *Proceedings of the Sixth Named Entity Workshop*, pages 34–40.

Forms of Anaphoric Reference to Organisational Named Entities:
Hoping to widen appeal, they diversified

Christian Hardmeier[1]   **Luca Bevacqua**[2]   **Sharid Loáiciga**[3]   **Hannah Rohde**[2]

[1]Department of Linguistics and Philology, Uppsala University
[2]Department of Linguistics and English Language, University of Edinburgh
[3]CLASP, University of Gothenburg

`christian.hardmeier@lingfil.uu.se`   `lbevacqu@ed.ac.uk`
`sharid.loaiciga@gu.se`   `hannah.rohde@ed.ac.uk`

Abstract

Proper names of organisations are a special case of collective nouns. Their meaning can be conceptualised as a collective unit or as a plurality of persons, permitting different morphological marking of anaphoric pronouns. This paper explores the variability of references to organisation names with 1) a corpus analysis and 2) two crowd-sourced story continuation experiments. The first shows the bias for singular vs. plural conceptualisation depends on the level of formality of a text. In the second, we observe a strong preference for plural *they* typical of informal speech. This preference is reduced for edited corpus data compared with constructed sentences.

1 Introduction

The names of organisations such as political bodies or companies are often made-up words (e. g., "Intel", "Novartis") or acronyms (e. g., "EU", "Unesco"). They differ from other noun phrases in that they offer very little information about their grammatical properties such as number or, in languages where this is relevant, gender. Such names are a special case of the broader category of collective nouns, which also includes common nouns such as "team" or "committee", and they can be conceptualised in different ways by focusing on the collective as a singular unit or on the plurality of people which the organisation is comprised of. When they occur as antecedents of referring expressions, names of organisations are a challenge for natural language processing (NLP) because they can trigger different types of morphological marking on the anaphoric elements. Moreover, the preference for certain types of agreement varies across different genres and, we expect, different languages. The experiments presented here address English only and serve as a pilot study for an investigation of reference to organisations across multiple languages.

Via a corpus analysis of the OntoNotes corpus (Pradhan et al., 2013) and two crowd-sourced story continuation experiments, we study how organisational named entities are referenced after their introduction in a discourse. Specifically, we consider anaphoric expressions coreferent with the proper name of an organisation that are separated from their antecedent by a sentence boundary, but no intervening mentions belonging to the same coreference chain. The expressions are categorised into four classes: repetition of the proper name (*name*), paraphrastic noun phrases with a common noun such as "the company" (*noun*), and forms of the pronouns *it* and *they*. The pronominal case is informative to speakers' choice between a conceptualisation as singular (*it*) or plural (*they*).

2 Related literature

Morphological agreement with collective nouns has received some attention in English linguistics, but most research focuses on the agreement of verbs rather than pronouns, and – to an even larger extent – on collective common nouns such as "team", which are formally singular but can trigger plural agreement, rather than proper names.

There is broad agreement that American English prefers singular verb agreement with collective nouns, whereas notional concord with plural forms is not uncommon in British English (Fries, 1988; Bock et al., 2006; Hundt, 2009). Other varieties of English range in between (Hundt, 2006). Shift towards singular agreement is considered to be an ongoing diachronic process (Hundt, 2009), but the extent to which plural verb agreement with collectives is disappearing among younger speakers of British English is disputed (Fries, 1988).

Proceedings of the Seventh Named Entities Workshop, pages 36–40
Melbourne, Australia, July 20, 2018. ©2018 Association for Computational Linguistics

	it	they	name	noun	other	total
bc	8	15	59	10	13	105
bn	11	12	146	44	12	225
mz	17	11	91	24	4	147
nw	76	11	926	193	36	1242
tc	2	3	7	0	0	12
wb	6	4	52	8	4	74
	120	56	1281	279	69	1805

Table 1: Reference types per genre in OntoNotes

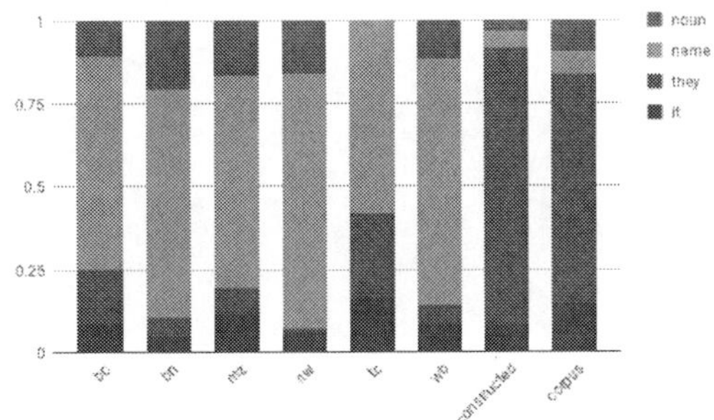

Bars 1–6: OntoNotes (Section 3)
Bars 7–8: Continuation studies (Section 5)

Figure 1: Proportions of reference types

The situation for pronouns is different. Pronouns following collective nouns are more likely to receive plural marking than verbs (Hundt, 2006, 2009), particularly in speech (Levin, 2001), and there is psycholinguistic evidence of processing differences favouring syntactic (singular) agreement for verbs and notional (plural) concord for pronouns (Bock et al., 2006). Singular and plural agreement can also co-occur with the same mention ("mixed concord"), typically involving a singular verb and a plural pronoun (Hundt, 2009).

3 Corpus analysis

3.1 Corpus and extraction

The OntoNotes corpus (Pradhan et al., 2013) contains about 1.7 million words of annotated English text predominantly of American origin from different genres, or data sources: *newswire* (nw), *broadcast news* (bn), *broadcast conversation* (bc), *magazine* (mz), *telephone conversation* (tc), *web data* (wb) and *pivot text* (pt).[1] We extract examples using the gold-standard annotations of coreference and named entity type. Each example is a pair of mentions belonging to the same coreference chain. To ensure that the corpus analysis is comparable with the continuation studies described in Section 5, we only extract pairs of mentions in adjacent sentences, excluding both pairs of mentions in the same sentence and pairs with intervening sentences. A pair of mentions is extracted if the two mentions are neighbouring members of the same coreference chain (i. e., no mentions of the same chain occur in between) and the first mention is annotated as a named entity of type ORG.

3.2 Overview

Table 1 and the first six bars of Figure 1 show the distribution of reference types for the different OntoNotes genres. The size of the individual subcorpora varies substantially and so does the number of examples that can be extracted from each. The smallest non-empty sample ($N = 12$) is from the *telephone conversations* (tc) subcorpus, the largest ($N = 1242$) is from *Newswire*.

The most common type of reference, making up 58–75% of the examples in all subcorpora, is a repetition of the name. Paraphrasing noun phrases are more common in *broadcast news* (19.6%), *magazine* (16.3%) and *newswire* (15.5%) than in *web data* (10.8%) and *broadcast conversation* (9.5%). Many examples in the *other* category are instances of the first-person pronoun *we* that occur when a representative of the organisation is quoted or speaking. The relative frequency of pronominal references (*it* and *they*) varies considerably between genres. It is greatest in *telephone conversations*, where 5 out of 12 references are of this type. In *newswire* (7%) and *broadcast news* (10.2%), pronominal references are much less common. *Web data* (13.5%), *magazine* (19.0%) and *broadcast conversation* (21.9%) are in between. Among the pronominal references, we observe large differences in the preference for *it* vs. *they* across subcorpora, with numbers ranging from 34.8% *it* in *broadcast conversation* to 87.4% in *newswire*.

4 The effect of formality

In this section, we examine the hypothesis that the cross-corpus variation in the conceptualisation of organisations as singular or plural can be explained by the different levels of *formality* of the texts.

---

[1] The pt subcorpus contains excerpts of the Bible and is not used in this paper.

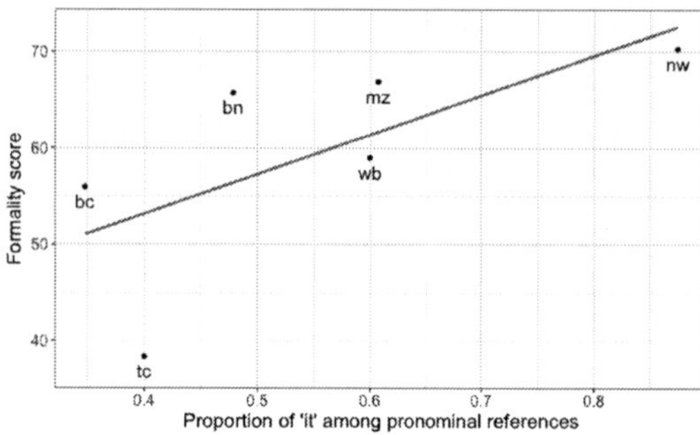

Figure 2: Formality score and prevalence of *it* in OntoNotes subcorpora

4.1 Measuring formality

To measure the formality of discourse, we use an automatic metric proposed by Heylighen and Dewaele (2002). The metric is called *F-score* by the original authors, but we use *Formality score* to avoid confusion with the entirely unrelated F-score derived from precision and recall. The fundamental assumption of Heylighen and Dewaele (2002) is an opposition between *formality* and *contextuality*, with the claim that more formal texts prefer more absolute and less context-dependent forms of expression, which is reflected in lexical choice. The authors identify two (non-exhaustive) subsets of the lexicon that they call *formal* or *non-deictic* and *deictic*, respectively. This distinction is then operationalised via part-of-speech (POS) categories with nouns, adjectives, prepositions and articles taken to be non-deictic, and pronouns, verbs, adverbs and interjections as deictic. The score is calculated as:

$$F = 100 \cdot \frac{N_{\text{formal}} - N_{\text{deictic}}}{2N} + 50 \qquad (1)$$

where N_{formal} and N_{deictic} are the counts of formal and deictic tokens and N is the total corpus size.

4.2 Choice of referring expression

Since the number of pronouns in a corpus enters the computation of the Formality score through the N_{deictic} term, we must exercise care when we measure referential preferences so that we do not use a metric that is correlated by construction with the Formality score. The preference among pronominal references between the conceptualisation of organisation as singular versus collective entities can be measured as the proportion of references with *it* among third-person pronominal references, i. e., $N_{it}/(N_{it}+N_{they})$. As both *it* and *they* are counted as

pronouns in the Formality score, their proportion can be measured independently from the score.

Figure 2 plots the proportion of *it* among pronominal references (*x*-axis) against the Formality score (*y*-axis). The ranking predicted by the Formality score seems intuitively reasonable: The *newswire, magazine* (two edited written genres) and *broadcast news* (prepared speech in a very formal setting) genres are identified as most formal, whereas *telephone conversations* are predicted to be least formal. The Pearson correlation coefficient between the Formality score and the proportion of *it* vs. *they* is 0.67, which fails to reach significance ($p = 0.146$). However, the Spearman rank correlation reaches a value of $\rho = 0.886$, which is significantly different from 0 ($p < 0.05$). This confirms that formality is a relevant factor to explain the language-internal variation in the number marking of pronouns with organisational antecedents, as was suggested for collective nouns more generally by Hundt (2009).

5 Continuation experiments

Two story-continuation studies presented participants with prompts to elicit entity coreference.

5.1 Study 1: Constructed stimuli

Materials   The 16 experimental items consisted of a context sentence and a prompt. The first sentence introduced a named entity in the subject position of the matrix clause with some additional contextual information, followed by a prompt with a discourse adverbial or other connective (e.g., *In the following years, Because of this*). The named entities belonged to four categories: names of companies, publishers, sport teams and music bands.

The experimental items were interleaved with 48 filler items. They included 20 fillers composed of a sentence introducing two animate or inanimate entities, followed by an adverbial prompt, 24 items for an unrelated production experiment involving the coreference of the pronouns *it* and *this*, and 4 catch trials with a straightforward correct response, which were mentioned in the instructions.

Participants   Twenty-seven monolingual American English speakers aged 19–63 (mean age 36, $\sigma = 11.2$; 15 male) were recruited from Amazon's Mechanical Turk (Munro et al., 2010; Gibson et al., 2011). All had US IP addresses and received \$4 for an estimated 30-minute task.

	it	they	name	noun	total
Study 1	32	307	19	12	370
Study 2	24	113	11	16	164
	56	420	30	28	534

Table 2: Reference types in the continuations

Procedure The continuations were collected via a web-based interface that participants accessed directly from Amazon's Mechanical Turk. The website displayed a background questionnaire, a consent form and an instructions page, and then proceeded to display one item at a time with a text box for participants to write their continuations.

Analysis The continuations were annotated for referent type, using the same labels as in the corpus analysis, plus *other* for continuations in which the named entity was not mentioned in any way. One of the authors of the paper annotated the whole set of continuations, and two others labelled half of it. The annotations did not present any real case of disagreement among the authors.

Results 50 out of 420 continuations were excluded because they were labelled as *other*. This left 370 labelled annotation for the analysis. The results are shown in Table 2 and Figure 1. It is striking that the participants produced an extremely high number of pronominal continuations, most of them with *they* (accounting for 83% of the referential types vs. only 3.1% in the OntoNotes data). By contrast, the *name* category occurred only infrequently (5.1% of types vs. 71% in OntoNotes).

5.2 Study 2: Corpus stimuli

Materials The 24 target passages were extracted from the data described in Section 3.1. They were interleaved with 76 filler items. 24 of these were extracted from the ParCorFull corpus (Lapshinova-Koltunski et al., 2018). These fillers mentioned a range of referents; the sentence continuation prompt was an adverbial expression (e.g., *Eventually*). 48 additional fillers were items of the aforementioned unrelated production experiment, and a final 4 fillers repeated the catch trials from Study 1.

Participants Nineteen monolingual English-speaking participants aged 23–44 (mean age 30, $\sigma = 6.5$; 13 male) were recruited as in Study 1, and received \$7 for an estimated 50-minute task.

Procedure and Analysis Identical to Study 1.

Results 43 out of 207 continuations were labelled *other* and excluded from the data set. This left 164 continuations labelled for referential type. The results are shown in Table 2 and Figure 1. While the continuations produced in this study still contain a much larger number of pronominal references than the OntoNotes examples, the proportion of pronouns (83.5%) is considerably lower than in Study 1 (91.6%), and the proportion of *it* among pronominal references is higher (17.5% vs. 9.4%). The difference between the distributions observed in Studies 1 and 2 is statistically significant ($\chi^2 = 145.71$; $p < 0.001$) in a χ^2 test with Monte Carlo simulation (Hope, 1968).

6 Conclusions

Focusing on pronouns referring to proper names, our study confirms a number of results suggested by earlier research concentrating primarily on collective common nouns and verb agreement (Hundt, 2009). There is significant language-internal variation in English in how speakers and writers refer to organisational named entities. In the OntoNotes corpus data, the most frequent way of referring to an organisation is by repeating its name. The number of pronominal references and their distribution among *it* and *they* varies greatly across genres. As suggested by Hundt (2009), we find a correlation between the level of formality of a text and the prevalence of singular pronominal references.

In the story continuation studies, we observe a distribution of reference types that is more extreme in its preference for *they* than even the most informal OntoNotes genres. This suggests that the patterns we obtain in this type of study are more representative of informal and spoken language than of more formal written genres, despite the written modality of the task. As a result, we cannot automatically generalise the findings from these studies across different genres. However, the combination of crowd-sourced continuation study and corpus analysis provides us with a useful baseline in terms of both methods and results for a planned cross-lingual study of reference to named entities.

Acknowledgements

Christian Hardmeier was supported by the Swedish Research Council under grant 2017-930, *Neural Pronoun Models for Machine Translation*. Hannah Rohde was supported via a Leverhulme Trust Prize in Languages & Literatures.

References

Kathryn Bock, Sally Butterfield, Anne Cutler, J. Cooper Cutting, Kathleen M. Eberhard, and Karin R. Humphreys. 2006. Number agreement in British and American English: Disagreeing to agree collectively. *Language*, 82(1):64–113.

Udo Fries. 1988. The crew have abandoned the ship: Concord with collective nouns revisited. *AAA: Arbeiten aus Anglistik und Amerikanistik*, 13(2):99–104.

Edward Gibson, Steve Piantadosi, and Kristina Fedorenko. 2011. Using Mechanical Turk to obtain and analyze English acceptability judgments. *Language and Linguistics Compass*, 5(8):509–524.

Francis Heylighen and Jean-Marc Dewaele. 2002. Variation in the contextuality of language: An empirical measure. *Foundations of Science*, 7:293–340.

Adery C. A. Hope. 1968. A simplified Monte Carlo significance test procedure. *Journal of the Royal Statistical Society. Series B (Methodological)*, 30(3):582–598.

Marianne Hundt. 2006. The committee has/have decided… On concord patterns with collective nouns in inner- and outer-circle varieties of English. *Journal of English Linguistics*, 34(3):206–232.

Marianne Hundt. 2009. Concord with collective nouns in Australian and New Zealand English. In Pam Peters et al., editors, *Comparative studies in Australian and New Zealand English: Grammar and beyond*, pages 207–224. John Benjamins.

Ekaterina Lapshinova-Koltunski, Christian Hardmeier, and Pauline Krielke. 2018. ParCorFull: a parallel corpus annotated with full coreference. In *Proceedings of 11th Language Resources and Evaluation Conference*, pages 00–00, Miyazaki, Japan. European Language Resources Association (ELRA). To appear.

Magnus Levin. 2001. *Agreement with collective nouns in English*. Ph.D. thesis, Lund University.

R. Munro, S. Bethard, V. Kuperman, V.T. Lai, R. Melnick, C. Potts, T. Schnoebelen, and H. Tily. 2010. Crowdsourcing and language studies: the new generation of linguistic data. In *Proceedings of the NAACL HLT 2010 Workshop on Creating Speech and Language Data with Amazon's Mechanical Turk*, pages 122–130. Association for Computational Linguistics.

Sameer Pradhan, Alessandro Moschitti, Nianwen Xue, Hwee Tou Ng, Anders Björkelund, Olga Uryupina, Yuchen Zhang, and Zhi Zhong. 2013. Towards robust linguistic analysis using ontonotes. In *Proceedings of the Seventeenth Conference on Computational Natural Language Learning*, pages 143–152, Sofia, Bulgaria. Association for Computational Linguistics.

Named-Entity Tagging and Domain adaptation for
Better Customized Translation

Zhongwei Li[1,2], Xuancong Wang[1], Ai Ti Aw[1]
Eng Siong Chng[2], Haizhou Li[1,3]
[1]Human Language Technology Department, Institute for Infocomm Research (I²R), Singapore
{li-z,wangxc,aaiti}@i2r.a-star.edu.sg
[2]School of Computer Science and Engineering, Nanyang Technological University, Singapore
[3]ECE Dept, National University of Singapore, Singapore

Abstract

Customized translation need pay special attention to the target domain terminology especially the named-entities for the domain. Adding linguistic features to neural machine translation (NMT) has been shown to benefit translation in many studies. In this paper, we further demonstrate that adding named-entity (NE) feature with named-entity recognition (NER) into the source language produces better translation with NMT. Our experiments show that by just including the different NE classes and boundary tags, we can increase the BLEU score by around 1 to 2 points using the standard test sets from WMT2017. We also show that adding NE tags using NER and applying in-domain adaptation can be combined to further improve customized machine translation.

1 Introduction

As generic machine translation cannot deal well with the translation with local or specific domain context, customized machine translation is adopted to focus on the terminology of local or domain context especially for named-entities translation.

Neural machine translation (NMT) (Sutskever et al., 2014; Bahdanau et al., 2014; Luong et al., 2015) is a more recent and effective approach than the traditional statistical machine translation (SMT). It uses a large recurrent neural network (RNN) to encode a source sentence into a vector, and uses another large network to generate sentence in the target language one word at a time using the source sentence embedding and the attention mechanism.

NMT has achieved impressive result by learning the translation as an end-to-end model (Wu et al., 2016; Zhou et al. 2017; Gehring et al. 2017). Conventional NMT systems do not use linguistic features explicitly. They expect the NMT model to learn these complex sentence structures and linguistic features from big data as word embedding vectors. However, because of uneven data distribution and high linguistic complexity, there is no guarantee that NMT can capture this information and produce proper translation in all cases, especially for those terms which do not occur very often.

Recently, researchers have shown the potential benefit of explicitly encoding the linguistic features into NMT. Sennrich and Haddow (2016) proposed to include linguistic features (part-of-speech tag, lemmatized form and dependency label, morphology) at NMT source encoder side. Roee et al. (2017) instead incorporated syntactic information of target language as linearized, lexicalized constituency trees into NMT target decoder side. Their experiments showed adding linguistic information at both the source and target side can be beneficial for NMT. Based on these findings, in this paper, we propose to incorporate named-entity (NE) features to further improve neural machine translation.

Named entities play a crucial role in many monolingual and multilingual Natural Language Processing (NLP) tasks. Proper NE identification will enhance the sentence structure understanding for NMT, and thus give better translation of the named entities as well as the whole sentence.

Proceedings of the Seventh Named Entities Workshop, pages 41–46
Melbourne, Australia, July 20, 2018. ©2018 Association for Computational Linguistics

In general, named entities are more difficult to translate for NMT than SMT. This is because and NMT is weaker in translating less frequent words as compared to SMT. In addition, since there are different types of named entities, e.g. Person, Place, Organization, etc., so linguistically and logically speaking, the translation mechanisms for different types of named entities are also different. Unlike other words or phrases which occur more frequent in the training corpus, NE expressions are quite flexible, they can be composed of any character or word; moreover, in real-world applications, new named entities can emerge every day. Thus, NMT need to pay special attention to named entities to enhance the overall translation quality. Without NE context information, it is difficult to know the meaning of the words or entities with different meaning under ambiguous situation (我 喜欢 秋月。秋月 can be interpreted as person name or natural phenomenon. 三十六行 can be interpreted as a number entity or an idiomatic expression). It is also very difficult to translate number entities under never seen or rare situation (百分之 8 千点零零七).

There are many domain-based or location-based named entities. These named entities are often rare words in the document, and generally NMT cannot produce good translation for these local contexts with local named entities. Identifying local named entities and generating their translation with local context is also a challenging task which we will address in this paper. (e.g., the English name for 张志贤 is 'Teo Chee Hean' in Singapore while it's pinyin translation is 'Zhang Zhi Xian' in China)

To address the NE translation issue, some researchers work on separate models or methods while others incorporate these separate models/methods with the main NMT models (Li et al., 2016; Wang et al., 2017). They use NER to identify and align the NE pairs at both of source and target sentences, then NE pairs are replaced with NE tags for training the model; at reference stage the NE tags at target are replaced by the separate NE translation model or bilingual NE dictionary. The disadvantages of the replacement methods include NE information loss and NE alignment errors.

To avoid the complexity and disadvantages of separate model training and integration, in this paper, we add the NE type information and boundary information directly to the source sentence by a NER tool, we hope NMT will learn and understand the sentence better with this additional NE information. NE classification based on context information is important for NMT to reduce translation error under various ambiguous situations. A named entity can consist of a single word or several words, the boundary tag feature of the named entity will inform NMT model to treat these words as a single entity during translation.

Since named entities often contain local names or domain-specific names, however, the amount of local or domain-specific training data is often small. Thus, in this paper we apply domain adaptation together with named entity features to make further improvement for local context or domain-specific translation.

2 Neural Machine Translation

Machine Translation (MT) translates text sentences from a source language to a target language. SMT systems use phrases as atomic units. It obtains phrase pairs by training on large parallel corpora. NMT is a new approach in which we train a single, large neural network to maximize the translation performance. Our baseline system is based on attention-based encoder-decoder neural network model (Cho et al., 2015).

The encoder, which is often implemented as a bidirectional recurrent network with long short-term memory units (LSTM) (Hochreiter and Schmidhuber, 1997), first reads a source sentence represented as a sequence of words $x = (x_1, x_2, \dots x_n)$. The encoder calculates a forward sequence of hidden states and a backward sequence of hidden states. These forward and backward hidden states are concatenated to obtain the sequence of bidirectional hidden states as $\mathbf{h} = (h_1, h_2, \dots h_n)$.

The decoder is implemented as a conditional recurrent language model that predicts a target sequence $y = (y_1, y_2, \dots y_m)$ given the input sequence $x = (x_1, x_2, \dots x_n)$. Each word y_i is predicted based on the decoder hidden state s_i, the previous word y_{i-1}, and a context vector c_i. c_i is a time-dependent content vector that is computed as a weighted-sum of the hidden states of $\mathbf{h}$: $c_i = \sum_j a_{i,j} h_j$. The weight $a_{i,j}$ of each hidden state h_j is computed by the attention model which models the probability that y_j is aligned to x_i.

The details of the attention-based multi-layer bidirectional-LSTM encoder-decoder NMT model can be found at (Cho et al., 2015). Figure 1 shows the overall system architecture.

3 NMT with NE Features and Domain Adaptation

Our main innovation over the standard sequence-to-sequence NMT model is a very simple and straight-forward way to add NE information of the source language. Compared with NE tag replacement and alignment methods (Li et al., 2016; Wang et al., 2017), our method just insert NE tags in the source sentences, there is no information loss and NE alignment issues. Since our approach does not modify the main NMT model structure, thus, our method can be applied to any sequence-to-sequence NMT model. In our model, apart from the original words in the sentence, we generate and insert NE tags which include both the NE class and NE boundary type for each NE into the sentence, thus we present the NMT encoder with the combined sentence sequence with additional NE tags.

The NE tags can be applied to both word-based and character-based source input of any language. For Chinese-to-English translation, the Chinese input can be either a word sequence or a character sequence, the English side is still word-based tokens. We segment all the unknown words as a sequence of subword units using the byte-pair encoding (Sennrich et al., 2016b).

3.1 Named-Entity Tags

For every NE in the source sentence we generate the NE class tags using the third-party tool, Stanford NER (Jenny et al., 2005):

- NE class for NE (PERSON, ORG, GPE, MISC, etc)[1]

- NE class and boundary tags: <PERSON> </PERSON> [2]

We add these NE tags to the corresponding NE of the source sentence, so as to produce the combined sentence sequence with additional NE tags.

When the source language is English, we apply subword split (@@ is the subword connector) for

---

[1] ORG: Organization Entity, GPE: Geo-Political Entity
[2] <PERSON>: Start of PERSON, </PERSON>: End of PERSON

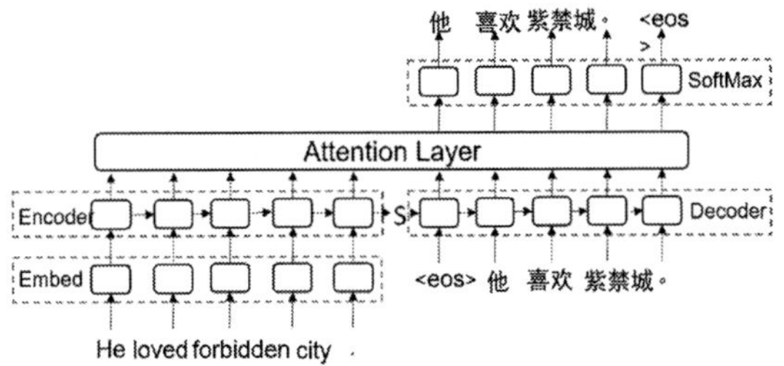

Figure 1: System Architecture

the out of vocabulary (OOV) words after tokenization:

Original Source:
```
Patrick Roy resigns as Avalanche coach
```
Words and subwords with NE tags[3]:
```
<PERSON> Patrick Roy </PERSON> re-
signs <ORG> Avalan @@che </ORG>
coach
```

When the source language is Chinese, we can use either word-based input or character-based input. To generate character-based input sequence for the Chinese sentence, we just split all Chinese word tokens into character tokens (English tokens are not split).

Original Source:
凯发集团成功进军中国
Words with NE tags:
<ORG> 凯发 集团 </ORG> 成功 进军 中国
Characters with NE tags:
<ORG> 凯 发 集 团 </ORG> 成 功 进 军 中 国

3.2 Preprocessing Pipeline

We design and develop the preprocessing pipeline to augment the source sequences with NE tags. It is applied on all the training set, the development set, and the test set. The preprocessing pipeline can also be used for the online translation system. The workflow of the pipeline is shown in Figure 2

The preprocessing pipeline includes the following modules:

Tokenizer: The input sentence is tokenized as word tokens.

NE Tagger: the NE tagger identifies the named entities in the sentence, and assigns the NE classes.

Subword/Chracter Splitter: We split the OOV words as subword units using byte-pair encoding (Sennrich et al., 2016b); for the Chinese

---

[3] *Words and subwords with NE tags are shown in blue color*

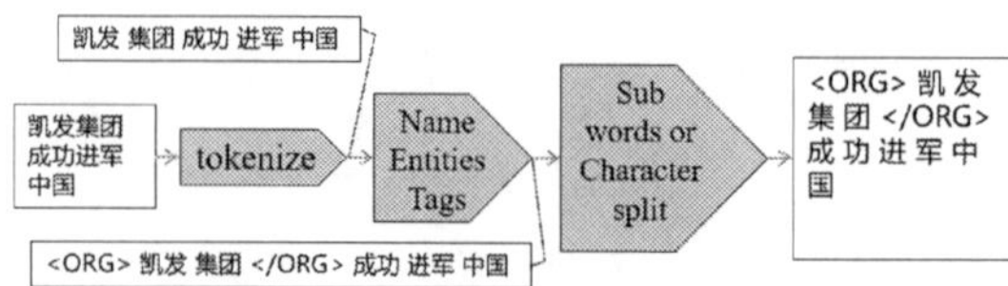

Figure 2: Preprocess Pipeline.

character-based system, we split each word as a character sequence.

Our pipeline framework is very flexible as the software components in the pipeline can be easily replaced by other software components with similar functions, for example we can, for better performance, choose different tokenizers based on the input language. For the same reason, we can switch to a different NE tagger, splitter for a different input language.

4 Experiments & Results

We have conducted our experiments with bi-direction translation between Chinese/English languages pair.

4.1 Datasets

We select the first 7 million Chinese-English sentence pairs from United Nations Parallel Corpus v1.0 (Ziemski et al., 2015), and data from LDC for the training corpus, we also select some in-domain data from local context for domain adaption training. After filtering out the long sentences (Chinese character length > 60 or number of English words > 60), the total number of sentence pairs for training is around 7 million. Table 1 shows the corpus sources for training.

Corpus	# of sentence pairs (K)	# of characters (M)
UNPCv1	6,453	1,722
LDC2017T05	63	16
LDC2017T06	6	1
LDC2006E26	35	9
In-domain	188	42
Total	6,745	1,790

Table 1: Training Data Corpus Selection.

We use the tuning sets with in-domain content for the model tuning. We use the standard test set from WMT 17 (http://www.statmt.org/wmt17/) to evaluate our model performance and compare with other models using same test set.

4.2 Data processing

We tokenize Chinese sentences using tools THU-LAC from Tsinghua University NLP (Zhongguo Li et al., 2009) (http://thulac.thunlp.org/), and tokenize English sentences using scripts from Moses (http://www.statmt.org/moses/). We use Stanford Named Entity Recognizer (NER) (Jenny et al., 2005) for NE Tagging for all the training, development and test data.

For character-based system, we also split every Chinese sentence as a character sequence (English words in Chinese sentences are not split into characters, but are split into subword units when OOV tokens are encountered), while the English side is still word-based. To enable open vocabulary translation, we used subword units obtained via Byte-Pair Encoding (Sennrich et al., 2016b) learning 60,000 merge operations on both Chinese and English training data.

4.3 Baseline Models

In this paper, we implement our experiment based on OpenNMT-py [4] (Klein et al., 2017) using PyTorch [5] (The PyTorch Developers, 2017). It is an open-source (MIT) neural machine translation system using Python. We train the model on one GPU: Nvidia P40. We use mini-batches of size 64, a maximum sequence length of 60, word embedding of size 600, NE boundary embedding of size 5, NE class embedding of size 10, hidden layers of size 1024, 4-layer bi-directional LSTM encoder and 4-layer uni-directional LSTM decoder. We use adam optimizer (Kingma et al., 2015) for training, we apply a dropout probability of 0.2 between LSTM stacks.

Baselines: The baseline system we trained for Chinese-to-English (ZH→EN) translation is a character-based model without any additional features, in which the Chinese source is split into characters and English is word-based with OOVs split into subword units. For ZH→EN, the performance of the character-based model is better than the word-based model. The baseline system we trained for EN→ZH translation is a word-based model, in which both source and target sentences are word tokens with OOVs split into sub-

---

[4] https://github.com/OpenNMT/OpenNMT-py
[5] http://pytorch.org/

word units. We found that for the baseline system without any additional linguistic features, the character-based model produces better translation than the word-based model.

Models with NE Tags: In our experiments, we train both word-based and character-based models with NE features. We found that when NE features are added, the word-based model performs better than the character-based model for both ZH→EN and EN→ZH translation.

4.4 Test Results

We calculate the performance matrix using the evaluation script *multi-bleu.perl* from Moses (Koehn et al., 2007). Two test sets are used for the evaluation; one is the standard news test set (newstest2017) from WMT 2017, while the other is our in-domain test set. Table 2 shows the performance metrics for WMT 2017 news test set for both ZH→EN and EN→ZH translation.

Models	ZH → EN	EN → ZH
Baseline	18.23	27.82
+ NE	19.92	30.38

Table 2: BLEU scores for WMT 2017 test sets

As shown in Table 2, we can see the performance improvement (around 1 BLEU score) for both directions (ZH→EN, EN→ZH) after adding NE features compared to the best baseline model.

We also apply the in-domain adaptation to the models by continue training on the in-domain data for 2-5 additional training epochs. Table 3 shows the test results for our in-domain test data.

Models	ZH → EN	EN → ZH
Baseline	14.32	21.87
+ NE	15.46	23.72
+ Adaptation	16.35	25.03

Table 3: BLEU scores for in-domain test sets

In Table 3, we show the same performance improvement when adding NE features with in-domain translation, and we also obtain further improvement for our in-domain translation by domain adaptation on top of the models with NE improvement.

5   Conclusion and Future Work

In this paper, we introduce an innovative and simple method to combine NE features and domain adaptation with NMT to improve customization translation. We add NE tags for every NE in the input sequence and pass the combined sequence to the encoder of the NMT framework. Our experiments on Chinese-to-English and English-to-Chinese translation show that adding NE features can significantly improve the performance of neural machine translation. The idea is language independent and applicable to other language pairs. Our method can also be applied to other NMT models such as the convolutional sequence-to-sequence model (Jonas Gehring et al. 2017) or the attention-only model (Vaswani et al. 2017). We also show that domain adaptation can also be applied to this method with additional improvement for in-domain text translation.

We believe that the results can be further improved by adding NE information at the target decoder side of NMT. In the future, we will explore new experiments and develop new methods to utilize the NE features to benefit translation at both source and target sides.

References

Bahdanau, Dzmitry, Cho, Kyunghyun, and Bengio, Yoshua. Neural machine translation by jointly learning to align and translate. arXiv preprint arXiv:1409.0473, 2014.

Guillaume Klein, Yoon Kim, Yuntian Deng, Jean Senellart, and Alexander M. Rush. 2017. OpenNMT: Open-source toolkit for neural machine translation. CoRR abs/1701.02810.

Jenny Rose Finkel, Trond Grenager, and Christopher Manning.2005. Incorporating Non-local Information into Information Extraction Systems by Gibbs Sampling. *Proceedings of the 43nd Annual Meeting of the Association for Computational Linguistics* (ACL 2005), pp. 363-370.

Jie Zhou, Ying Cao, Xuguang Wang, Peng Li, and Wei Xu. 2016. Deep Recurrent Models with FastForward Connections for Neural Machine Translation. TACL 4:371–383.

Jonas Gehring, Michael Auli, David Grangier, Denis Yarats, and Yann N. Dauphin. 2017. Convolutional Sequence to Sequence Learning. CoRR abs/1705.03122

Kristina Toutanova, Dan Klein, Christopher Manning, and Yoram Singer. 2003. Feature-Rich Part-of-Speech Tagging with a Cyclic Dependency Network. In Proceedings of HLT-NAACL 2003, pp. 252-259.

Kingma, Diederik P. and Jimmy Ba. 2015. "Adam: A Method for Stochastic Optimization." The International Conference on Learning Representations. San Diego, California, USA.

Koehn, Philipp, Hieu Hoang, Alexandra Birch, Chris Callison-Burch, Marcello Federico, Nicola Bertoldi, Brooke Cowan, Wade Shen, Christine Moran, Richard Zens, Chris Dyer, Ond˘rej Bojar, Alexandra Constantin, and Evan Herbst. 2007. "Moses: Open Source Toolkit for Statistical Machine Translation." Proceedings of the ACL-2007 Demo and Poster Sessions, 177–180. Prague, Czech Republic.

Kyunghyun Cho, Aaron Courville, and Yoshua Bengio. 2015. Describing multimedia content using attention-based encoder-decoder networks. *IEEE Transactions on Multimedia* 17(11):1875–1886

Li, Xiaoqing; Zhang, Jiajun; Zong, Chengqing. Neural Name Translation Improves Neural Machine Translation. arXiv eprint arXiv:1607.01856, 2016.

Luong, Minh-Thang, Pham, Hieu, and Manning, Christopher D. Effective approaches to attention-based neural machine translation. In Proc. of EMNLP, 2015.

Matthew D. Zeiler. 2012. ADADELTA: An Adaptive Learning Rate Method. *CoRR*, abs/1212.5701.

Rico Sennrich and Barry Haddow. 2016a. Linguistic input features improve neural machine translation. *In Proceedings of the First Conference on Machine Translation.* Association for Computational Linguistics, Berlin, Germany, pages 83–91. http://www.aclweb.org/anthology/W16-2209.

Rico Sennrich, Barry Haddow, and Alexandra Birch. 2016b. Neural machine translation of rare words with subword units. *In Proceedings of the 54th Annual Meeting of the Association for Computational Linguistics* (Volume 1: Long Papers). Association for Computational Linguistics, Berlin, Germany, pages 1715–1725.

Rico Sennrich, Alexandra Birch, Anna Currey, Ulrich Germann, Barry Haddow, Kenneth Heafield, Antonio Valerio Miceli Barone, and Philip Williams. 2017. The University of Edinburgh's Neural MT Systems for WMT17. In Proceedings of the Second Conference on Machine Translation, Volume 2: Shared Task Papers. Copenhagen, Denmark.

Roee Aharoni and Yoav Goldberg. 2017. Towards string-to-tree neural machine translation. *In Proceedings of the 55th Annual Meeting of the Association for Computational Linguistics.*

Sepp Hochreiter and Jurgen Schmidhuber. 1997. Long short-term memory. *Neural Comput.* 9(8):1735–1780.

Sutskever, Ilya, Vinyals, Oriol, and Le, Quoc V. Sequence to Sequence Learning with Neural Networks. In Proc. of NIPS, pp. 3104–3112, 2014.

The PyTorch Developers. Pytorch. http://pytorch.org, 2017.

Vaswani, Ashish, Noam Shazeer, Niki Parmar, Jakob Uszkoreit, Llion Jones, Aidan N. Gomez, Łukasz Kaiser, and Illia Polosukhin. "Attention is all you need." In Advances in Neural Information Processing Systems, pp. 6000-6010. 2017.

Wang, Yuguang, Shanbo Cheng, Liyang Jiang, Jiajun Yang, Wei Chen, Muze Li, Lin Shi, Yanfeng Wang and Hongtao Yang. "Sogou Neural Machine Translation Systems for WMT17." WMT (2017).

Wu, Yonghui, Schuster, Mike, Chen, Zhifeng, Le, Quoc V, Norouzi, Mohammad, Macherey, Wolfgang, Krikun, Maxim, Cao, Yuan, Gao, Qin, Macherey, Klaus, et al. Google's Neural Machine Translation System: Bridging the Gap between Human and Machine Translation. arXiv preprint arXiv:1609.08144, 2016.

Ziemski, M., Junczys-Dowmunt, M., and Pouliquen, B. (2015). The united nations parallel corpus v1.0. In International Conference on Language Resources and Evaluation (LREC).

Zhongguo Li, Maosong Sun. Punctuation as Implicit Annotations for Chinese Word Segmentation. *Computational Linguistics,* vol. 35, no. 4, pp. 505-512, 2009.

Whitepaper on NEWS 2018 Shared Task on Machine Transliteration

Nancy Chen[†], Xiangyu Duan[‡], Min Zhang[‡], Rafael E. Banchs[η], Haizhou Li[⋆]

[†]Singapore University of Technology and Design, Singapore
[‡]Soochow University, China 215006
[η]Nanyang Technological University, Singapore
[⋆]National University of Singapore, Singapore

Abstract

Transliteration is defined as the phonetic translation of names across languages. Transliteration of Named Entities (NEs) is a necessary subtask in many applications, such as machine translation, corpus alignment, cross-language IR, information extraction and automatic lexicon acquisition. All such systems call for high-performance transliteration, which is the focus of the shared task in NEWS 2018.

1 Task Description

The objective of the Shared Task on Named Entity Transliteration at NEWS 2018 is to promote machine transliteration research by providing a common benchmarking platform for the research community to evaluate state-of-the-art approaches to this problem. The task is to develop machine transliteration and/or back-transliteration systems in one or more of the provided language pairs.

For each language pair, training and development data sets containing source and target name pairs are released for participating teams to train their systems. At the evaluation time, test sets of source names only will be released, on which participants are expected to produce a ranked list of transliteration and/or back-transliteration candidates in the target language. The results will be automatically evaluated by using the same metrics used in previous editions of the shared task.

This year's shared task focuses mainly on "standard" submissions, i.e. output results from systems that have been trained only with the data provided by the shared task organizing team. This will ensure that all results for the same task are comparable across the different systems. Participants may submit several "standard" runs for each of the task they participate in. Those participants interested in submitting "non-standard" runs, i.e.

output results from systems that use additional data during the training phase, still will be able to do so. However such runs will be evaluated and reported separately.

2 Important Dates

Train/Development data release	12 March 2018
Test data release	07 May 2018
Results Submission Due	14 May 2018
Task (short) Papers Due	21 May 2018
Acceptance Notification	28 May 2018
Camera-Ready Deadline	04 June 2018
Workshop Date	20 July 2018

3 Participation

1. Registration (12 March 2018). Prospective participants are to register through the NEWS 2018 website by requesting the datasets from 12 March onwards.

2. Train/Development Data (12 March 2018). Registered participants are to obtain train and development data from the shared task registration form and/or the designated copyright owners of databases. All registered participants are required to participate in the evaluation of at least one language pair, submit the results, prepare a short paper and attend the workshop at ACL 2018.

3. Test Data (07 May 2018). The test data would be released on 07 May 2018, and the participants have a maximum of 7 days to submit their results to the competition site. NEWS 2018 shared task will be run on CodaLab. Participants need to create a codalab account and register into the NEWS 2018 competition in order to be able to submit their system results. Only "standard" runs will be

Proceedings of the Seventh Named Entities Workshop, pages 47–54
Melbourne, Australia, July 20, 2018. ©2018 Association for Computational Linguistics

processed this year. According to this, participants are required to use only the training and development data provided within the shared task to train their systems.

Participants can submit several runs for each individual language pair at the competition site. However, the total number of submissions per language pair will be limited to a maximum of 3 submissions per day, with a total maximum of 15 submissions during the whole period of the competition. From all submissions done to each individual language pair, each participant must select one to be posted on the leaderboard. Results on the leaderboard (by the last day of the shared task on 14 May 2018) will constitute the final official results of the shared task.

Each submission must be saved in a file named "results.xml" and submitted into the system in a ".zip" compressed file format. Each "results.xml" file can contain up to 10 output candidates in a ranked list for each corresponding input entry in the test file (refer to Appendix B for more details on file formating and naming conventions).

Those participants interested in submitting "non-standard" runs, i.e. transliteration results from systems that use additional data during the training phase, still will be able to do so. However such runs will be evaluated and reported separately (please contact the organizers).

4. Results (14 May 2018). Leaderboard results, as on 14 May 2018, will be considered the official evaluation results of the NEWS 2018 shared task. These results will be published on the workshop website and proceedings.

Note that only the scores (evaluation metrics) of the participating systems on each language pair will be published, and no explicit reference to the participating teams will be provided. Furthermore, all participants should agree on not to reveal identities of other participants in any of their publications unless permission from the other respective participants is granted. By default, all participants remain anonymous in published results. Participating teams are allowed to reveal only their own identity in their publications.

5. Shared Task Short Papers (21 May 2018). Each participant is required to submit a 4-page system paper (short paper) describing their system, the used approach, submissions and results. Peer reviews will be conducted to improve paper quality and readability and make sure the authors' ideas and methods can be understood by the workshop participants.

We are aiming at accepting all system papers, and selected ones will be presented orally in the workshop. All participants are required to register and attend the workshop to present their work. All paper submission and reviews will be managed electronically through https://www.softconf.com/acl2018/NEWS/.

4   Language Pairs

The different evaluation tasks within the NEWS 2018 shared task focus on transliteration and/or back-transliteration of personal and place names from a source language into a target language as summarized in Table 1. This year, the shared task offers 19 evaluation tasks, including 9 transliteration tasks, 6 back-transliteration tasks and 4 hybrid tasks. NEWS 2018 will release training, development and testing data for each of the language pairs. Within the 19 evaluation tasks, NEWS 2018 includes the 14 tasks that were evaluated in the previous year editions. In such cases, the training and development datasets are augmented versions of the previous year ones. New test dataset will be used in NEWS 2018 evaluations.

The names given in the training sets for Thai (T-EnTh & B-ThEn), Persian (T-EnPe & B-PeEn), Chinese (T-EnCh & B-ChEn), Hebrew (T-EnHe & B-HeEn), Vietnamese (T-EnVi), Japanese (T-EnJa) and Korean (T-EnKo) are Western names and their respective transliterations.

The training sets in the Persian (T-PeEn & B-EnPe) tasks are names of Persian origin. The training set in the English to Japanese Kanji (B-JnJk) task consists only of native Japanese names. The training set in the Arabic to English (T-ArEn) task consists only of native Arabic names. Finally, the training sets for the English to Indian languages Hindi (M-EnHi), Tamil (M-EnTa), Kannada (M-EnKa) and Bangla (M-EnBa) tasks consist of a mix of both Indian and Western names.

Name origin	Source script	Target script	Type of Task	Dataset Size			Task ID
				Train	Dev	Test	
Western	English	Thai	Transliteration	30781	1000	1000	T-EnTh
Western	Thai	English	Back-transliteration	27273	1000	1000	B-ThEn
Western	English	Persian	Transliteration	13386	1000	1000	T-EnPe
Western	Persian	English	Back-transliteration	15677	1000	1000	B-PeEn
Western	English	Chinese	Transliteration	41318	1000	1000	T-EnCh
Western	Chinese	English	Back-transliteration	32002	1000	1000	B-ChEn
Western	English	Vietnamese	Transliteration	3256	500	500	T-EnVi
Mixed	English	Hindi	Mixed trans/back	12937	1000	1000	M-EnHi
Mixed	English	Tamil	Mixed trans/back	10957	1000	1000	M-EnTa
Mixed	English	Kannada	Mixed trans/back	10955	1000	1000	M-EnKa
Mixed	English	Bangla	Mixed trans/back	13623	1000	1000	M-EnBa
Western	English	Hebrew	Transliteration	10501	1000	1000	T-EnHe
Western	Hebrew	English	Back-transliteration	9447	1000	1000	B-HeEn
Western	English	Japanese Katakana	Transliteration	28828	1000	1000	T-EnJa
Japanese	English	Japanese Kanji	Back-transliteration	10514	1000	1000	B-JnJk
Western	English	Korean Hangul	Transliteration	7387	1000	1000	T-EnKo
Arabic	Arabic	English	Transliteration	31354	1000	1000	T-ArEn
Persian	Persian	English	Transliteration	6000	1000	1000	T-PeEn
Persian	English	Persian	Back-transliteration	11204	1000	1000	B-EnPe

Table 1: Source and target languages for the shared task on transliteration.

5 Standard Datasets

Training Data (Parallel)

Paired names between source and target languages; size 3K – 41K.

Training data is used for training a basic transliteration system.

Development Data (Parallel)

Paired names between source and target languages; size 1K (500 for T-EnVi).

Development data is in addition to the training data, which is used for fine-tuning the system parameters, in case of need. Participants are allowed to use it as part of the training data for their final submissions.

Testing Data

Source names only; size 1K (500 for T-EnVi). This is a held-out set, which will be used for evaluating the quality of the transliterations.

Participants will need to obtain licenses from the respective copyright owners of the different datasets and/or agree to the terms and conditions of use that are given on the downloading website (Li et al., 2004; MSRI, 2010; CJKI, 2010). NEWS 2018 will provide the contact details for each dataset group.

The data would be provided in Unicode UTF-8 encoding, in XML format. The results are expected to be submitted in UTF-8 encoding also in XML format. The required XML format details are available in the Appendix A.

Note that name pairs are distributed as-is, as provided by the respective creators. While the datasets are mostly manually checked, there may be still inconsistencies (that is, non-standard usage, region-specific usage, errors, etc.) or incompleteness (that is, not all right variations may be covered). The participants are allowed to use any method of their preference to further clean up the data provided:

- For any participant conducting a manual clean up, we appeal that such data be provided back to the organizers for redistribution to all the participating groups in that language pair. Such sharing benefits all participants!

- If automatic clean up were used, such clean up will be considered part of the system implementation, and hence it is not required to be shared with all participants.

All participants are required to use only the dataset (parallel names) provided by the shared task organizers for training their systems. This "standard" submission procedure will ensure a fair evaluation in term of score comparison across the different systems. Those participants wanting to additionally evaluate "non-standard" runs need to contact the organizers

6 Evaluation Metrics

As in previous editions of the shared task, the quality of the submitted results will be evaluated by using the following 4 metrics. Each individual name result might include up to 10 output candidates in a ranked list.

Since a given source name may have multiple correct target transliterations, all these alternatives are treated equally in the evaluation. That is, any of these alternatives are considered as a correct transliteration, and the first correct transliteration in the ranked list is accepted as a correct hit.

The following notation is further assumed:

N : Total number of names (source words) in the test set.

n_i : Number of reference transliterations for i-th name in the test set ($n_i \geq 1$).

$r_{i,j}$: j-th reference transliteration for i-th name in the test set.

$c_{i,k}$: k-th candidate transliteration (system output) for i-th name in the test set ($1 \leq k \leq 10$).

K_i : Number of candidate transliterations produced by a transliteration system.

1. Word Accuracy in Top-1 (ACC) Also known as Word Error Rate. It measures correctness of the first transliteration candidate in the candidate list produced by a transliteration system. $ACC = 1$ means that all top candidates are correct transliterations i.e. they match one of the references, and $ACC = 0$ means that none of the top candidates are correct.

$$ACC = \frac{1}{N} \sum_{i=1}^{N} \left\{ \begin{array}{l} 1 \text{ if } \exists\, r_{i,j} : r_{i,j} = c_{i,1}; \\ 0 \text{ otherwise} \end{array} \right\} \tag{1}$$

2. Fuzziness in Top-1 (Mean F-score) The mean F-score measures how different, on average, the top transliteration candidate is from its closest reference. F-score for each source word is a function of Precision and Recall and equals 1 when the top candidate matches one of the references, and 0 when there are no common characters between the candidate and any of the references.

Precision and Recall are calculated based on the length of the Longest Common Subsequence between a candidate and a reference:

$$LCS(c, r) = \frac{1}{2} \left(|c| + |r| - ED(c, r) \right) \tag{2}$$

where ED is the edit distance and $|x|$ is the length of x. For example, the longest common subsequence between "abcd" and "afcde" is "acd" and its length is 3. The best matching reference, that is, the reference for which the edit distance has the minimum value, is taken for calculation. If the best matching reference is given by

$$r_{i,m} = \arg\min_{j} \left(ED(c_{i,1}, r_{i,j}) \right) \tag{3}$$

then Recall, Precision and F-score for i-th word are calculated as follows:

$$R_i = \frac{LCS(c_{i,1}, r_{i,m})}{|r_{i,m}|} \tag{4}$$

$$P_i = \frac{LCS(c_{i,1}, r_{i,m})}{|c_{i,1}|} \tag{5}$$

$$F_i = 2 \frac{R_i \times P_i}{R_i + P_i} \tag{6}$$

- The length is computed in distinct Unicode characters.

- No distinction is made among different character types of a language (e.g. vowel vs. consonants vs. combining diereses etc.)

3. Mean Reciprocal Rank (MRR) Measures traditional MRR *for any right answer* produced by the system, from among the candidates. $1/MRR$ tells approximately the average rank of the correct transliteration. MRR closer to 1 implies that the correct answer is mostly produced close to the top of the n-best lists.

$$RR_i = \left\{ \begin{array}{l} \min_j \frac{1}{j} \text{ if } \exists r_{i,j}, c_{i,k} : r_{i,j} = c_{i,k}; \\ 0 \text{ otherwise} \end{array} \right\} \tag{7}$$

$$MRR = \frac{1}{N} \sum_{i=1}^{N} RR_i \tag{8}$$

4. MAP$_{ref}$ Measures tightly the precision in the n-best candidates for i-th source name, for which reference transliterations are available. If all of the references are produced, then the MAP is 1. Let's denote the number of correct candidates for the i-th source word in k-best list as $num(i, k)$. MAP$_{ref}$ is then given by

$$MAP_{ref} = \frac{1}{N} \sum_{i}^{N} \frac{1}{n_i} \left(\sum_{k=1}^{n_i} num(i, k) \right) \tag{9}$$

7 Paper Format

Paper submissions to NEWS 2018 should follow the ACL 2018 paper submission policy, including paper format, blind review policy and title and author conventions. Full papers (research papers) must be in two-column format without exceeding eight (8) pages of content plus two (2) extra pages for references and short papers (research and shared task papers) must also be in two-column format without exceeding four (4) pages content plus two (2) extra pages for references. Submission must conform to the official ACL 2018 style guidelines. For details, please refer to the ACL 2018 website: http://acl2018.org/call-for-papers/.

8 Contact Us

If you have any questions about the share task and the datasets, please contact any of the workshop organizers. Contact information is available at the NEWS 2018 website http://workshop.colips.org/news2018/contact.html

References

[CJKI2010] CJK Institute. 2010. http://www.cjk.org/.

[Li et al.2004] Haizhou Li, Min Zhang, and Jian Su. 2004. A joint source-channel model for machine transliteration. In *Proc. 42nd ACL Annual Meeting*, pages 159–166, Barcelona, Spain.

[MSRI2010] MSRI. 2010. Microsoft Research India. http://research.microsoft.com/india.

[AILab2018] Artificial Intelligence Laboratory (AILab) 2018. Ho Chi Minh City University of Science (VNU-HCMUS). https://www.ailab.hcmus.edu.vn/

[Cao et al.2010] Nam X. Cao, Nhut M. Pham, Quan H. Vu. 2010. Comparative analysis of transliteration techniques based on statistical machine translation and joint-sequence model. In *Proc. Symposium on Information and Comunication Technology*, pages 59–63, ACM.

[Ngo et al.2015] Hoang Gia Ngo, Nancy F. Chen, Nguyen Binh Minh, Bin Ma, Haizhou Li. 2015. Phonology-Augmented Statistical Transliteration for Low-Resource Languages. Interspeech, 2015.

A Appendix: Data Formats

- File Naming Conventions:
  ```
  NEWS18_Z-XXYY_trn.xml
  NEWS18_Z-XXYY_dev.xml
  ```

  - Z: Type of task (T: transliteration, B: back-transliteration, M: mixed)
  - XX: Source Language
  - YY: Target Language

- File formats:
  All data will be made available in XML formats as illustrated in Figure 1.

- Data Encoding Formats:
  The data will be in Unicode UTF-8 encoding files without byte-order mark, and in the XML format specified.

B Appendix: Submission of Results

- File Naming Conventions:
  Each submission must be saved in a file named "results.xml" and submitted into the NEWS 2018 CodaLab competition in a ".zip" compressed file. Each "results.xml" file can contain up to 10 output candidates in a ranked list for each corresponding input entry in the test file.

- File formats:
  All data will be provided in XML formats as illustrated in Figure 2.

- Data Encoding Formats:
  The results are expected to be submitted in UTF-8 encoded files without byte-order mark only, and in the XML format specified.

```xml
<?xml version = "1.0" encoding = "UTF-8"?>

<TransliterationCorpus
    CorpusFormat = "UTF-8"
    CorpusID = "[task_id]"
    CorpusSize = "[total_number_of_names_in_file]"
    CorpusType = "[Training|Development]"
    NameSource = "[name_origin]"
    SourceLang = "[source_language]"
    TargetLang = "[target_language]">

    <Name ID="1">
        <SourceName>[source_name_1]</SourceName>
        <TargetName ID="1">[target_name_1_1]</TargetName>
        <TargetName ID="2">[target_name_1_2]</TargetName>
        ...
        <TargetName ID="n">[target_name_1_n]</TargetName>
    </Name>

    <Name ID="2">
        <SourceName>[source_name_2]</SourceName>
        <TargetName ID="1">[target_name_2_1]</TargetName>
        <TargetName ID="2">[target_name_2_2]</TargetName>
        ...
        <TargetName ID="k">[target_name_2_k]</TargetName>
    </Name>

    ...
    <!-- rest of the names to follow -->
    ...

</TransliterationCorpus>
```

Figure 1: Example of training and development data format.

```xml
<?xml version="1.0" encoding="UTF-8"?>

<TransliterationTaskResults
    SourceLang = "[source_language]"
    TargetLang = "[target_language]"
    GroupID = "[your_institution_name]"
    RunID = "[your_submission_number]"
    RunType = "Standard"
    Comments = "[your_comments_here]"
    TaskID = "[task_id]">

    <Name ID="1">
        <SourceName>[test_name_1]</SourceName>
        <TargetName ID="1">[your_system_result_1_1]</TargetName>
        <TargetName ID="2">[your_system_result_1_2]</TargetName>
        ...
        <TargetName ID="10">[your_system_result_1_10]</TargetName>
    </Name>

    <Name ID="2">
        <SourceName>[test_name_2]</SourceName>
        <TargetName ID="1">[your_system_result_2_1]</TargetName>
        <TargetName ID="2">[your_system_result_2_2]</TargetName>
        ...
        <TargetName ID="10">[your_system_result_2_10]</TargetName>
    </Name>


    ...
    <!-- All names in test corpus to follow -->
    ...

</TransliterationTaskResults>
```

Figure 2: Example of submission result format.

Report of NEWS 2018 Named Entity Transliteration Shared Task

Nancy Chen[1], Rafael E. Banchs[2], Min Zhang[3], Xiangyu Duan[3], Haizhou Li[4]

[1] Singapore University of Technology and Design, Singapore

nancychen@alum.mit.edu

[2] Nanyang Technological University, Singapore

rbanchs@ntu.edu.sg

[3] Soochow University, China

{minzhang,xiangyuduan}@suda.edu.cn

[4] National University of Singapore, Singapore

haizhou.li@nus.edu.sg

Abstract

This report presents the results from the Named Entity Transliteration Shared Task conducted as part of The Seventh Named Entities Workshop (NEWS 2018) held at ACL 2018 in Melbourne, Australia. Similar to previous editions of NEWS, the Shared Task featured 19 tasks on proper name transliteration, including 13 different languages and two different Japanese scripts. A total of 6 teams from 8 different institutions participated in the evaluation, submitting 424 runs, involving different transliteration methodologies. Four performance metrics were used to report the evaluation results. The NEWS shared task on machine transliteration has successfully achieved its objectives by providing a common ground for the research community to conduct comparative evaluations of state-of-the-art technologies that will benefit the future research and development in this area.

1   Introduction

Names play an important role in the performance of most natural language processing and information retrieval applications. They are also critical in cross-lingual applications such as machine translation and cross-language information retrieval, as it has been shown that system performance correlates positively with the quality of name conversion across languages (Demner-Fushman and Oard 2002, Mandl and Womser-Hacker 2005, Hermjakob et al. 2008, Udupa et al. 2009). Bilingual dictionaries constitute the traditional source of information for name conversion across languages, however they offer very limited support as in most languages names are continuously emerging and evolving.

All of the above points to the critical need for robust machine transliteration methods and systems. Significant efforts has been conducted by the research community to address the problem of machine transliteration (Knight and Graehl 1998, Meng et al. 2001, Li et al. 2004, Zelenko and Aone 2006, Sproat et al. 2006, Sherif and Kondrak 2007, Hermjakob et al. 2008, Al-Onaizan and Knight 2002, Goldwasser and Roth 2008, Goldberg and Elhadad 2008, Klementiev and Roth 2006, Oh and Choi 2002, Virga and Khudanpur 2003, Wan and Verspoor 1998, Kang and Choi 2000, Gao et al. 2004, Li et al. 2009a, Li et al. 2009b). These efforts fall into three main categories: grapheme-based, phoneme-based and hybrid methods. Grapheme based methods (Li et al. 2004) treat transliteration as a direct orthographic mapping and only uses orthography-related features while phoneme-based methods (Knight and Graehl 1998) make use of phonetic correspondences to generate the transliteration. The hybrid approach refers to the combination of several different models or knowledge sources to support the transliteration generation process. Recently, neural network approaches have been explored with varying successes, depending on the size of the training data.

The first machine transliteration shared task (Li et al. 2009a, Li et al. 2009b) was organized and conducted as part of NEWS 2009 at ACL-IJCNLP 2009. It was the first time that common benchmarking data in diverse language pairs was provided for evaluating state-of-the-art machine transliteration. While the focus of the 2009 shared task was on establishing the quality metrics and on setting up a baseline for transliteration quality based on those metrics, the 2010 shared task (Li et al. 2010a, Li et al. 2010b) fo-

Proceedings of the Seventh Named Entities Workshop, pages 55–73
Melbourne, Australia, July 20, 2018. ©2018 Association for Computational Linguistics

cused on expanding the scope of the transliteration generation task to about a dozen languages and on exploring the quality of the task depending on the direction of transliteration.

In NEWS 2011 (Zhang et al. 2011a, Zhang et al. 2011b), the focus was on significantly increasing the hand-crafted parallel corpora of named entities to include 14 different language pairs from 11 language families, and on making them available as the common dataset for the shared task.

The NEWS 2018 Shared Task on Named Entity Transliteration has been a continued effort for evaluating machine transliteration performance following the NEWS edition of 2012 (Zhang et al. 2012), 2015 (Zhang et al. 2015) and 2016 (Duan et al. 2016).

In this paper, we present in full detail the results of NEWS 2018 Named Entity Transliteration Shared Task. The rest of the paper is structured as follows. Section 2 provides as short review of the main characteristics of the machine transliteration task and the corpora used for it. Section 3 reviews the four metrics used for the evaluations. Section 4 reports specific details about participation in the shared task, and section 5 presents and discusses the evaluation results. Finally, section 6 presents our main conclusions and future plans.

2 Shared Task on Transliteration

Transliteration, sometimes also called Romanization, especially if Latin Scripts are used for target strings (Halpern 2007), deals with the conversion of names between two languages and/or script systems. Within the context of this transliteration shared task, we are aiming not only at addressing the name conversion process but also its practical utility for downstream applications, such as machine translation and cross-language information retrieval.

In this context, we adopt the same definition of transliteration as proposed during NEWS 2009 (Li et al. 2009a): transliteration is understood as the conversion of a given name in the source language (a text string in the source writing system or orthography) to a name in the target language (another text string in the target writing system or orthography) conditioned to the following specific requirements regarding the name representation in the target language:

- it is phonetically equivalent to the source name,
- it conforms to the phonology of the target language, and
- it matches the user intuition on its equivalence with respect to the source language name.

Following previous editions of NEWS some back-transliteration tasks are considered. Back-transliteration attempts to restore transliterated names back into their original source language. NEWS 2018 included a total of six back-transliteration tasks.

2.1 Shared Task Description

As in previous editions of the workshop series, the shared task in NEWS 2018 consists of developing machine transliteration systems in one or more of the specified language pairs. Each language pair of the shared task consists of a source and a target language, implicitly specifying the transliteration direction. Training and development data in each of the language pairs was made available to all registered participants for developing their transliteration systems.

At the evaluation time, hand-crafted test sets of source names were released to the participants, who were required to produce a ranked list of transliteration candidates in the target language for each source name. The system outputs were tested against their corresponding reference sets (which may include multiple correct transliterations for some source names). The performance of a system is quantified using multiple metrics (defined in Section 3).

In this edition of the workshop, only *standard* runs (restricted to the train and development data provided) were considered. No other data or linguistic resources were allowed for standard runs. This ensures parity between systems and enables meaningful comparison of performance of various algorithmic approaches in a given language pair. Participants were allowed to submit one or more standard runs for each task they participated in. If more than one standard runs were submitted, it was required to select one as the "primary" run by publishing it into the leaderboard. The primary runs are the ones used to compare results across different systems.

The NEWS 2018 Shared Task was run on CodaLab (http://codalab.org/).

2.2 Shared Task Corpora

Two specific constraints were considered when selecting languages for the shared task: language diversity and data availability. To make the shared task interesting and to attract wider participation, it is important to ensure a reasonable variety of linguistic diversity, orthography and geography. Following NEWS 2016, the tasks were grouped into five categories based on the specific organizations providing the datasets. The 19 tasks for NEWS 2018 are shown in Tables 1.a-e. In addition to the 14 tasks from NEWS 2016, five new tasks (highlighted in *italics*) have been included this year. This year, new evaluation data was generated and used.

Task ID	Type	Origin	Source	Target
T-EnTh	Trans.	Western	English	Thai
B-ThEn	Back.	Western	Thai	English

Table 1.a: NEWS 2018 Dataset_01

Task ID	Type	Origin	Source	Target
T-EnPe	trans.	western	English	Persian
B-PeEn	*back.*	*western*	*Persian*	*English*

Table 1.b: NEWS 2018 Dataset_02

Task ID	Type	Origin	Source	Target
T-EnCh	trans.	western	English	Chinese
B-ChEn	back.	western	Chinese	English
T-EnVi	*trans.*	*western*	*English*	*Vietnamese*

Table 1.c: NEWS 2018 Dataset_03

Task ID	Type	Origin	Source	Target
M-EnHi	mixed	mixed	English	Hindi
M-EnTa	mixed	mixed	English	Tamil
M-EnKa	mixed	mixed	English	Kannada
M-EnBa	mixed	mixed	English	Bangla
T-EnHe	trans.	western	English	Hebrew
B-HeEn	*back.*	*western*	*Hebrew*	*English*

Table 1.d: NEWS 2018 Dataset_04

Task ID	Type	Origin	Source	Target
T-EnJa	trans.	western	English	Katakana
B-JnJk	back.	japanese	English	Kanji
T-EnKo	trans.	western	English	Hangul
T-ArEn	trans.	arabic	Arabic	English
T-PeEn	*trans.*	*persian*	*Persian*	*English*
T-EnPe	*back.*	*persian*	*English*	*Persian*

Table 1.e: NEWS 2018 Dataset_05

In Tables 1.a-e, *Type* refers to the type of task (transliteration, back-transliteration or mixed); *Origin* refers to the origin of the names; and *Source/Target* refer to the source/target scripts.

3 Evaluation Metrics and Rationale

The participants have been asked to submit standard and, optionally, non-standard runs. One of the standard runs must be named as the primary submission, which was the one used for the performance summary. Each run must contain a ranked list of up to ten candidate transliterations for each source name. The submitted results are compared to the ground truth (reference transliterations) using four evaluation metrics capturing different aspects of transliteration performance. The four considered evaluation metrics are

- Word Accuracy in Top-1 (ACC),
- Fuzziness in Top-1 (Mean F-score) (Powers 2011),
- Mean Reciprocal Rank (MRR) (Voorhees 1999), and
- Mean Average Precision (MAP_{ref}) (Powers 2011).

In the next subsections, we present a brief description of the four considered evaluation metrics. The following notation is further assumed:

- N: Total number of names (source words) in the test set,
- n_i: Number of reference transliterations for i-th name in the test set ($n_i \geq 1$),
- $r_{i,j}$: j-th reference transliteration for i-th name in the test set,
- $c_{i,k}$: k-th candidate transliteration (system output) for i-th name in the test set ($1 \leq k \leq 10$),
- K_i: Number of candidate transliterations produced by a transliteration system.

3.1 Word Accuracy in Top-1 (ACC)

Also known as Word Error Rate, it measures correctness of the first transliteration candidate in the candidate list produced by a transliteration system. $ACC = 1$ means that all top candidates are correct transliterations; i.e. they match one of the references, and $ACC = 0$ means that none of the top candidates are correct.

$$ACC = \frac{1}{N}\sum_{i=1}^{N}\left\{ \begin{array}{l} 1 \; if \; \exists r_{i,j} : r_{i,j} = c_{i,1} \; ; \\ 0 \; otherwise \end{array} \right\} \qquad (Eq.1)$$

3.2 Fuzziness in Top-1 (Mean F-score)

The Mean F-score measures how different, on average, the top transliteration candidate is from its closest reference. F-score for each source word is a function of Precision and Recall and equals 1 when the top candidate matches one of the references, and 0 when there are no common characters between the candidate and any of the references.

Precision and Recall are calculated based on the length of the Longest Common Subsequence (LCS) between a candidate and a reference:

$$LCS(c,r) = \tfrac{1}{2}\big(|c| + |r| - ED(c,r)\big) \qquad \text{(Eq.2)}$$

where ED is the edit distance and $|x|$ is the length of x. For example, the longest common subsequence between "abcd" and "afcde" is "acd" and its length is 3. The best matching reference, i.e. the reference for which the edit distance has the minimum, is taken for calculation. If the best matching reference is given by

$$r_{i,m} = \arg\min_j\big(ED(c_{i,1}, r_{i,j})\big) \qquad \text{(Eq.3)}$$

the Recall, Precision and F-score for the i-th word are calculated as:

$$R_i = \frac{LCS(c_{i,1}, r_{i,m})}{|r_{i,m}|} \qquad \text{(Eq.4)}$$

$$P_i = \frac{LCS(c_{i,1}, r_{i,m})}{|c_{i,1}|} \qquad \text{(Eq.5)}$$

$$F_i = 2\frac{R_i \times P_i}{R_i + P_i} \qquad \text{(Eq.6)}$$

The lengths are computed with respect to distinct Unicode characters, and no distinctions are made for different character types of a language (e.g. vowel vs. consonant vs. combining diereses).

3.3 Mean Reciprocal Rank (MRR)

Measures traditional MRR for any right answer produced by the system, from among the candidates. 1/MRR tells approximately the average rank of the correct transliteration. MRR closer to 1 implies that the correct answer is mostly produced close to the top of the n-best lists.

$$RR_i = \begin{cases} \min_j \tfrac{1}{j} & if\ \exists r_{i,j}, c_{i,k} : r_{i,j} = c_{i,k}\ ; \\ 0 & otherwise \end{cases} \qquad \text{(Eq.7)}$$

$$MRR = \tfrac{1}{N}\sum_{i=1}^{N} RR_i \qquad \text{(Eq.8)}$$

3.4 Mean Average Precision (MAP$_{ref}$)

This metric measures tightly the precision in the n-best candidates for i-th source name, for which reference transliterations are available. If all of the references are produced, then the MAP is 1. If we denote the number of correct candidates for the i-th source word in k-best list as $num(i,k)$, then MAP$_{ref}$ is given by:

$$MAP_{ref} = \tfrac{1}{N}\sum_{i=1}^{N}\tfrac{1}{n_i}\Big(\sum_{k=1}^{n_i} num(i,k)\Big) \qquad \text{(Eq.9)}$$

4 Participation in the Shared Task

A total of six teams from eight different institutions participated in the NEWS 2018 Shared Task. More specifically, the participating teams were from University of Alberta (UALB), University of Edinburgh (EDI), University of Jadavpur and Universitat des Saarlandes (UJUS), Universite du Quebec a Montreal (UQAM), and team SINGA (from National University of Singapore and Singapore University of Technology and Design) and WIPO (World Intellectual Property Organization)[1].

In total, we received 424 standard runs. Table 2 summarizes the number of standard runs and the teams participated in each task.

Task	Std	Teams Participating
T-EnPe	13	UALB, EDI, UJUS, SINGA
B-ThEn	30	UALB, EDI, SINGA
T-EnTh	31	UALB, EDI, UJUS, SINGA
T-EnHe	27	UALB, EDI, UJUS, SINGA
M-EnBa	27	UALB, EDI, UJUS, SINGA
M-EnKa	29	UALB, EDI, UJUS, SINGA
M-EnTa	28	UALB, EDI, UJUS, SINGA
M-EnHi	30	UALB, EDI, UJUS, SINGA
T-ArEn	14	UALB, SINGA
B-JnJk	6	UALB
T-EnJa	17	UALB, SINGA
T-EnKo	15	UALB, SINGA
B-ChEn	29	UALB, EDI, UJUS, SINGA
T-EnCh	27	UALB, EDI, UJUS, WIPO, SINGA
T-PeEn	16	UALB, EDI, UJUS, SINGA
T-EnVi	29	UQAM, UALB, EDI, UJUS, SINGA
B-HeEn	29	UALB, EDI, UJUS, SINGA
B-EnPe	17	UALB, EDI, UJUS, SINGA
B-PeEn	10	EDI, SINGA
Overall	424	-

Table 2: Number of standard (Std) runs submitted, and teams participating in each task.

Table 2 shows that the most popular task continues to be the transliteration from English to Chinese (Zhang et al. 2012), followed by Chinese to English, English to Hindi, and English to Tamil.

5 Task Results and Analysis

In this section, we present the official results of the shared task along with brief descriptions of

---

[1] This last team did not submit a system paper, but we are including their submission result for the sake of completeness.

the different participant systems and some recommendations for future improvements.

5.1 Shared Task Results

Figure 1 summarizes the results of the NEWS 2018 Shared Task. In the figure, only F-scores over the NEWS 2018 evaluation test set for all primary standard submissions are depicted. A total of 66 primary standard submissions were received.

Most language pairs are able to achieve close to 80% or more in terms of F-score for at least some systems. An intriguing observation from Figure 1 is that for the language pair English-Chinese, the back-transliteration task from Chinese to English performs at least 15% better than the transliteration task from English to Chinese.

It also can be observed from the table that results for the T-EnPe and the B-PeEn tasks (western names) are significantly low. This resulted from a mismatch on scripting conventions used for the Persian language between the original train and development sets and the newly developed test set.

A much more comprehensive presentation of results for the NEWS 2018 Shared Task is provided in the Appendix at the end of this paper, where the resulting scores are reported for all received submissions for all four metrics, including non-primary submissions. All results are presented in 19 tables, each of which reports the scores for one transliteration task. In the tables, all primary standard runs are highlighted in bold-italic fonts.

5.2 Participant Systems

This year, the SINGA team (Snigdha et al. 2018) provided two baseline systems using Sequitur and Moses (phrase-based machine translation). All other systems used some version of neural modeling. It is interesting to note that non-neural systems by SINGA, while not the highest in performance, are generally comparable to neural systems or system combinations which include neural models.

Regarding the systems participating in this year evaluation, the UALB's system (Najafi et al. 2018) was based on multiple system combinations. They presented experimental results involving five different well-known transliteration approaches: DirecTL+(Jiampojamarn et al. 2009), Sequitur (Bisani and Ney 2008), OpenNMT (Klein et al. 2017), BaseNMT (Sutskever et al. 2014), and RL-NMT (Najafi et al., 2018). They

showed improvements of up to 8% absolute over a baseline system by using system combination.

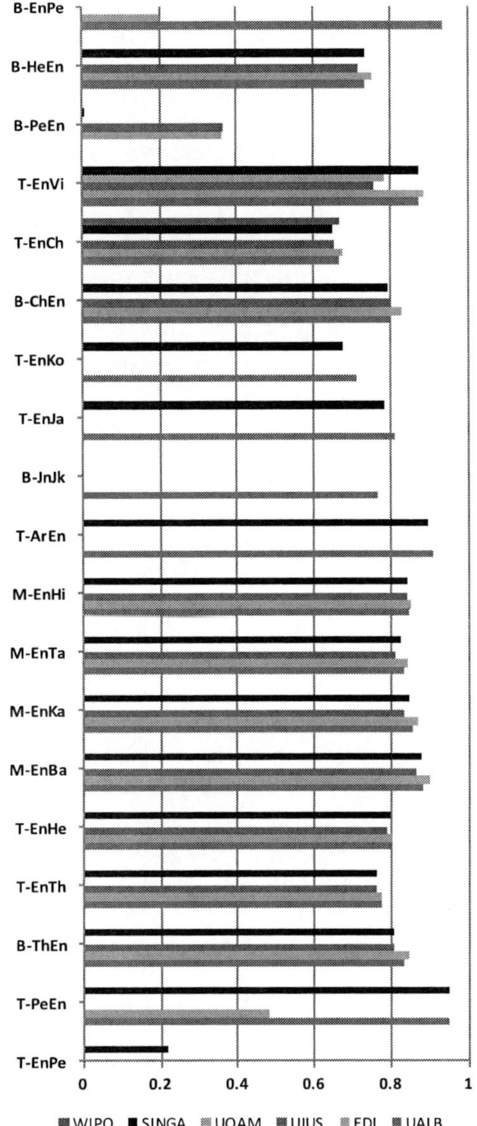

Figure 1: Mean F-scores (Top-1) on the evaluation set for all primary submissions and tasks.

The UJUS system (Kundu et al. 2018) used an RNN-based NMT framework and a CNN-based NMT framework, where both byte-pair encoding and character-based segmentation were employed for both cases. They also adopted an ensemble method to choose the hypothesis that has the highest frequency of occurrence to further improve accuracy.

The EDI system (Grundkiewicz et al. 2018) system uses a deep attention RNN encoder decoder model, which employed neural machine translation techniques such as dropout regularization, model ensembling, and re-scoring with right-left models. The EDI system is competitive, outperforming other teams in most of the tasks it participated in.

The UQAM system (Le et al. 2018) aligned the sequences in the English Vietnamese language pair before an RNN based machine transliteration system was trained.

5.3 Issues and Recommendations

In this section, we report some issues encountered during the shared task execution along with recommendations for future improvement of the Shared Task on Named Entity Transliteration.[2]

- As mentioned in section 5.1, scripting discrepancies between the train/dev data and the test data occurred for Persian characters in the T-EnPe and B-PeEn tasks. Specifically, the newly developed test set happens to contain a mixture of the Persian and Arabic scripts, which includes visually similar characters that have distinct encodings. This dataset will be revised to resolve this problem for the next evaluation campaign.

- Some of the datasets for the shared task are available under specific licensing agreements that have to be undertaken directly by the participants from the data providers. The organizing team will explore alternative means to offer all the datasets in the shared task under a unique centralized licensing agreement, which should be ideally free of cost for the participants.

- Some of the participants experienced failures and delays during submissions to the CodaLab system. Most of these problems are due to server overloads. The organizing team will contact CodaLab support to see how these problems can be fully resolved, or at least minimized, in the future editions of the shared task.

- Participants also believe that better publicity for the shared task would result in increased participation in the task. NEWS workshop organizers receive a significant number of request for dataset and information about the shared task throughout the year. However, the total number of participants in the shared task does not reflect such actual interests from the research community on the data and the tasks. Publicity strategies and shared task timelines will be revised accordingly.

6   Conclusions

The Shared Task on Named Entity Transliteration in NEWS 2018 has shown that the research community has a continued interest in this area. This report summarizes the results of the NEWS 2018 Shared Task.

We are pleased to report a comprehensive set of machine transliteration approaches and their evaluation results from 6 teams from 8 different institutions that participated in the shared task. This year, we received 424 runs in total. Most of the current state-of-the-art in machine transliteration is represented in the systems that have participated in the shared task.

Encouraged by the continued success of the NEWS workshop series, we plan to continue this event in the future to further promoting machine transliteration research and development.

Acknowledgments

The organizers of the NEWS 2018 Shared Task would like to thank the Institute for Infocomm Research (Singapore), National University of Singapore, Artificial Intelligence Laboratory at the Ho Chi Minh City University of Science (AILab, VNU-HCMUS, Vietnam), Microsoft Research India, the Computer Science & Engineering Department of Jadavpur University (India), the CJK Institute (Japan), the National Electronics and Computer Technology Center (NECTEC, Thailand) and Sarvnaz Karim (RMIT, Australia) for providing the corpora and technical support. Without those, the Shared Task would not be possible. In addition, we want to thank Grandee Lee and Snigdha Singhania for their help and support with CodaLab and the baseline systems, respectively. We also want to thank all programme committee members for their valuable comments that improved the quality of the shared task papers and, finally, we wish to thank all participants for their active participation, which have made again the NEWS 2018 edition of the Shared Task on Named Entity Transliteration a successful competition.

References

Y. Al-Onaizan, K. Knight. 2002. Machine transliteration of names in arabic text. In Proc. ACL-2002Workshop: Computational Apporaches to Semitic Languages, Philadelphia, PA, USA.

---

[2] The organizers would like to thank all the participants, especially the University of Alberta team, for their valuable feedback and suggestions.

M. Bisani, H. Ney. 2008. Joint sequence models for grapheme-to-phoneme conversion. Speech Communication, 50(5):434–451.

CJKI. 2010. CJK Institute. http://www.cjk.org/.

D. Demner-Fushman, D.W. Oard. 2002. The effect of bilingual term list size on dictionary-based cross-language information retrieval. In Proc. 36-th Hawaii Int'l. Conf. System Sciences, volume 4, page 108.2.

W. Gao, K.F. Wong, W. Lam. 2004. Phoneme-based transliteration of foreign names for OOV problem. In Proc. IJCNLP, pages 374–381, Sanya, Hainan, China.

Y. Goldberg, M. Elhadad. 2008. Identification of transliterated foreign words in Hebrew script. In Proc. CICLing, volume LNCS 4919, pages 466–477.

D. Goldwasser, D. Roth. 2008. Transliteration as constrained optimization. In Proc. EMNLP, pages 353–362.

R. Grundkiewicz and K. Heafield. 2018. Neural Machine Translation Techniques for Named Entity Transliteration. In Proc. Named Entities Workshop at ACL 2018.

J. Halpern. 2007. The challenges and pitfalls of Arabic romanization and arabization. In Proc. Workshop on Comp. Approaches to Arabic Scriptbased Lang.

U. Hermjakob, K. Knight, H. Daum. 2008. Name translation in statistical machine translation: Learning when to transliterate. In Proc. ACL, Columbus, OH, USA, June.

S. Jiampojamarn, C. Cherry, G. Kondrak. 2010. Integrating joint n-gram features into a discriminative training framework. In Proceedings of NAACL-2010, Los Angeles, CA, June. Association for Computational Linguistics.

B.J. Kang, K.S. Choi. 2000. English-Korean automatic transliteration/ backtransliteration system and character alignment. In Proc. ACL, pages 17–18, Hong Kong.

G. Klein, Y. Kim, Y. Deng, J. Senellart, and A. M. Rush. 2017. Opennmt: Open-source toolkit for neural machine translation. In Proc. ACL.

A. Klementiev, D. Roth. 2006. Weakly supervised named entity transliteration and discovery from multilingual comparable corpora. In Proc. 21st Int'l Conf Computational Linguistics and 44th Annual Meeting of ACL, pages 817–824, Sydney, Australia, July.

K. Knight, J. Graehl. 1998. Machine transliteration. Computational Linguistics, 24(4).

P. Koehn, H. Hoang, A. Birch, C. Callison-Burch, M. Federico, N. Bertoldi, B. Cowan, W. Shen, C. Moran, R. Zens, C. Dyer, O. Bojar, A. Constantin, E. Herbst. 2007. Moses: Open source toolkit for statistical machine translation. In Proceedings of the 45th Annual Meeting of the Association for Computational Linguistics Companion Volume Proceedings of the Demo and Poster Sessions, pages 177–180, Prague, Czech Republic.

A. Kumaran, T. Kellner. 2007. A generic framework for machine transliteration. In Proc. SIGIR, pages 721–722.

S. Kundu, S. Paul, S. Pal. 2018. A Deep Learning Based Approach to Transliteration. In Proc. Named Entities Workshop at ACL 2018.

N. T. Le and F. Sadat. 2018. Low-Resource Machine Transliteration Using Recurrent Neural Networks of Asian Languages. In Proc. Named Entities Workshop at ACL 2018.

H. Li, M. Zhang, J. Su. 2004. A joint source-channel model for machine transliteration. In Proc. 42nd ACL Annual Meeting, pages 159–166, Barcelona, Spain.

H. Li, A. Kumaran, V. Pervouchine, M. Zhang. 2009a. Report of NEWS 2009 machine transliteration shared task. In Proc. Named Entities Workshop at ACL 2009.

H. Li, A. Kumaran, M. Zhang, V. Pervouchine. 2009b. ACL-IJCNLP 2009 Named Entities Workshop - Shared Task on Transliteration. In Proc. Named Entities Workshop at ACL 2009.

H. Li, A. Kumaran, M. Zhang, V. Pervouchine. 2010a. Report of news 2010 transliteration generation shared task. In Proc. Named Entities Workshop at ACL 2010.

H. Li, A. Kumaran, M. Zhang, V. Pervouchine. 2010b. Whitepaper of news 2010 shared task on transliteration generation. In Proc. Named Entities Workshop at ACL 2010.

T. Mandl, C. Womser-Hacker. 2005. The effect of named entities on effectiveness in cross-language information retrieval evaluation. In Proc. ACM Symp. Applied Comp., pages 1059–1064.

H.M. Meng, W.K. Lo, B. Chen, K. Tang. 2001. Generate phonetic cognates to handle name entities in English-Chinese cross-language spoken document retrieval. In Proc. ASRU.

MSRI. 2009. Microsoft Research India. http://research.microsoft.com/india.

S. Najafi, Bradley Hauer, Rashed Rubby Riyadh, Lyeuan Yu, Gregorz Kondrak. 2018. Comparison of Assorted Models of Transliteration. In Proc. Named Entities Workshop at ACL 2018.

J.H. Oh, K.S. Choi. 2002. An English-Korean transliteration model using pronunciation and contextual rules. In Proc. COLING 2002, Taipei, Taiwan.

D. M. W. Powers. (2011). "Evaluation: From Precision, Recall and F-Measure to ROC, Informedness, Markedness & Correlation" (PDF). Journal of Machine Learning Technologies. 2 (1): 37–63.

T. Sherif, G. Kondrak. 2007. Substringbased transliteration. In Proc. 45th Annual Meeting of the ACL, pages 944–951, Prague, Czech Republic, June.

S. Singhania, M. Nguyen, H. G. Ngo, N. F. Chen. 2018. Statistical Machine Transliteration Baselines for NEWS 2018. In Proc. Named Entities Workshop at ACL 2018.

R. Sproat, T. Tao, C.X. Zhai. 2006. Named entity transliteration with comparable corpora. In Proc. 21st Int'l Conf Computational Linguistics and 44th Annual Meeting of ACL, pages 73–80, Sydney, Australia.

I. Sutskever, Oriol Vinyals, and Quoc V Le. 2014. Sequence to sequence learning with neural networks. In Advances in Neural Information Processing Systems 27, pages 3104–3112.

R. Udupa, K. Saravanan, A. Bakalov, A. Bhole. 2009. "They are out there, if you know where to look": Mining transliterations of OOV query terms for cross-language information retrieval. In LNCS: Advances in Information Retrieval, volume 5478, pages 437–448. Springer Berlin / Heidelberg.

P. Virga, S. Khudanpur. 2003. Transliteration of proper names in cross-lingual information retrieval. In Proc. ACL MLNER, Sapporo, Japan.

E. M. Voorhees. 1999. Proceedings of the 8th Text Retrieval Conference. TREC-8 Question Answering Track Report. pp. 77–82.

S. Wan, C.M. Verspoor. 1998. Automatic English-Chinese name transliteration for development of multilingual resources. In Proc. COLING, pages 1352–1356.

D. Zelenko, C. Aone. 2006. Discriminative methods for transliteration. In Proc. EMNLP, pages 612–617, Sydney, Australia, July.

M. Zhang, A. Kumaran, H. Li. 2011a. Whitepaper of news 2011 shared task on machine transliteration. In Proc. Named Entities Workshop at IJCNLP 2011.

M. Zhang, H. Li, A. Kumaran, M. Liu. 2011b. Report of news 2011 machine transliteration shared task. In Proc. Named Entities Workshop at IJCNLP 2011.

M. Zhang, H. Li, A. Kumaran, M. Liu. 2012. Report of NEWS 2012 Machine Transliteration Shared Task. Proceedings of the 50th Annual Meeting of the Association for Computational Linguistics, pages 10–20, Jeju, Republic of Korea.

Appendix: Evaluation Results

Team	Test Set	Accuracy	F-score	MRR	MAP
EDI	**NEWS18**	**0.0010 (1)**	**0.2111 (4)**	**0.0044 (3)**	**0.0010 (1)**
EDI	NEWS18	0.0010 (1)	0.2063 (5)	0.0041 (4)	0.0010 (1)
UALB	**NEWS18**	**0.0010 (1)**	**0.2056 (6)**	**0.0010 (5)**	**0.0010 (1)**
UALB	NEWS18	0.0010 (1)	0.2042 (7)	0.0051 (1)	0.0010 (1)
UALB	NEWS18	0.0010 (1)	0.2034 (8)	0.0051 (1)	0.0010 (1)
UALB	NEWS18	0.0010 (1)	0.2012 (9)	0.0044 (2)	0.0010 (1)
SINGA	**NEWS18**	**0.0010 (1)**	**0.2167 (1)**	**0.0010 (5)**	**0.0010 (1)**
SINGA	NEWS18	0.0010 (1)	0.2167 (1)	0.0010 (5)	0.0010 (1)
SINGA	NEWS18	0.0010 (1)	0.2167 (1)	0.0010 (5)	0.0010 (1)
UJUS	**NEWS18**	**0.0010 (1)**	**0.2145 (2)**	**0.0010 (5)**	**0.0010 (1)**
UJUS	NEWS18	0.0010 (1)	0.2137 (3)	0.0010 (5)	0.0010 (1)
UJUS	NEWS18	0.0010 (1)	0.1928 (11)	0.0010 (5)	0.0010 (1)
UJUS	NEWS18	0.0000 (2)	0.1987 (10)	0.0000 (6)	0.0000 (2)

Table A1: Results for the English to Persian transliteration task (T-EnPe) on Evaluation Test. Numbers in parentheses refer to the ranking of the submitted system.

Team	Test Set	Accuracy	F-score	MRR	MAP
EDI	**NEWS18**	**0.0033 (2)**	**0.3590 (2)**	**0.0086 (2)**	**0.0030 (2)**
EDI	NEWS18	0.0022 (3)	0.3235 (4)	0.0053 (3)	0.0019 (3)
EDI	NEWS18	0.0000 (4)	0.0014 (8)	0.0000 (4)	0.0000 (4)
SINGA	**NEWS18**	**0.0000 (4)**	**0.0098 (5)**	**0.0000 (4)**	**0.0000 (4)**
SINGA	NEWS18	0.0000 (4)	0.0077 (6)	0.0000 (4)	0.0000 (4)
SINGA	NEWS18	0.0000 (4)	0.0074 (7)	0.0000 (4)	0.0000 (4)
SINGA	NEWS18	0.0000 (4)	0.0074 (7)	0.0000 (4)	0.0000 (4)
UJUS	**NEWS18**	**0.0088 (1)**	**0.3662 (1)**	**0.0088 (1)**	**0.0078 (1)**
UJUS	NEWS18	0.0000 (4)	0.3573 (3)	0.0000 (4)	0.0000 (4)
UJUS	NEWS18	0.0000 (4)	0.3573 (3)	0.0000 (4)	0.0000 (4)

Table A2: Results for the Persian to English transliteration task (B-PeEn) on Evaluation Test. Numbers in parentheses refer to the ranking of the submitted system.

Team	Test Set	ACC	F-score	MRR	MAP$_{ref}$
EDI	**NEWS18**	**0.0010 (12)**	**0.4817 (12)**	**0.0022 (13)**	**0.0012 (13)**
EDI	NEWS18	0.0000 (13)	0.0014 (13)	0.0000 (14)	0.0000 (14)
EDI	NEWS18	0.0000 (13)	0.0000 (14)	0.0000 (14)	0.0000 (14)
UALB	**NEWS18**	**0.6880 (1)**	**0.9515 (1)**	**0.7755 (3)**	**0.6081 (1)**
UALB	NEWS18	0.6820 (2)	0.9498 (3)	0.7777 (2)	0.6050 (2)
UALB	NEWS18	0.6800 (3)	0.9508 (2)	0.7780 (1)	0.6049 (3)
UALB	NEWS18	0.6450 (6)	0.9462 (5)	0.7476 (6)	0.5786 (4)
UALB	NEWS18	0.6440 (7)	0.9429 (7)	0.7546 (4)	0.5748 (5)
UALB	NEWS18	0.6380 (8)	0.9420 (8)	0.7516 (5)	0.5721 (6)
UALB	NEWS18	0.5070 (9)	0.9174 (9)	0.5070 (10)	0.4368 (9)
UALB	NEWS18	0.3930 (10)	0.9094 (10)	0.5075 (9)	0.3486 (10)
SINGA	**NEWS18**	**0.6580 (4)**	**0.9476 (4)**	**0.6580 (7)**	**0.5701 (7)**
SINGA	NEWS18	0.6560 (5)	0.9437 (6)	0.6560 (8)	0.5663 (8)

SINGA	NEWS18	0.6560 (5)	0.9437 (6)	0.6560 (8)	0.5663 (8)
SINGA	NEWS18	0.2460 (11)	0.9019 (11)	0.4812 (11)	0.2363 (11)
SINGA	NEWS18	0.2460 (11)	0.9019 (11)	0.2460 (12)	0.2060 (12)

Table A3: Results for the Persian to English transliteration task (T-PeEn) on Evaluation Test. Numbers in parentheses refer to the ranking of the submitted system.

Team	Test Set	Accuracy	F-score	MRR	MAP
EDI	**NEWS18**	**0.2367 (1)**	**0.8405 (1)**	**0.3291 (1)**	**0.2367 (1)**
EDI	NEWS18	0.2155 (2)	0.8361 (2)	0.3148 (2)	0.2155 (2)
EDI	NEWS18	0.0544 (21)	0.4591 (26)	0.0687 (23)	0.0544 (21)
EDI	NEWS18	0.0504 (22)	0.4577 (27)	0.0658 (24)	0.0504 (22)
UALB	**NEWS18**	**0.2135 (3)**	**0.8348 (3)**	**0.3078 (3)**	**0.2135 (3)**
UALB	NEWS18	0.2105 (4)	0.8314 (5)	0.3016 (5)	0.2105 (4)
UALB	NEWS18	0.2064 (5)	0.8332 (4)	0.3019 (4)	0.2064 (5)
UALB	NEWS18	0.1974 (6)	0.8271 (7)	0.2873 (6)	0.1974 (6)
UALB	NEWS18	0.1934 (7)	0.8304 (6)	0.2638 (9)	0.1934 (7)
UALB	NEWS18	0.1853 (8)	0.8175 (11)	0.2700 (8)	0.1853 (8)
UALB	NEWS18	0.1813 (11)	0.8217 (9)	0.1813 (13)	0.1813 (11)
UALB	NEWS18	0.1793 (12)	0.8159 (13)	0.2586 (10)	0.1793 (12)
SINGA	**NEWS18**	**0.1833 (9)**	**0.8260 (8)**	**0.1833 (11)**	**0.1833 (9)**
SINGA	NEWS18	0.1833 (9)	0.8260 (8)	0.1833 (11)	0.1833 (9)
SINGA	NEWS18	0.1833 (9)	0.8173 (12)	0.1833 (11)	0.1833 (9)
SINGA	NEWS18	0.1823 (10)	0.8126 (14)	0.2735 (7)	0.1823 (10)
SINGA	NEWS18	0.1813 (11)	0.7996 (20)	0.1813 (13)	0.1813 (11)
SINGA	NEWS18	0.1601 (16)	0.8176 (10)	0.1601 (18)	0.1601 (16)
SINGA	NEWS18	0.1581 (17)	0.7930 (23)	0.1581 (19)	0.1581 (17)
SINGA	NEWS18	0.0000 (23)	0.7668 (24)	0.0000 (25)	0.0000 (23)
UJUS	**NEWS18**	**0.1823 (10)**	**0.8076 (17)**	**0.1823 (12)**	**0.1823 (10)**
UJUS	NEWS18	0.1793 (12)	0.8100 (16)	0.1793 (14)	0.1793 (12)
UJUS	NEWS18	0.1702 (13)	0.8039 (18)	0.1702 (15)	0.1702 (13)
UJUS	NEWS18	0.1641 (14)	0.8109 (15)	0.1641 (16)	0.1641 (14)
UJUS	NEWS18	0.1631 (15)	0.7954 (22)	0.1631 (17)	0.1631 (15)
UJUS	NEWS18	0.1541 (18)	0.8006 (19)	0.1541 (20)	0.1541 (18)
UJUS	NEWS18	0.1460 (19)	0.7995 (21)	0.1460 (21)	0.1460 (19)
UJUS	NEWS18	0.1339 (20)	0.7591 (25)	0.1339 (22)	0.1339 (20)

Table A4: Results for the English to Tamil transliteration task (M-EnTa) on Evaluation Test. Numbers in parentheses refer to the ranking of the submitted system.

Team	Test Set	Accuracy	F-score	MRR	MAP
EDI	**NEWS18**	**0.3333 (2)**	**0.8515 (1)**	**0.4455 (1)**	**0.3333 (2)**
EDI	NEWS18	0.3283 (3)	0.8501 (2)	0.4426 (2)	0.3283 (3)
EDI	NEWS18	0.0400 (25)	0.4488 (27)	0.0568 (26)	0.0400 (25)
UALB	**NEWS18**	**0.3243 (4)**	**0.8472 (4)**	**0.4287 (4)**	**0.3243 (4)**
UALB	NEWS18	0.3233 (5)	0.8472 (5)	0.3935 (8)	0.3233 (5)
UALB	NEWS18	0.3223 (6)	0.8474 (3)	0.4291 (3)	0.3223 (6)
UALB	NEWS18	0.3193 (7)	0.8438 (6)	0.4235 (5)	0.3193 (7)
UALB	NEWS18	0.3033 (11)	0.8374 (16)	0.4083 (7)	0.3033 (11)
UALB	NEWS18	0.2943 (15)	0.8407 (12)	0.2943 (18)	0.2943 (15)
UALB	NEWS18	0.2683 (19)	0.8347 (20)	0.3873 (9)	0.2683 (19)
UALB	NEWS18	0.2543 (21)	0.8290 (21)	0.3741 (10)	0.2543 (21)
UALB	NEWS18	0.0000 (27)	0.0509 (29)	0.0000 (28)	0.0000 (27)
SINGA	**NEWS18**	**0.3343 (1)**	**0.8383 (14)**	**0.3343 (11)**	**0.3343 (1)**

SINGA	NEWS18	0.3333 (2)	0.8426 (8)	0.3333 (12)	0.3333 (2)
SINGA	NEWS18	0.3153 (8)	0.8417 (9)	0.3153 (13)	0.3153 (8)
SINGA	NEWS18	0.3143 (9)	0.8407 (11)	0.4167 (6)	0.3143 (9)
SINGA	NEWS18	0.3113 (10)	0.8369 (17)	0.3113 (14)	0.3113 (10)
SINGA	NEWS18	0.3013 (12)	0.8377 (15)	0.3013 (15)	0.3013 (12)
SINGA	NEWS18	0.3013 (12)	0.8377 (15)	0.3013 (15)	0.3013 (12)
SINGA	NEWS18	0.0010 (26)	0.3856 (28)	0.0010 (27)	0.0010 (26)
SINGA	NEWS18	0.0000 (27)	0.7784 (26)	0.0000 (28)	0.0000 (27)
UJUS	**NEWS18**	**0.2993 (13)**	**0.8401 (13)**	**0.2993 (16)**	**0.2993 (13)**
UJUS	NEWS18	0.2963 (14)	0.8429 (7)	0.2963 (17)	0.2963 (14)
UJUS	NEWS18	0.2923 (16)	0.8408 (10)	0.2923 (19)	0.2923 (16)
UJUS	NEWS18	0.2833 (17)	0.8359 (18)	0.2833 (20)	0.2833 (17)
UJUS	NEWS18	0.2773 (18)	0.8347 (19)	0.2773 (21)	0.2773 (18)
UJUS	NEWS18	0.2553 (20)	0.8195 (24)	0.2553 (22)	0.2553 (20)
UJUS	NEWS18	0.2502 (22)	0.8275 (22)	0.2502 (23)	0.2502 (22)
UJUS	NEWS18	0.2472 (23)	0.8223 (23)	0.2472 (24)	0.2472 (23)
UJUS	NEWS18	0.2312 (24)	0.7982 (25)	0.2312 (25)	0.2312 (24)

Table A5: Results for the English to Hindi transliteration task (M-EnHi) on Evaluation Test. Numbers in parentheses refer to the ranking of the submitted system.

Team	Test Set	Accuracy	F-score	MRR	MAP
EDI	**NEWS18**	**0.3404 (1)**	**0.8673 (1)**	**0.4588 (1)**	**0.3404 (1)**
EDI	NEWS18	0.3343 (2)	0.8638 (2)	0.4504 (2)	0.3343 (2)
EDI	NEWS18	0.0251 (23)	0.4087 (28)	0.0361 (25)	0.0251 (23)
EDI	NEWS18	0.0221 (24)	0.4091 (27)	0.0342 (26)	0.0221 (24)
UALB	**NEWS18**	**0.3042 (3)**	**0.8569 (3)**	**0.4198 (3)**	**0.3042 (3)**
UALB	NEWS18	0.3022 (4)	0.8563 (4)	0.4152 (4)	0.3022 (4)
UALB	NEWS18	0.2912 (5)	0.8528 (5)	0.4077 (5)	0.2912 (5)
UALB	NEWS18	0.2831 (8)	0.8486 (6)	0.4043 (6)	0.2831 (8)
UALB	NEWS18	0.2510 (15)	0.8391 (11)	0.3433 (10)	0.2510 (15)
UALB	NEWS18	0.2369 (16)	0.8405 (10)	0.3691 (8)	0.2369 (16)
UALB	NEWS18	0.2339 (17)	0.8385 (12)	0.2339 (20)	0.2339 (17)
UALB	NEWS18	0.2199 (19)	0.8362 (14)	0.3502 (9)	0.2199 (19)
SINGA	**NEWS18**	**0.2851 (6)**	**0.8453 (7)**	**0.2851 (11)**	**0.2851 (6)**
SINGA	NEWS18	0.2851 (6)	0.8422 (9)	0.3899 (7)	0.2851 (6)
SINGA	NEWS18	0.2841 (7)	0.8439 (8)	0.2841 (12)	0.2841 (7)
SINGA	NEWS18	0.2841 (7)	0.8439 (8)	0.2841 (12)	0.2841 (7)
SINGA	NEWS18	0.2781 (9)	0.8279 (20)	0.2781 (13)	0.2781 (9)
SINGA	NEWS18	0.2711 (10)	0.8313 (18)	0.2711 (14)	0.2711 (10)
SINGA	NEWS18	0.2691 (11)	0.8362 (13)	0.2691 (15)	0.2691 (11)
SINGA	NEWS18	0.0000 (25)	0.7809 (26)	0.0000 (27)	0.0000 (25)
UJUS	**NEWS18**	**0.2671 (12)**	**0.8298 (19)**	**0.2671 (16)**	**0.2671 (12)**
UJUS	NEWS18	0.2651 (13)	0.8338 (17)	0.2651 (17)	0.2651 (13)
UJUS	NEWS18	0.2641 (14)	0.8345 (16)	0.2641 (18)	0.2641 (14)
UJUS	NEWS18	0.2369 (16)	0.8192 (21)	0.2369 (19)	0.2369 (16)
UJUS	NEWS18	0.2239 (18)	0.8087 (24)	0.2239 (21)	0.2239 (18)
UJUS	NEWS18	0.2179 (20)	0.8346 (15)	0.2179 (22)	0.2179 (20)
UJUS	NEWS18	0.2108 (21)	0.8169 (23)	0.2108 (23)	0.2108 (21)
UJUS	NEWS18	0.1867 (22)	0.8169 (22)	0.1867 (24)	0.1867 (22)
UJUS	NEWS18	0.1867 (22)	0.7911 (25)	0.1867 (24)	0.1867 (22)

Table A6: Results for the English to Kannada transliteration task (M-EnKa) on Evaluation Test. Numbers in parentheses refer to the ranking of the submitted system.

Team	Test Set	Accuracy	F-score	MRR	MAP
EDI	**NEWS18**	**0.4610 (1)**	**0.9006 (1)**	**0.5927 (1)**	**0.4610 (1)**
EDI	NEWS18	0.4560 (2)	0.8994 (2)	0.5907 (2)	0.4560 (2)
EDI	NEWS18	0.4560 (2)	0.8994 (2)	0.5907 (2)	0.4560 (2)
UALB	**NEWS18**	**0.4120 (3)**	**0.8812 (5)**	**0.5312 (3)**	**0.4120 (3)**
UALB	NEWS18	0.4080 (4)	0.8840 (3)	0.5295 (4)	0.4080 (4)
UALB	NEWS18	0.4070 (5)	0.8827 (4)	0.5284 (5)	0.4070 (5)
UALB	NEWS18	0.3780 (10)	0.8701 (9)	0.5093 (7)	0.3780 (10)
UALB	NEWS18	0.3580 (12)	0.8680 (13)	0.4511 (10)	0.3580 (12)
UALB	NEWS18	0.3400 (14)	0.8714 (7)	0.4746 (8)	0.3400 (14)
UALB	NEWS18	0.3350 (15)	0.8701 (10)	0.4698 (9)	0.3350 (15)
UALB	NEWS18	0.3270 (17)	0.8635 (14)	0.3270 (20)	0.3270 (17)
UALB	NEWS18	0.3270 (17)	0.8635 (14)	0.3270 (20)	0.3270 (17)
SINGA	**NEWS18**	**0.4070 (5)**	**0.8793 (6)**	**0.4070 (11)**	**0.4070 (5)**
SINGA	NEWS18	0.4060 (6)	0.8682 (12)	0.4060 (12)	0.4060 (6)
SINGA	NEWS18	0.3950 (7)	0.8684 (11)	0.5126 (6)	0.3950 (7)
SINGA	NEWS18	0.3950 (7)	0.8684 (11)	0.3950 (13)	0.3950 (7)
SINGA	NEWS18	0.3930 (8)	0.8626 (16)	0.3930 (14)	0.3930 (8)
SINGA	NEWS18	0.3820 (9)	0.8713 (8)	0.3820 (15)	0.3820 (9)
SINGA	NEWS18	0.0010 (20)	0.3629 (24)	0.0010 (23)	0.0010 (20)
SINGA	NEWS18	0.0000 (21)	0.8215 (22)	0.0000 (24)	0.0000 (21)
UJUS	**NEWS18**	**0.3820 (9)**	**0.8618 (18)**	**0.3820 (15)**	**0.3820 (9)**
UJUS	NEWS18	0.3780 (10)	0.8621 (17)	0.3780 (16)	0.3780 (10)
UJUS	NEWS18	0.3760 (11)	0.8606 (19)	0.3760 (17)	0.3760 (11)
UJUS	NEWS18	0.3430 (13)	0.8631 (15)	0.3430 (18)	0.3430 (13)
UJUS	NEWS18	0.3340 (16)	0.8540 (20)	0.3340 (19)	0.3340 (16)
UJUS	NEWS18	0.2550 (18)	0.8291 (21)	0.2550 (21)	0.2550 (18)
UJUS	NEWS18	0.1180 (19)	0.7507 (23)	0.1180 (22)	0.1180 (19)

Table A7: Results for the English to Bangla (Bengali) transliteration task (M-EnBa) on Evaluation Test. Numbers in parentheses refer to the ranking of the submitted system.

Team	Test Set	Accuracy	F-score	MRR	MAP
UQAM	**NEWS18**	**0.0260 (16)**	**0.7831 (15)**	**0.0311 (18)**	**0.0260 (16)**
UQAM	NEWS18	0.0240 (17)	0.7502 (17)	0.0292 (20)	0.0240 (17)
UQAM	NEWS18	0.0240 (17)	0.7480 (18)	0.0309 (19)	0.0240 (17)
UQAM	NEWS18	0.0120 (19)	0.7423 (19)	0.0195 (23)	0.0120 (19)
EDI	**NEWS18**	**0.5020 (1)**	**0.8893 (1)**	**0.6046 (1)**	**0.5020 (1)**
EDI	NEWS18	0.5020 (1)	0.8893 (1)	0.6046 (1)	0.5020 (1)
EDI	NEWS18	0.4940 (2)	0.8858 (3)	0.5935 (3)	0.4940 (2)
EDI	NEWS18	0.4900 (3)	0.8885 (2)	0.5967 (2)	0.4900 (3)
UALB	**NEWS18**	**0.4540 (5)**	**0.8719 (5)**	**0.5447 (4)**	**0.4540 (5)**
UALB	NEWS18	0.4360 (7)	0.8641 (7)	0.5345 (6)	0.4360 (7)
UALB	NEWS18	0.4280 (9)	0.8605 (8)	0.5266 (7)	0.4280 (9)
UALB	NEWS18	0.4200 (10)	0.8592 (9)	0.5228 (8)	0.4200 (10)
UALB	NEWS18	0.3960 (11)	0.8533 (12)	0.4952 (9)	0.3960 (11)
UALB	NEWS18	0.3960 (11)	0.8525 (13)	0.4897 (10)	0.3960 (11)
UALB	NEWS18	0.3400 (12)	0.8448 (14)	0.4047 (14)	0.3400 (12)
UALB	NEWS18	0.0080 (20)	0.6021 (24)	0.0080 (24)	0.0080 (20)
SINGA	**NEWS18**	**0.4580 (4)**	**0.8583 (11)**	**0.4580 (11)**	**0.4580 (4)**
SINGA	NEWS18	0.4500 (6)	0.8730 (4)	0.4500 (12)	0.4500 (6)
SINGA	NEWS18	0.4500 (6)	0.8730 (4)	0.4500 (12)	0.4500 (6)
SINGA	NEWS18	0.4500 (6)	0.8658 (6)	0.5377 (5)	0.4500 (6)
SINGA	NEWS18	0.4500 (6)	0.8658 (6)	0.4500 (12)	0.4500 (6)

Team	Test Set	Accuracy	F-score	MRR	MAP
SINGA	NEWS18	0.4340 (8)	0.8587 (10)	0.4340 (13)	0.4340 (8)
SINGA	NEWS18	0.0260 (16)	0.6764 (22)	0.0260 (21)	0.0260 (16)
SINGA	NEWS18	0.0220 (18)	0.6690 (23)	0.0220 (22)	0.0220 (18)
UJUS	**NEWS18**	**0.2000 (13)**	**0.7560 (16)**	**0.2000 (15)**	**0.2000 (13)**
UJUS	NEWS18	0.1780 (14)	0.7399 (20)	0.1780 (16)	0.1780 (14)
UJUS	NEWS18	0.0940 (15)	0.6774 (21)	0.0940 (17)	0.0940 (15)
UJUS	NEWS18	0.0080 (20)	0.5863 (25)	0.0080 (24)	0.0080 (20)
UJUS	NEWS18	0.0080 (20)	0.5088 (26)	0.0080 (24)	0.0080 (20)

Table A8: Results for the English to Vietnamese transliteration task (T-EnVi) on Evaluation Test. Numbers in parentheses refer to the ranking of the submitted system.

Team	Test Set	Accuracy	F-score	MRR	MAP
EDI	**NEWS18**	**0.1670 (1)**	**0.7740 (4)**	**0.2547 (2)**	**0.1670 (2)**
EDI	NEWS18	0.1650 (3)	0.7728 (6)	0.2533 (3)	0.1650 (4)
EDI	NEWS18	0.1640 (5)	0.7760 (1)	0.2487 (4)	0.1640 (5)
EDI	NEWS18	0.1610 (6)	0.7712 (8)	0.2479 (5)	0.1610 (6)
UALB	**NEWS18**	**0.1660 (2)**	**0.7740 (5)**	**0.2352 (6)**	**0.1660 (3)**
UALB	NEWS18	0.1660 (2)	0.7654 (9)	0.2310 (9)	0.1660 (3)
UALB	NEWS18	0.1640 (5)	0.7712 (7)	0.2340 (7)	0.1640 (5)
UALB	NEWS18	0.1610 (6)	0.7745 (2)	0.2335 (8)	0.1610 (6)
UALB	NEWS18	0.1600 (7)	0.7606 (13)	0.2306 (10)	0.1600 (7)
UALB	NEWS18	0.1550 (8)	0.7596 (15)	0.1550 (16)	0.1550 (8)
UALB	NEWS18	0.1530 (9)	0.7627 (10)	0.2242 (11)	0.1530 (9)
UALB	NEWS18	0.1480 (10)	0.7615 (11)	0.2000 (15)	0.1480 (10)
UALB	NEWS18	0.1450 (11)	0.7586 (17)	0.2177 (12)	0.1450 (11)
UALB	NEWS18	0.1450 (11)	0.7578 (19)	0.1450 (17)	0.1450 (11)
UALB	NEWS18	0.1400 (16)	0.7590 (16)	0.2076 (14)	0.1400 (16)
SINGA	**NEWS18**	**0.1430 (13)**	**0.7578 (18)**	**0.2115 (13)**	**0.1430 (13)**
SINGA	NEWS18	0.1430 (13)	0.7578 (18)	0.1430 (19)	0.1430 (13)
SINGA	NEWS18	0.1420 (14)	0.7542 (21)	0.1420 (20)	0.1420 (14)
SINGA	NEWS18	0.1410 (15)	0.7604 (14)	0.1410 (21)	0.1410 (15)
SINGA	NEWS18	0.1390 (17)	0.7511 (22)	0.1390 (22)	0.1390 (17)
SINGA	NEWS18	0.1380 (18)	0.7481 (24)	0.1380 (23)	0.1380 (18)
SINGA	NEWS18	0.0380 (26)	0.4580 (29)	0.0380 (31)	0.0380 (26)
UJUS	**NEWS18**	**0.1450 (11)**	**0.7610 (12)**	**0.1450 (17)**	**0.1450 (11)**
UJUS	NEWS18	0.1440 (12)	0.7551 (20)	0.1440 (18)	0.1440 (12)
UJUS	NEWS18	0.1350 (19)	0.7484 (23)	0.1350 (24)	0.1350 (19)
UJUS	NEWS18	0.1300 (20)	0.7449 (25)	0.1300 (25)	0.1300 (20)
UJUS	NEWS18	0.1270 (21)	0.7383 (26)	0.1270 (26)	0.1270 (21)
UJUS	NEWS18	0.1080 (22)	0.7164 (27)	0.1080 (27)	0.1080 (22)
UJUS	NEWS18	0.0760 (23)	0.6632 (28)	0.0760 (28)	0.0760 (23)
UJUS	NEWS18	0.0750 (24)	0.3984 (30)	0.0750 (29)	0.0750 (24)
UJUS	NEWS18	0.0700 (25)	0.3947 (31)	0.0700 (30)	0.0700 (25)

Table A9: Results for the English to Thai transliteration task (T-EnTh) on Evaluation Test. Numbers in parentheses refer to the ranking of the submitted system.

Team	Test Set	Accuracy	F-score	MRR	MAP
UALB	**NEWS18**	**0.3400 (1)**	**0.7113 (1)**	**0.4301 (1)**	**0.3400 (1)**
UALB	NEWS18	0.3400 (1)	0.7110 (2)	0.4273 (2)	0.3400 (1)
UALB	NEWS18	0.3190 (2)	0.6954 (3)	0.4106 (3)	0.3190 (2)
UALB	NEWS18	0.2790 (6)	0.6775 (5)	0.3688 (5)	0.2790 (6)
UALB	NEWS18	0.2780 (7)	0.6822 (4)	0.3669 (6)	0.2780 (7)
UALB	NEWS18	0.2680 (9)	0.6672 (8)	0.3368 (7)	0.2680 (9)

UALB	NEWS18	0.2450 (11)	0.6286 (9)	0.3329 (8)	0.2450 (11)
UALB	NEWS18	0.2450 (11)	0.6286 (9)	0.3329 (8)	0.2450 (11)
UALB	NEWS18	0.0070 (12)	0.2646 (13)	0.0070 (14)	0.0070 (12)
SINGA	**NEWS18**	**0.3110 (3)**	**0.6093 (10)**	**0.3788 (4)**	**0.3110 (3)**
SINGA	NEWS18	0.3110 (3)	0.6093 (10)	0.3110 (9)	0.3110 (3)
SINGA	NEWS18	0.2910 (4)	0.5877 (11)	0.2910 (10)	0.2910 (4)
SINGA	NEWS18	0.2860 (5)	0.5836 (12)	0.2860 (11)	0.2860 (5)
SINGA	NEWS18	0.2730 (8)	0.6770 (6)	0.2730 (12)	0.2730 (8)
SINGA	NEWS18	0.2590 (10)	0.6747 (7)	0.2590 (13)	0.2590 (10)

Table A10: Results for the English to Korean Hangul transliteration task (T-EnKo) on Evaluation Test. Numbers in parentheses refer to the ranking of the submitted system.

Team	Test Set	ACC	F-score	MRR	MAP$_{ref}$
UALB	**NEWS18**	**0.3904 (1)**	**0.8098 (1)**	**0.5157 (1)**	**0.3893 (1)**
UALB	NEWS18	0.3844 (2)	0.8078 (3)	0.5116 (2)	0.3825 (2)
UALB	NEWS18	0.3814 (3)	0.8093 (2)	0.5110 (3)	0.3815 (3)
UALB	NEWS18	0.3684 (4)	0.8029 (5)	0.4979 (4)	0.3688 (4)
UALB	NEWS18	0.3644 (5)	0.8030 (4)	0.4977 (5)	0.3625 (5)
UALB	NEWS18	0.3594 (6)	0.8009 (7)	0.4924 (6)	0.3583 (6)
UALB	NEWS18	0.3504 (7)	0.8024 (6)	0.4897 (7)	0.3490 (7)
UALB	NEWS18	0.3463 (8)	0.7936 (8)	0.3463 (11)	0.3428 (8)
UALB	NEWS18	0.3293 (11)	0.7803 (15)	0.4258 (10)	0.3296 (11)
UALB	NEWS18	0.3203 (12)	0.7828 (12)	0.4602 (8)	0.3209 (13)
UALB	NEWS18	0.3033 (15)	0.7806 (14)	0.3033 (16)	0.3003 (16)
SINGA	**NEWS18**	**0.3393 (9)**	**0.7829 (11)**	**0.3393 (12)**	**0.3363 (9)**
SINGA	NEWS18	0.3313 (10)	0.7851 (9)	0.3313 (13)	0.3286 (12)
SINGA	NEWS18	0.3313 (10)	0.7848 (10)	0.4536 (9)	0.3322 (10)
SINGA	NEWS18	0.3183 (13)	0.7807 (13)	0.3183 (14)	0.3153 (14)
SINGA	NEWS18	0.3043 (14)	0.7745 (16)	0.3043 (15)	0.3008 (15)
SINGA	NEWS18	0.2913 (16)	0.7737 (17)	0.2913 (17)	0.2880 (17)

Table A11: Results for the English to Japanese Katakana transliteration task (T-EnJa) on Evaluation Test. Numbers in parentheses refer to the ranking of the submitted system.

Team	Test Set	ACC	F-score	MRR	MAP$_{ref}$
EDI	**NEWS18**	**0.1836 (1)**	**0.8042 (1)**	**0.2855 (1)**	**0.1807 (1)**
EDI	NEWS18	0.1778 (2)	0.8033 (2)	0.2776 (2)	0.1750 (2)
UALB	**NEWS18**	**0.1702 (4)**	**0.7983 (6)**	**0.1702 (12)**	**0.1663 (6)**
UALB	NEWS18	0.1702 (4)	0.7983 (6)	0.1702 (12)	0.1663 (6)
UALB	NEWS18	0.1683 (5)	0.7952 (12)	0.2741 (3)	0.1673 (5)
UALB	NEWS18	0.1683 (5)	0.7946 (13)	0.2600 (6)	0.1659 (7)
UALB	NEWS18	0.1683 (5)	0.7940 (14)	0.2555 (7)	0.1659 (7)
UALB	NEWS18	0.1625 (8)	0.7965 (9)	0.2627 (5)	0.1611 (13)
UALB	NEWS18	0.1606 (9)	0.7969 (8)	0.2636 (4)	0.1587 (15)
UALB	NEWS18	0.1530 (10)	0.7962 (11)	0.2211 (9)	0.1501 (17)
UALB	NEWS18	0.1530 (10)	0.7962 (11)	0.2211 (9)	0.1501 (17)
SINGA	**NEWS18**	**0.1778 (2)**	**0.7982 (7)**	**0.1778 (10)**	**0.1740 (3)**

SINGA	NEWS18	0.1759 (3)	0.8000 (4)	0.1759 (11)	0.1721 (4)
SINGA	NEWS18	0.1683 (5)	0.7986 (5)	0.1683 (13)	0.1649 (9)
SINGA	NEWS18	0.1683 (5)	0.7964 (10)	0.1683 (13)	0.1654 (8)
SINGA	NEWS18	0.1644 (7)	0.8002 (3)	0.2484 (8)	0.1620 (11)
SINGA	NEWS18	0.1644 (7)	0.8002 (3)	0.1644 (15)	0.1611 (13)
SINGA	NEWS18	0.0000 (15)	0.7373 (24)	0.0000 (22)	0.0000 (22)
UJUS	**NEWS18**	**0.1663 (6)**	**0.7884 (15)**	**0.1663 (14)**	**0.1630 (10)**
UJUS	NEWS18	0.1644 (7)	0.7825 (17)	0.1644 (15)	0.1611 (13)
UJUS	NEWS18	0.1644 (7)	0.7812 (18)	0.1644 (15)	0.1616 (12)
UJUS	NEWS18	0.1625 (8)	0.7843 (16)	0.1625 (16)	0.1592 (14)
UJUS	NEWS18	0.1606 (9)	0.7789 (19)	0.1606 (17)	0.1573 (16)
UJUS	NEWS18	0.1453 (11)	0.7519 (23)	0.1453 (18)	0.1424 (18)
UJUS	NEWS18	0.1377 (12)	0.7560 (22)	0.1377 (19)	0.1348 (19)
UJUS	NEWS18	0.1300 (13)	0.7746 (20)	0.1300 (20)	0.1286 (20)
UJUS	NEWS18	0.1205 (14)	0.7691 (21)	0.1205 (21)	0.1185 (21)

Table A12: Results for the English to Hebrew transliteration task (T-EnHe) on Evaluation Test. Numbers in parentheses refer to the ranking of the submitted system

Team	Test Set	ACC	F-score	MRR	MAP_{ref}
WIPO	**NEWS18**	**0.2820 (4)**	**0.6686 (4)**	**0.4040 (4)**	**0.2820 (4)**
EDI	**NEWS18**	**0.3040 (1)**	**0.6791 (1)**	**0.4364 (2)**	**0.3040 (1)**
EDI	NEWS18	0.3030 (2)	0.6776 (3)	0.4267 (3)	0.3030 (2)
EDI	NEWS18	0.3010 (3)	0.6785 (2)	0.4383 (1)	0.3010 (3)
UALB	**NEWS18**	**0.2820 (4)**	**0.6680 (5)**	**0.3854 (5)**	**0.2820 (4)**
UALB	NEWS18	0.2750 (5)	0.6634 (6)	0.3771 (6)	0.2750 (5)
UALB	NEWS18	0.2750 (5)	0.6634 (6)	0.3771 (6)	0.2750 (5)
UALB	NEWS18	0.2710 (6)	0.6627 (7)	0.2710 (12)	0.2710 (6)
UALB	NEWS18	0.2600 (12)	0.6516 (10)	0.3664 (8)	0.2600 (12)
UALB	NEWS18	0.2560 (13)	0.6513 (12)	0.3646 (9)	0.2560 (13)
UALB	NEWS18	0.2460 (14)	0.6435 (19)	0.3108 (10)	0.2460 (14)
UALB	NEWS18	0.2280 (18)	0.6288 (21)	0.2280 (21)	0.2280 (18)
SINGA	**NEWS18**	**0.2750 (5)**	**0.6512 (13)**	**0.2750 (11)**	**0.2750 (5)**
SINGA	NEWS18	0.2700 (7)	0.6515 (11)	0.3736 (7)	0.2700 (7)
SINGA	NEWS18	0.2700 (7)	0.6515 (11)	0.2700 (13)	0.2700 (7)
SINGA	NEWS18	0.2670 (8)	0.6461 (17)	0.2670 (14)	0.2670 (8)
SINGA	NEWS18	0.2630 (9)	0.6489 (15)	0.2630 (15)	0.2630 (9)
SINGA	NEWS18	0.2620 (10)	0.6509 (14)	0.2620 (16)	0.2620 (10)
UJUS	**NEWS18**	**0.2610 (11)**	**0.6603 (8)**	**0.2610 (17)**	**0.2610 (11)**
UJUS	NEWS18	0.2610 (11)	0.6566 (9)	0.2610 (17)	0.2610 (11)
UJUS	NEWS18	0.2440 (15)	0.6443 (18)	0.2440 (18)	0.2440 (15)
UJUS	NEWS18	0.2400 (16)	0.6475 (16)	0.2400 (19)	0.2400 (16)
UJUS	NEWS18	0.2370 (17)	0.6358 (20)	0.2370 (20)	0.2370 (17)
UJUS	NEWS18	0.1870 (19)	0.6086 (22)	0.1870 (22)	0.1870 (19)
UJUS	NEWS18	0.1590 (20)	0.3497 (24)	0.1590 (23)	0.1590 (20)
UJUS	NEWS18	0.1540 (21)	0.3495 (25)	0.1540 (24)	0.1540 (21)

| UJUS | NEWS18 | 0.0410 (22) | 0.4569 (23) | 0.0410 (25) | 0.0410 (22) |

Table A13: Results for the English to Chinese transliteration task (T-EnCh) on Evaluation Test. Numbers in parentheses refer to the ranking of the submitted system.

Team	Test Set	ACC	F-score	MRR	MAP$_{ref}$
UALB	**NEWS18**	**0.3940 (1)**	**0.9087 (1)**	**0.3940 (9)**	**0.0586 (9)**
UALB	NEWS18	0.3910 (2)	0.9029 (2)	0.4949 (2)	0.1880 (1)
UALB	NEWS18	0.3900 (3)	0.9029 (3)	0.5012 (1)	0.1822 (2)
UALB	NEWS18	0.3730 (5)	0.9007 (4)	0.4688 (3)	0.1816 (3)
UALB	NEWS18	0.3730 (5)	0.8995 (5)	0.4632 (4)	0.1787 (5)
UALB	NEWS18	0.3630 (6)	0.8972 (7)	0.4559 (5)	0.1797 (4)
UALB	NEWS18	0.3520 (7)	0.8936 (9)	0.4413 (7)	0.1707 (6)
UALB	NEWS18	0.3300 (9)	0.8817 (10)	0.4167 (8)	0.1366 (8)
SINGA	**NEWS18**	**0.3750 (4)**	**0.8976 (6)**	**0.4552 (6)**	**0.1671 (7)**
SINGA	NEWS18	0.3750 (4)	0.8976 (6)	0.3750 (10)	0.0561 (10)
SINGA	NEWS18	0.3380 (8)	0.8964 (8)	0.3380 (11)	0.0507 (11)
SINGA	NEWS18	0.2910 (10)	0.8656 (12)	0.2910 (12)	0.0442 (12)
SINGA	NEWS18	0.2740 (11)	0.8645 (13)	0.2740 (13)	0.0413 (13)
SINGA	NEWS18	0.2620 (12)	0.8762 (11)	0.2620 (14)	0.0390 (14)

Table A14: Results for the Arabic to English transliteration task (T-ArEn) on Evaluation Test. Numbers in parentheses refer to the ranking of the submitted system.

Team	Test Set	ACC	F-score	MRR	MAP$_{ref}$
EDI	**NEWS18**	**0.3280 (2)**	**0.8454 (2)**	**0.4286 (2)**	**0.3278 (2)**
EDI	NEWS18	0.3050 (4)	0.8444 (3)	0.4101 (3)	0.3051 (4)
UALB	**NEWS18**	**0.3119 (3)**	**0.8089 (10)**	**0.3645 (8)**	**0.3118 (3)**
UALB	NEWS18	0.2840 (5)	0.8321 (4)	0.3741 (4)	0.2840 (5)
UALB	NEWS18	0.2819 (6)	0.8318 (5)	0.3732 (5)	0.2819 (6)
UALB	NEWS18	0.2729 (7)	0.8295 (6)	0.3657 (6)	0.2729 (7)
UALB	NEWS18	0.2715 (8)	0.8215 (9)	0.2715 (12)	0.2713 (8)
UALB	NEWS18	0.2687 (9)	0.8251 (8)	0.3645 (7)	0.2687 (9)
UALB	NEWS18	0.2617 (12)	0.8251 (7)	0.3529 (9)	0.2617 (12)
UALB	NEWS18	0.2212 (19)	0.8032 (16)	0.3081 (11)	0.2214 (19)
UALB	NEWS18	0.2031 (21)	0.8033 (15)	0.2712 (13)	0.2031 (22)
UALB	NEWS18	0.1298 (24)	0.7555 (24)	0.1786 (25)	0.1298 (25)
UALB	NEWS18	0.0223 (27)	0.0752 (29)	0.0292 (29)	0.0223 (28)
UALB	NEWS18	0.0223 (27)	0.0752 (29)	0.0292 (29)	0.0223 (28)
SINGA	**NEWS18**	**0.2554 (13)**	**0.7731 (22)**	**0.3308 (10)**	**0.2554 (13)**
SINGA	NEWS18	0.2554 (13)	0.7731 (22)	0.2554 (16)	0.2554 (13)
SINGA	NEWS18	0.2505 (14)	0.7376 (25)	0.2505 (17)	0.2505 (14)
SINGA	NEWS18	0.2338 (16)	0.7315 (26)	0.2338 (19)	0.2338 (16)
SINGA	NEWS18	0.2289 (17)	0.8067 (12)	0.2289 (20)	0.2289 (17)
SINGA	NEWS18	0.2233 (18)	0.8041 (14)	0.2233 (21)	0.2233 (18)
SINGA	NEWS18	0.0621 (26)	0.5045 (27)	0.0621 (28)	0.0621 (27)
UJUS	**NEWS18**	**0.2680 (10)**	**0.8079 (11)**	**0.2680 (14)**	**0.2678 (10)**
UJUS	NEWS18	0.2673 (11)	0.8046 (13)	0.2673 (15)	0.2671 (11)

UJUS	NEWS18	0.2352 (15)	0.8005 (17)	0.2352 (18)	0.2350 (15)
UJUS	NEWS18	0.2289 (17)	0.7987 (18)	0.2289 (20)	0.2289 (17)
UJUS	NEWS18	0.2212 (19)	0.7906 (19)	0.2212 (22)	0.2210 (20)
UJUS	NEWS18	0.2114 (20)	0.7881 (20)	0.2114 (23)	0.2113 (21)
UJUS	NEWS18	0.1989 (22)	0.7776 (21)	0.1989 (24)	0.1987 (23)
UJUS	NEWS18	0.1689 (23)	0.7588 (23)	0.1689 (26)	0.1689 (24)
UJUS	NEWS18	0.0984 (25)	0.2960 (28)	0.0984 (27)	0.0982 (26)

Table A15: Results for the Thai to English back-transliteration task (B-ThEn) on Evaluation Test. Numbers in parentheses refer to the ranking of the submitted system.

Team	Test Set	ACC	F-score	MRR	MAP$_{ref}$
UALB	**NEWS18**	**0.5930 (1)**	**0.7678 (1)**	**0.6669 (1)**	**0.3740 (3)**
UALB	NEWS18	0.5690 (2)	0.7543 (2)	0.6492 (2)	0.3840 (1)
UALB	NEWS18	0.5650 (3)	0.7529 (3)	0.6459 (3)	0.3813 (2)
UALB	NEWS18	0.5530 (4)	0.7388 (4)	0.6399 (4)	0.3546 (4)
UALB	NEWS18	0.4660 (5)	0.6919 (5)	0.4660 (6)	0.1941 (6)
UALB	NEWS18	0.3850 (6)	0.6622 (6)	0.4837 (5)	0.2442 (5)

Table A16: Results for the English to Japanese Kanji back-transliteration task (B-JnJk) on Evaluation Test. Numbers in parentheses refer to the ranking of the submitted system.

Team	Test Set	ACC	F-score	MRR	MAP$_{ref}$
EDI	**NEWS18**	**0.1525 (2)**	**0.7532 (1)**	**0.2306 (1)**	**0.1521 (2)**
EDI	NEWS18	0.1068 (3)	0.7454 (2)	0.1803 (3)	0.1068 (3)
UALB	**NEWS18**	**0.1729 (1)**	**0.7240 (10)**	**0.2181 (2)**	**0.1725 (1)**
UALB	NEWS18	0.0915 (5)	0.7316 (8)	0.0915 (14)	0.0915 (5)
UALB	NEWS18	0.0881 (6)	0.7337 (4)	0.1505 (5)	0.0881 (6)
UALB	NEWS18	0.0864 (7)	0.7331 (5)	0.1498 (6)	0.0864 (7)
UALB	NEWS18	0.0864 (7)	0.7319 (6)	0.1494 (7)	0.0864 (7)
UALB	NEWS18	0.0780 (9)	0.7316 (7)	0.1477 (8)	0.0780 (9)
UALB	NEWS18	0.0780 (9)	0.7300 (9)	0.1436 (9)	0.0780 (9)
UALB	NEWS18	0.0678 (12)	0.7234 (11)	0.1148 (11)	0.0678 (12)
UALB	NEWS18	0.0644 (13)	0.7194 (13)	0.1261 (10)	0.0644 (13)
UALB	NEWS18	0.0644 (13)	0.7129 (17)	0.1035 (12)	0.0644 (13)
SINGA	**NEWS18**	**0.0949 (4)**	**0.7135 (16)**	**0.1560 (4)**	**0.0949 (4)**
SINGA	NEWS18	0.0949 (4)	0.7135 (16)	0.0949 (13)	0.0949 (4)
SINGA	NEWS18	0.0915 (5)	0.7339 (3)	0.0915 (14)	0.0915 (5)
SINGA	NEWS18	0.0915 (5)	0.6757 (27)	0.0915 (14)	0.0915 (5)
SINGA	NEWS18	0.0864 (7)	0.6730 (28)	0.0864 (15)	0.0864 (7)
SINGA	NEWS18	0.0678 (12)	0.7205 (12)	0.0678 (20)	0.0678 (12)
SINGA	NEWS18	0.0000 (17)	0.6819 (24)	0.0000 (25)	0.0000 (17)
UJUS	**NEWS18**	**0.0831 (8)**	**0.7157 (14)**	**0.0831 (16)**	**0.0831 (8)**
UJUS	NEWS18	0.0780 (9)	0.7147 (15)	0.0780 (17)	0.0780 (9)
UJUS	NEWS18	0.0746 (10)	0.7122 (19)	0.0746 (18)	0.0746 (10)
UJUS	NEWS18	0.0712 (11)	0.7026 (21)	0.0712 (19)	0.0712 (11)
UJUS	NEWS18	0.0678 (12)	0.7031 (20)	0.0678 (20)	0.0678 (12)
UJUS	NEWS18	0.0644 (13)	0.7006 (22)	0.0644 (21)	0.0644 (13)

UJUS	NEWS18	0.0610 (14)	0.7129 (18)	0.0610 (22)	0.0610 (14)
UJUS	NEWS18	0.0610 (14)	0.6788 (26)	0.0610 (22)	0.0610 (14)
UJUS	NEWS18	0.0593 (15)	0.6945 (23)	0.0593 (23)	0.0593 (15)
UJUS	NEWS18	0.0508 (16)	0.6818 (25)	0.0508 (24)	0.0508 (16)

Table A17: Results for the Hebrew to English back-transliteration task (B-HeEn) on Evaluation Test. Numbers in parentheses refer to the ranking of the submitted system.

Team	Test Set	ACC	F-score	MRR	MAP_{ref}
EDI	**NEWS18**	**0.0000 (14)**	**0.1996 (15)**	**0.0008 (16)**	**0.0000 (15)**
EDI	NEWS18	0.0000 (14)	0.1950 (16)	0.0007 (17)	0.0000 (15)
UALB	**NEWS18**	**0.6350 (1)**	**0.9363 (3)**	**0.7601 (1)**	**0.6348 (1)**
UALB	NEWS18	0.6300 (2)	0.9369 (2)	0.7576 (2)	0.6298 (2)
UALB	NEWS18	0.6240 (3)	0.9373 (1)	0.7555 (3)	0.6232 (3)
UALB	NEWS18	0.6120 (4)	0.9323 (6)	0.7223 (8)	0.6122 (4)
UALB	NEWS18	0.6120 (4)	0.9303 (7)	0.7426 (4)	0.6115 (5)
UALB	NEWS18	0.5990 (6)	0.9336 (4)	0.7304 (5)	0.5982 (7)
UALB	NEWS18	0.5980 (7)	0.9335 (5)	0.7304 (6)	0.5972 (8)
UALB	NEWS18	0.5920 (8)	0.9296 (8)	0.7250 (7)	0.5915 (9)
UALB	NEWS18	0.5840 (9)	0.9286 (9)	0.7204 (9)	0.5835 (10)
UALB	NEWS18	0.5320 (11)	0.9199 (11)	0.5320 (13)	0.5315 (12)
UALB	NEWS18	0.5060 (12)	0.9142 (13)	0.5060 (14)	0.5055 (13)
SINGA	**NEWS18**	**0.6100 (5)**	**0.9286 (10)**	**0.6100 (10)**	**0.6095 (6)**
SINGA	NEWS18	0.5560 (10)	0.9183 (12)	0.5560 (11)	0.5555 (11)
SINGA	NEWS18	0.3520 (13)	0.8776 (14)	0.5502 (12)	0.3518 (14)
SINGA	NEWS18	0.3520 (13)	0.8776 (14)	0.3520 (15)	0.3518 (14)

Table A18: Results for the English to Persian back-transliteration task (B-EnPe) on Evaluation Test. Numbers in parentheses refer to the ranking of the submitted system.

Team	Test Set	ACC	F-score	MRR	MAP_{ref}
EDI	**NEWS18**	**0.2760 (2)**	**0.8300 (1)**	**0.3860 (1)**	**0.2760 (2)**
EDI	NEWS18	0.2530 (3)	0.8257 (2)	0.3570 (3)	0.2530 (3)
UALB	**NEWS18**	**0.3000 (1)**	**0.8011 (8)**	**0.3741 (2)**	**0.3002 (1)**
UALB	NEWS18	0.2100 (4)	0.8024 (4)	0.3002 (4)	0.2100 (4)
UALB	NEWS18	0.2100 (4)	0.8024 (4)	0.3002 (4)	0.2100 (4)
UALB	NEWS18	0.2090 (5)	0.8023 (6)	0.2968 (6)	0.2090 (5)
UALB	NEWS18	0.2090 (5)	0.8023 (6)	0.2968 (6)	0.2090 (5)
UALB	NEWS18	0.2080 (6)	0.8034 (3)	0.2991 (5)	0.2080 (6)
UALB	NEWS18	0.1920 (9)	0.8024 (5)	0.1920 (10)	0.1920 (9)
UALB	NEWS18	0.1160 (22)	0.7672 (20)	0.1900 (12)	0.1160 (22)
UALB	NEWS18	0.0940 (24)	0.6607 (25)	0.1444 (22)	0.0940 (24)
SINGA	**NEWS18**	**0.1960 (7)**	**0.7636 (23)**	**0.1960 (8)**	**0.1960 (7)**
SINGA	NEWS18	0.1950 (8)	0.7840 (18)	0.2889 (7)	0.1950 (8)
SINGA	NEWS18	0.1950 (8)	0.7840 (18)	0.1950 (9)	0.1950 (8)
SINGA	NEWS18	0.1820 (12)	0.7561 (24)	0.1820 (14)	0.1820 (12)
SINGA	NEWS18	0.1790 (13)	0.7917 (11)	0.1790 (15)	0.1790 (13)

SINGA	NEWS18	0.1750 (14)	0.7850 (16)	0.1750 (16)	0.1750 (14)
SINGA	NEWS18	0.0100 (25)	0.3440 (26)	0.0100 (26)	0.0100 (25)
UJUS	**NEWS18**	**0.1910 (10)**	**0.8003 (9)**	**0.1910 (11)**	**0.1910 (10)**
UJUS	NEWS18	0.1900 (11)	0.8014 (7)	0.1900 (13)	0.1900 (11)
UJUS	NEWS18	0.1820 (12)	0.7962 (10)	0.1820 (14)	0.1820 (12)
UJUS	NEWS18	0.1600 (15)	0.7849 (17)	0.1600 (17)	0.1600 (15)
UJUS	NEWS18	0.1540 (16)	0.7875 (13)	0.1540 (18)	0.1540 (16)
UJUS	NEWS18	0.1520 (17)	0.7850 (15)	0.1520 (19)	0.1520 (17)
UJUS	NEWS18	0.1490 (18)	0.7879 (12)	0.1490 (20)	0.1490 (18)
UJUS	NEWS18	0.1470 (19)	0.7857 (14)	0.1470 (21)	0.1470 (19)
UJUS	NEWS18	0.1330 (20)	0.7656 (22)	0.1330 (23)	0.1330 (20)
UJUS	NEWS18	0.1280 (21)	0.7670 (21)	0.1280 (24)	0.1280 (21)
UJUS	NEWS18	0.1120 (23)	0.7736 (19)	0.1120 (25)	0.1120 (23)

Table A19: Results for the Chinese to English back-transliteration task (B-ChEn) on Evaluation Test. Numbers in parentheses refer to the ranking of the submitted system.

Statistical Machine Transliteration Baselines for NEWS 2018

Snigdha Singhania[1], Minh Nguyen[1], Hoang Gia Ngo[1], Nancy F. Chen[2]

[1]National University of Singapore, Singapore
{singhaniasnigdha,nguyen.binh.minh92,ngohgia}@u.nus.edu
[2]Singapore University of Technology and Design, Singapore
nancychen@alum.mit.edu

Abstract

This paper reports the results of our transliteration experiments conducted on NEWS 2018 Shared Task dataset. We focus on creating the baseline systems trained using two open-source, statistical transliteration tools, namely Sequitur and Moses. We discuss the pre-processing steps performed on this dataset for both the systems. We also provide a re-ranking system which uses top hypotheses from Sequitur and Moses to create a consolidated list of transliterations. The results obtained from each of these models can be used to present a good starting point for the participating teams.

1 Introduction

Transliteration is defined as the phonetic translation of words across languages (Knight and Graehl, 1998; Li et al., 2009). It can be considered as a machine translation problem at the character level. Transliteration converts words written in one writing system (source language, e.g., English) into phonetically equivalent words in another writing system (target language, e.g., Hindi) and is often used to translate foreign names of people, locations, organizations, and products (Gia et al., 2015). With names comprising over 75 percent of the unseen words (Bhargava and Kondrak, 2011), they are a challenging problem in machine translation, multilingual information retrieval, corpus alignment and other natural language processing applications. More so, studies suggest that cross-lingual information retrieval performances can improve by as much as 50 percent if the system is provided with suitably transliterated named entities (Larkey et al., 2003).

In this paper, we run two baseline transliteration experiments and report our results on the NEWS 2018 Shared Task dataset. A re-ranking model using linear regression has also been provided in an attempt to combine hypotheses from both the baselines. Song et al. (2010) proposed that the performance of a transliteration system is expected to improve when the output candidates are re-ranked, as the Shared Task considers only the top-1 hypothesis when evaluating a system. Our re-ranking approach which uses the union of Sequitur and Moses hypotheses results in the top-1 word accuracy for all language pairs to be either an improvement or lie in their respective Moses and Sequitur accuracy range, excluding English-to-Thai, English-to-Chinese and English-to-Vietnamese where the results are relatively poorer.

The rest of this paper is structured as follows. Section 2 contains a summary of the datasets used for the transliteration task. Section 3 describes the two well-known statistical transliteration methods adopted; first, a joint-source channel approach using Sequitur, and second, a phrase-based statistical machine translation approach using Moses. Section 4 focuses on the experimental setup, re-ranking approach, and documents the results obtained. Finally, Section 5 summarizes the paper.

2 Data

The corpus sizes of each of the data partitions, namely training, development and test for the 19 language pairs used in the transliteration experiments is summarized in Table 1.

3 Methods

In this section, we describe the two software tools used for the transliteration experiment: Sequitur, which is based on the joint source-channel model

Proceedings of the Seventh Named Entities Workshop, pages 74–78
Melbourne, Australia, July 20, 2018. ©2018 Association for Computational Linguistics

Task ID	Training	Development	Test
T-EnTh	30781	1000	1000
B-ThEn	27273	1000	1433
T-EnPe	13386	1000	1000
B-PeEn	15677	1000	908
T-EnCh	41318	1000	1000
B-ChEn	32002	1000	1000
T-EnVi	3256	500	500
M-EnBa	13623	1000	1000
M-EnHi	12937	1000	1000
T-EnHe	10501	1000	523
M-EnKa	10955	1000	1000
M-EnTa	10957	1000	1000
B-HeEn	9447	1000	590
T-ArEn	31354	1000	1000
T-EnKo	7387	1000	1000
T-EnJa	28828	1000	1000
B-JnJk	10514	1000	1000
B-EnPe	11204	1000	1000
T-PeEn	6000	1000	1000

Table 1: Corpus Size for the 19 language pairs, where En: English, Th: Thai, Pe: Persian, Ch: Chinese, Vi: Vietnamese, Ba: Bangla, Hi: Hindi, He: Hebrew, Ka: Kannada, Ta: Tamil, Ar: Arabic, Ko: Korean, Ja: Japanese Katakana, Jn: English, Jk: Japanese Kanji.

and Moses, which adopts phrase-based statistical machine translation. It should be noted that identical settings were used for all 19 language pairs.

3.1 Joint Source-Channel Model

The Joint Source-Channel Model was first studied by Li et al. (2004), where a direct orthographic mapping was proposed for transliteration. Given a pair of languages, for example English and Hindi, where e and h are representative of their transliteration units, respectively; the transliteration process is nding the alignment for sub-sequences of the input string, E and the output string, H (Pervouchine et al., 2009), and can be represented for an n-gram model as

$$
\begin{aligned}
P(E, H) &= P(e_1, e_2, ..., e_k, h_1, h_2, ..., h_k) \\
&= P(<e_1, h_1>, ..., <e_k, h_k>) \\
&= \prod_{i=1}^{k} P(<e, h>_i \mid <e, h>_{i-n+1}^{i-1})
\end{aligned}
$$

(1)

where k is number of alignment units. $P(E, H)$ is, thus, the joint probability of the i-th alignment

pair, which depends on n previous pairs in the sequence.

Sequitur is a data-driven translation tool, originally developed for grapheme-to-phoneme conversion by Bisani and Ney (2008). It is applicable to several monotonous sequence translation tasks and hence is a popular tool in machine transliteration. It is different from many translation tools, as it is able to train a joint n-gram model from unaligned data. Higher order n-grams are trained iteratively from the smaller ones — first, a unigram model is trained, which is then used for a bigram model, and so on. We report results on a 5-gram Sequitur model in this paper.

3.2 Phrase-Based Statistical Machine Translation (PB-SMT)

Phrase-based machine translation model breaks the source sentence into phrases and translates these phrases in the target language before combining them to produce one final translated result (Brown et al., 1993; Collins, 2011). Its use can be extended in the field of transliteration — as transliteration is defined as a translation task at the character level (Koehn et al., 2007). The best transliteration sequence, H^{best}, in the target language is generated by multiplying the probabilities of the transliteration model, P and the language model, $P(E \mid H)$, along with their respective weights, α and β, as

$$
\begin{aligned}
H^{best} &= argmax_{H \in h} P(H|E) \\
&= argmax_{H \in h} \alpha P(E|H) \times \beta P(H)
\end{aligned}
$$

(2)

where h is the set of all phonologically correct words in the target orthography.

Moses is the statistical translation tool, which adopts the Phrase-Based Statistical Machine Translation approach. GIZA++ is used for aligning the word pairs and KenLM is used for creating the n-gram language models. We create 5-gram language models using the target language corpus. The decoders log-linear model is tuned using MERT.

3.3 Hypothesis Re-ranking

Song et al. (2010) proposed that re-ranking the output candidates is expected to boost transliteration accuracy, as the Shared Task considers only the top-1 hypothesis when evaluating the accuracy of the system. We adopt the following re-ranking approach in an attempt to improve over the individual Moses and Sequitur results.

Moses + Sequitur: We conduct an experiment to analyze the outcome when using hypotheses from both Sequitur and Moses, where a linear combination of their corresponding scores is used to rank the consolidated hypothesis list. The feature set consists of 10 scores from lexical reordering, language modelling, word penalty, phrase penalty, and translation from Moses and 1 confidence score from Sequitur. We use constrained decoding to obtain Moses scores for Sequitur transliterations which do not occur in the top-n Moses hypotheses. A linear regression model similar to that adopted by Shao et al. (2015) is used for re-ranking. For each transliteration, we use the edit distance of the hypothesis from the reference as the output of the linear regression model, following Wang et al. (2015). The hypotheses are ranked in increasing order of their calculated edit distance. The linear regression model can be mathematically represented using:

$$ED = c + \sum_{i=1}^{10} \alpha_i x_i \qquad (3)$$

where ED is the edit distance calculated by the regression model, c is the intercept, and α_i and x_i are the coefficient and value of the i-th feature. As the edit distance between the hypothesis and reference is a measure of their similarity, it is seen as an effective parameter which can be used to re-rank the different hypotheses. It should be noted that these re-ranking experiments were performed after the Shared Task deadline and are not included in the official results submitted to the workshop.

4 Experiments

4.1 Experimental Setup for Sequitur

As an inherent grapheme-to-phoneme converter, the target language is broken down into its phonetic letter representation (phonemes), which are individual target language characters in a transliteration task. An example from the English-Hindi corpus is shown in Figure 1.

Input (English)	Transliteration (Hindi)
AFRICA	अफ ़ ़ र ी क ा

Figure 1: An example of data pre-processing in Sequitur from the English-Hindi corpus where the English word is AFRICA and Hindi representation is अफ्रीका.

4.2 Experimental Setup for Moses

For this experiment, we augment word representations with boundary markers (ˆ for the start of the word and $ for the end of the word). Adding boundary markers ensures that character position is encoded in these word representations, which is otherwise ignored in PB-SMT models (Kunchukuttan and Bhattacharyya, 2015). This significantly improves transliteration accuracy for languages (e.g., all Indian languages) which have different characters for identical phonological symbols depending on where (initial, medial or terminal position) they occur in a word. Figure 2 shows an example of how the strings are represented after pre-processing for Moses.

Input (English)	Transliteration (Hindi)
ˆ A F R I C A $	ˆ अफ ़ ़ र ी क ा $

Figure 2: An example of data pre-processing (augmented with word boundary markers) in Moses from the English-Hindi corpus where the English word is *AFRICA* and Hindi representation is *अफ्रीका*.

4.3 Results

Results from Moses and Sequitur on the test set are included in Tables 2 and 3. Table 2 includes top-1 accuracy results, while Table 3 summarizes the mean F-scores, for outcomes from each of Sequitur, Moses, and the consolidated re-ranking model on the hidden test partition. The top-1 hypothesis from the (Moses + Sequitur) re-ranked model is found to be the top-1 Sequitur and top-1 Moses transliteration in 61.93% and 61.06% instances, on average; of which the Sequitur and Moses results are identical in 45.62% instances. 22.63% of the time, on average, the top-1 re-ranked hypothesis is neither the top-1 from Moses nor Sequitur. These numbers do not include the English-to-Persian and Persian-to-English (with Western names) datasets, on account of the encoding mismatch between their test set with their training and development set, which is discussed later in this section.

From observing the accuracy results reported in Table 2, Sequitur reports best results on 5 language pairs — English-to-Thai, English-to-Vietnamese, English-to-Tamil, English-to-Japanese and English-to-Persian (with Persian

Task ID	Sequitur	Moses	Re-ranked
T-EnTh	**14.10**	13.90	13.50
B-ThEn	22.33	22.89	**26.59**
T-EnPe	**0.10**	**0.10**	**0.10**
B-PeEn	0.00	**0.11**	**0.11**
T-EnCh	26.20	**26.30**	24.90
B-ChEn	17.50	17.90	**18.80**
T-EnVi	**45.00**	43.40	40.40
M-EnBa	38.20	40.70	**41.10**
M-EnHi	30.03	**33.33**	31.83
T-EnHe	16.83	**17.59**	17.40
M-EnKa	28.41	26.90	**30.02**
M-EnTa	**18.22**	16.01	17.73
B-HeEn	6.78	**9.16**	8.47
T-ArEn	33.80	35.00	**37.50**
T-EnKo	25.90	26.10	**29.20**
T-EnJa	**31.83**	29.13	31.73
B-JnJk	51.70	**60.30**	57.20
B-EnPe	**61.00**	55.60	57.10
T-PeEn	65.80	65.60	**66.40**

Table 2: Word accuracies (%) from Moses and Sequitur models reported on the test set.

Task ID	Sequitur	Moses	Re-ranked
T-EnTh	**0.759759**	0.751033	0.756556
B-ThEn	0.804144	0.806737	**0.823464**
T-EnPe	**0.216715**	0.200054	0.203888
B-PeEn	0.007387	**0.307681**	0.297896
T-EnCh	**0.650861**	0.648604	0.639682
B-ChEn	0.784957	0.792034	**0.805242**
T-EnVi	**0.872989**	0.858727	0.857129
M-EnBa	0.871288	**0.879262**	0.873197
M-EnHi	0.836694	0.842555	**0.843902**
T-EnHe	0.796416	0.799957	**0.801067**
M-EnKa	0.840973	0.836202	**0.848025**
M-EnTa	0.820962	0.817579	**0.822778**
B-HeEn	0.720478	0.733852	**0.739240**
T-ArEn	0.896376	0.896873	**0.900685**
T-EnKo	**0.674653**	0.671095	0.671618
T-EnJa	**0.780412**	0.773722	0. 777001
B-JnJk	0.759595	**0.785229**	0.771079
B-EnPe	**0.928553**	0.918301	0.925398
T-PeEn	**0.947587**	0.943719	0.946168

Table 3: Mean F-scores from Moses and Sequitur models reported on the test set.

names) while Moses works best for another 5 — namely, English-to-Chinese, English-to-Hindi, English-to-Hebrew, Hebrew-to-English, and English-to-Kanji. The combined re-ranking of Moses + Sequitur improves the top-1 accuracy for 7 language pairs, which are Thai-to-English, Chinese-to-English, English-to-Bengali, English-to-Kannada, Arabic-to-English, English-to-Korean and Persian-to-English (with Persian names).

Further, it is observed that English-to-Persian and Persian-to-English (with Western names) perform very poorly as 66.92% and 67.53% Persian characters in the test set, respectively, were not present in either the training or the development set. The model is thus unable to predict transliterations for these characters, which occurs very frequently in the test set and hence report 100% error rates. The same language pair, however, performs significantly better (55-65% accuracy) for Persian names where the test set introduces no new tokens from the data used to train the transliteration models.

5   Summary

The two systems based on the joint source-channel and phrase-based statistical approaches are baseline systems for the NEWS 2018 shared task. For all our experiments we have adopted a language independent approach, wherein each language pair is processed automatically from the character sequence representation supplied for the shared tasks, with no language specific treatment for any of the language pairs.

References

Aditya Bhargava and Grzegorz Kondrak. 2011. How do you pronounce your name?: improving g2p with transliterations. In *Proceedings of the 49th Annual Meeting of the Association for Computational Linguistics: Human Language Technologies-Volume 1*, pages 399–408. Association for Computational Linguistics.

Maximilian Bisani and Hermann Ney. 2008. Joint-sequence models for grapheme-to-phoneme conversion. *Speech communication*, 50(5):434–451.

Peter F Brown, Vincent J Della Pietra, Stephen A Della Pietra, and Robert L Mercer. 1993. The mathematics of statistical machine translation: Parameter estimation. *Computational linguistics*, 19(2):263–311.

Michael Collins. 2011. Statistical machine translation: Ibm models 1 and 2. *Columbia Columbia Univ.*

Ngo Hoang Gia, Nancy F Chen, Nguyen Binh Minh, Bin Ma, and Haizhou Li. 2015. Phonology-augmented statistical transliteration for low-resource languages. In *Sixteenth Annual Conference of the International Speech Communication Association*.

Kevin Knight and Jonathan Graehl. 1998. Machine transliteration. *Computational Linguistics*, 24(4):599–612.

Philipp Koehn, Hieu Hoang, Alexandra Birch, Chris Callison-Burch, Marcello Federico, Nicola Bertoldi, Brooke Cowan, Wade Shen, Christine Moran, Richard Zens, et al. 2007. Moses: Open source toolkit for statistical machine translation. In *Proceedings of the 45th annual meeting of the ACL on interactive poster and demonstration sessions*, pages 177–180. Association for Computational Linguistics.

Anoop Kunchukuttan and Pushpak Bhattacharyya. 2015. Data representation methods and use of mined corpora for indian language transliteration. In *Proceedings of the Fifth Named Entity Workshop*, pages 78–82.

Leah S Larkey, Nasreen AbdulJaleel, and Margaret Connell. 2003. What's in a name?: Proper names in arabic cross language information retrieval. In *ACL Workshop on Comp. Approaches to Semitic Languages*. Citeseer.

Haizhou Li, A Kumaran, Vladimir Vladimire Pervouchine, and Min Zhang. 2009. Report of news 2009 machine transliteration shared task. In *Proceedings of the 2009 Named Entities Workshop: Shared Task on Transliteration*, pages 1–18. Association for Computational Linguistics.

Haizhou Li, Min Zhang, and Jian Su. 2004. A joint source-channel model for machine transliteration. In *Proceedings of the 42nd Annual Meeting on association for Computational Linguistics*, page 159. Association for Computational Linguistics.

Vladimir Pervouchine, Haizhou Li, and Lin Bo. 2009. Transliteration alignment. In *Proceedings of the Joint Conference of the 47th Annual Meeting of the ACL and the 4th International Joint Conference on Natural Language Processing of the AFNLP: Volume 1-Volume 1*, pages 136–144. Association for Computational Linguistics.

Yan Shao, Jörg Tiedemann, and Joakim Nivre. 2015. Boosting english-chinese machine transliteration via high quality alignment and multilingual resources. In *Proceedings of the Fifth Named Entity Workshop*, pages 56–60.

Yan Song, Chunyu Kit, and Hai Zhou. 2010. Reranking with multiple features for better transliteration. In *Proceedings of the 2010 Named Entities Workshop*, pages 62–65. Association for Computational Linguistics.

Yu-Chun Wang, Chun-Kai Wu, and Richard Tzong-Han Tsai. 2015. Ncu iisr english-korean and english-chinese named entity transliteration using different grapheme segmentation approaches. In *Proceedings of the Fifth Named Entity Workshop*, pages 83–87.

A Deep Learning Based Approach to Transliteration

Soumyadeep Kundu[1], Sayantan Paul[1], Santanu Pal[2]

[1]Jadavpur University, Kolkata, India
[2]Universität des Saarlandes, Saarbrücken, Germany
`{soumyadeep1497, sayantanpaul98}@gmail.com`
`santanu.pal@uni-saarland.de`

Abstract

In this paper, we propose different architectures for language independent machine transliteration which is extremely important for natural language processing (NLP) applications. Though a number of statistical models for transliteration have already been proposed in the past few decades, we proposed some neural network based deep learning architectures for the transliteration of named entities. Our transliteration systems adapt two different neural machine translation (NMT) frameworks: recurrent neural network and convolutional sequence to sequence based NMT. It is shown that our method provides quite satisfactory results when it comes to multi lingual machine transliteration. Our submitted runs are an ensemble of different transliteration systems for all the language pairs. In the NEWS 2018 Shared Task on Transliteration, our method achieves top performance for the En–Pe and Pe–En language pairs and comparable results for other cases.

1   Introduction

Machine Transliteration is the process by which a word written in source language is transformed into a target language, accurately and unambiguously, by preserving the phonetic aspects and pronunciation. Generally named entities or proper nouns are transliterated from one orthographic system to another. Based on the phonetics of source and target languages, and using statistical and language-specific methods, many machine transliteration algorithms have been developed over the past few years. Transliteration is used as part of many multilingual applications (Koehn, 2009), corpus alignment, multilingual text processing, cross lingual information retrieval and extraction (Virga and Khudanpur, 2003; Fujii and Ishikawa, 2001), and most importantly it is used as a component of machine translation system. Also considering the presence of various languages and increasing number of multilingual speakers, there is an immense need for automated, machine learning based transliteration systems. Transliteration can also be used to handle words not present in vocabulary in machine translation systems (Hermjakob et al., 2008). The task of transliteration is quite challenging and a complicated one owing to the various types of difficulties that arise. Pronunciation varies between different languages, and different dialects of the same language, thus making the task of transliteration intricate. Moreover, the absence of character correspondences in many language pairs makes this task complex. So, these types of characters are needed to be tackled in different ways, sometimes these are omitted, and in most of the cases these are approximated and represented in the best possible way keeping the pronunciation intact. Studies have shown that Machine Transliteration have been done mainly with traditional and different statistical methods (Knight and Graehl, 1998; Nguyen et al., 2016; Rama and Gali, 2009). With the advent of deep learning techniques, few research attempts have been made using deep learning (Yan and Nivre, 2016; Rosca and Breuel, 2016; Finch et al., 2016). The deep learning frame-works used are similar to that of the Sequence to Sequence machine translation (Bahdanau et al., 2015; Cho et al., 2014b). In our work, we present a comprehensive study of deep learning techniques for Machine Transliteration. We present some segmentation techniques for Transliteration–Character based and Byte-Pair based. We also present different deep learning architectures for machine transliteration such as

79

Proceedings of the Seventh Named Entities Workshop, pages 79–83
Melbourne, Australia, July 20, 2018. ©2018 Association for Computational Linguistics

Reccurent Neural Network (RNN) Encoder Decoder framework and the Convolutional NMT framework. The Convolutional Sequence to Sequence (Conv Seq2Seq) framework is a relatively new framework when compared to the RNN based NMT framework. This is the first attempt to use Conv Seq2Seq framework in transliteration of named entities and we have successfully implemented this framework. We have also implemented an ensemble method, which is based on the frequency of occurrence of output words. This type of ensembling based on the frequency has never been used before in this domain.

In Section 2, we discuss about the different deep learning frameworks used for transliteration and then in Section 3, we present our experimental methodology. In Section 4, we discuss about the results and then we conclude with Section 5.

2 Proposed Work

We propose two architectures which we have used for machine transliteration. These are the RNN based NMT framework and the Convolutional Sequence to Sequence Neural Machine Translation (ConvS2S NMT) framework.

2.1 RNN based NMT framework

RNN based NMT frameworks are basically the Sequence-to-sequence models (Sutskever et al., 2014; Cho et al., 2014b) which have been highly successful in a wide range of tasks such as speech recognition, machine translation and text summarization. NMT model portrays a more accurate translation than phrase-based traditional translation systems by capturing the context of the source sentence. The NMT framework is basically an encoder-decoder framework. An NMT system encoder converts the source sentence into a vector that holds the meaning of the source sentence. The vector is then processed by the decoder to generate the translation output. Therefore, NMT oversees the locality problem in the translation, and captures long range dependencies like gender agreements and syntax structures, improving the overall fluency of the translation system. Encoders and decoders both use RNN models, though they might differ in directionality, such as unidirectional or bidirectional, single-layer or multi-layer, or on the types of units used in the RNN, such as a vanilla RNN, a Long Short Term Memory (LSTM) (Hochreiter and Schmidhuber, 1997), or a Gated

Recurrent Unit (GRU)(Cho et al., 2014a).

2.2 ConvS2S NMT framework

We adapt a convolutional neural network (CNN)-based sequence-to-sequence NMT with multi-hop attention mechanism between encoder and decoder (Gehring et al., 2017). Our CNN architecture computes the encoder state z and the decoder state h. We embed input units and their absolute positions as a combined input element representation f. We proceed with a similar CNN architecture to build the output element representation e for the decoder network. We use a multi-step attention mechanism that allows the network to look back multiple times into f in order to produce e. The encoder creates a vector representation of f units using a CNN, and the computations of every f units are done simultaneously. The CNN decoder produces e output units, one at a time at every step, using a multi-step attention mechanism.

The multi-step attention layer works as follows:

- The first layer determines a useful source context from f which is fed to the second layer.

- The second layer uses this information during attention weight computation and then propagates it to the next layer and so on.

- The decoder also has immediate access to the attention history of the previous time steps.

Source	Target	Dataset Size		
Language	Language	Train	Dev	Test
English	Thai	30781	1000	1000
Thai	English	27273	1000	1433
English	Persian	13386	1000	1000
Persian	English	15677	1000	908
English	Chinese	41318	1000	1000
Chinese	English	32002	1000	1000
English	Vietnamese	3256	500	500
English	Bangla	13623	1000	1000
English	Hindi	12937	1000	1000
English	Tamil	10957	1000	1000
English	Kannada	10955	1000	1000
English	Hebrew	10501	1000	523
Hebrew	English	9447	1000	590

Table 1: Source and Target languages for the NEWS 2018 Shared Task on Transliteration

3 Experimental Methodology

In our work, we have explored two different architectures for both character level and byte-pair level segmentation.

3.1 Corpora

The corpora as provided by NEWS 2018[1] consisted of paired names between source and target languages. The size of the datasets varies from 3K to 41K. This is used as our training set. Additionally, they have also provided a development dataset of 1000 paired names for each language pair, which we have used as validation data for hyper-tuning the different system parameters. The test set consisted of 500–1433 paired names, depending on the language pairs. The details of the corpora is shown in Table 1.

3.2 Data Preprocessing

We have visualized the Machine Transliteration as a Machine Translation task, where we segmented each word into different small units. Here we describe the ways we used to segment the words. These sequence of segmented words forms the basis of input to different architectures.

3.2.1 Character Based segmentation

In character level segmentation, we segment the input word as a sequence of character units. Here, characters are the smallest representable unit. For example, a word 'sourjyakta' will be segmented as 's-o-u-r-j-y-a-k-t-a', where the different segments are shown by a '-' sign.

3.2.2 Byte-Pair based segmentation

Byte Pair encoding is a simple data compression technique in which the most common pair of consecutive bytes of data are replaced with a byte that does not occur within the data. In this segmentation type, we divide the words into different subword units and these units form a sequence, which in turn represents the word. The subword units are generally character n-gram which are generated by a process described in (Sennrich et al., 2015). Character n-grams of variable lengths are produced. The training set is processed and all character n-grams with frequency greater than a certain threshold value are considered. Now, when an input word is considered, the word is searched according to these character n-grams and are segmented accordingly. For example, for a training sample, the most frequent character n-grams are 'sa', 'sou', 'ta', etc. An input word 'sourjyakta' will be segmented as 'sou-r-y-t-a-k-ta'. The segmentation is shown with the help of - sign. We can

see that, 'sou' and 'ta', being the frequent n grams are segmented accordingly.

3.3 Ensemble method

Based on different architectures, segmentation methods and hyper parameters, we have generated different test data results. Taking into account all the generated output results, we implement an ensemble technique based on the frequency of occurrence of the output words. Corresponding to each input word, we calculate the most occurring output word from all the generated results.

Suppose there are 6 different methods, giving 6 output results for an input. For example, for an input word, there are 6 output words ('amit', 'ameet', 'amit', 'amit', 'amet', 'amit') generated from 6 different methods. So, here we see that amit occurs 4 times, so it is the most occurring word. As it is the most occurring word, the probability of 'amit' being the correct output is quite high. The frequency based ensembling provides an increase in accuracy about 2–3% on an average.

3.4 Training and Hyper parameters

For each language pair, character based and byte-pair based models are trained separately. To segment the words into subword units using byte-pair model, we consider only the 100 most frequent character n-grams as the byte-pairs, evaluated from the training data. Here, we choose 100 as a parameter, after extensive experimentation.

3.4.1 Hyper-parameters for RNN based NMT

For the training of the Sequence to Sequence architecture, we consider a learning rate of 1, and trained the systems till they converged. We used a batch size of 64, Cross Entropy as loss function and Gradient Descent Optimizer as the optimizer. Generally, it took about 20-50 epochs for each of the models to converge, using a single GPU system. We used a unidirectional RNN encoder with an attention RNN decoder for the Seq2Seq NMT.

3.4.2 Hyper-parameters for ConvS2S based NMT

The convolutional Sequence to Sequence model uses 15 layers in both the encoder and decoder, both with 256 hidden units with a kernel width of 3 for each CNN layer. We set the batch size

---

[1] http://workshop.colips.org/news2018/dataset.html

Language Pairs	RNN Based NMT				ConvS2S NMT				Ensemble (Frequency based)	
	Byte-Pair		Character		Byte-Pair		Character			
	ACC	F-score	ACC	F-score	ACC	F-score	ACC	F-score	ACC	F-score
En–Ch	0.240	0.648	0.261	0.657	0.187	0.608	0.041	0.457	**0.261**	**0.660**
Ch–En	0.128	0.767	0.154	0.788	0.152	0.785	0.160	0.785	**0.191**	**0.800**
En–Th	0.130	0.749	**0.145**	**0.761**	0.076	0.663	0.108	0.716	0.144	0.755
Th–En	0.211	0.788	0.229	0.799	0.235	0.801	0.169	0.759	**0.268**	**0.809**
En–Pe	0.001	0.214	**0.001**	**0.215**	0.000	0.199	0.001	0.193	-	-
Pe–En	0.000	0.357	**0.009**	**0.366**	-	-	-	-	-	-
En–Vi	0.094	0.677	**0.200**	**0.756**	0.008	0.586	0.178	0.740	-	-
En–Ba	0.334	0.854	0.343	0.863	0.255	0.829	0.118	0.751	**0.382**	**0.862**
En–Hi	0.255	0.820	0.283	0.836	0.247	0.822	0.250	0.827	**0.299**	**0.840**
En - Ka	0.224	0.809	0.237	0.819	0.187	0.817	0.211	0.817	**0.265**	**0.839**
En–Ta	0.134	0.759	0.164	0.811	0.154	0.801	0.146	0.799	**0.182**	**0.808**
En–He	0.145	0.752	**0.166**	**0.788**	0.120	0.769	0.130	0.775	0.164	0.782
He - En	0.061	0.679	0.075	0.712	0.071	0.703	0.061	0.713	**0.083**	**0.716**

Table 2: Evaluation Results in terms of Top 1 accuracy and mean F-score

to 32 for training our models, and that took approximately 1–2 hours on a single GPU setting. Network parameters are optimized with the negative log-likelihood objective. During transliteration we set the beam size to 5. Other additional hyper-parameter settings are borrowed from Gehring et al. (2017).

3.5 Evaluation Metrics

As mentioned in the News 2018 Shared Task Whitepaper (Chen et al., 2018), there are 4 different evaluation metrics - Word Accuracy in Top-1 (ACC), Fuzziness in Top-1 (Mean F-score), Mean Reciprocal Rank (MRR) and MAP. All these metrics are explained in detail in (Chen et al., 2018).

4 Results

In this work, we implement 4 different systems for each language pair. Two systems are based on RNN based NMT framework whereas the other two systems are based on ConvS2S NMT framework and each framework are trained on two separate preprocessing methods i.e., character and byte-pair based segmentations. Additionally, we implement a frequency based ensemble technique using the results of these 4 systems. In NEWS 2018 Shared Task on Transliteration, we have participated in 13 language pairs i.e. English–Chinese (En–Ch), Chinese–English (Ch–En), English–Persian (En–Pe), Persian–English (Pe–En), English–Thai (En–Th), Thai–English (Th–En), English–Vietnamese (En–Vi), English–Bangla (En–Bn), English–Hindi (En–Hi), English–Kannada (En–Ka), English–Tamil (En–Ta), English–Hebrew (En–He) and Hebrew–English (He–En). The results of our sys-

tem for these 13 language pairs are shown in Table 2. From Table 2, we see that the sequence to sequence architecture with character level segmentation gave the maximum accuracy among all the methods for most of the language pairs. Also, on ensembling, there is a significant amount of increase in accuracy. Overall, ensembling gives the best results for most of the language pairs. For some of the language pairs like En–He, En–Th, En–Vi, En–Pe and Pe–En, the output results of the different methods are vary so much, therefore ensembling does not provide improvement in accuracy.

5 Conclusion and Future Work

Our work presented some different approaches to machine transliteration using deep learning and neural network architecture. The official evaluation results of the NEWS 2018 Shared Task show that we achieved state-of-the-art results in En-Pe and Pe-En, and for the other language pairs, our system achieved almost competitive results as other systems. Therefore, we can conclude that we have successfully applied different deep learning approaches to machine transliteration. In the future, we aim to explore more neural network architectures such as explore an ensemble of bidirectional encoder frameworks along with different types of cell units such as LSTM, vanilla RNN, GRU, along with extensive parameter estimation.

References

Dzmitry Bahdanau, Kyunghyun Cho, and Yoshua Bengio. 2015. Neural Machine Translation by Jointly Learning to Align and Translate. In *International*

Conference on Learning Representations (ICLR), San Diego, CA, USA.

Nancy Chen, Xiangyu Duan, Min Zhang, Rafael E Banchs, and Haizhou Li. 2018. Whitepaper on news 2018 shared task on machine transliteration.

Kyunghyun Cho, Bart van Merrienboer, Dzmitry Bahdanau, and Yoshua Bengio. 2014a. On the Properties of Neural Machine Translation: Encoder–Decoder Approaches. In *Proceedings of SSST-8, Eighth Workshop on Syntax, Semantics and Structure in Statistical Translation*, pages 103–111, Doha, Qatar. Association for Computational Linguistics.

Kyunghyun Cho, Bart Van Merriënboer, Caglar Gulcehre, Dzmitry Bahdanau, Fethi Bougares, Holger Schwenk, and Yoshua Bengio. 2014b. Learning phrase representations using rnn encoder-decoder for statistical machine translation. *arXiv preprint arXiv:1406.1078.*

Andrew Finch, Lemao Liu, Xiaolin Wang, and Eiichiro Sumita. 2016. Target-bidirectional neural models for machine transliteration. In *Proceedings of the Sixth Named Entity Workshop*, pages 78–82.

Atsushi Fujii and Tetsuya Ishikawa. 2001. Japanese/english cross-language information retrieval: Exploration of query translation and transliteration. *Computers and the Humanities*, 35(4):389–420.

Jonas Gehring, Michael Auli, David Grangier, Denis Yarats, and Yann N. Dauphin. 2017. Convolutional Sequence to Sequence Learning. *CoRR*, abs/1705.03122.

Ulf Hermjakob, Kevin Knight, and Hal Daumé III. 2008. Name translation in statistical machine translation-learning when to transliterate. *Proceedings of ACL-08: HLT*, pages 389–397.

Sepp Hochreiter and Jürgen Schmidhuber. 1997. Long Short-Term Memory. *Neural Comput.*, 9(8):1735–1780.

Kevin Knight and Jonathan Graehl. 1998. Machine transliteration. *Computational Linguistics*, 24(4):599–612.

Philipp Koehn. 2009. *Statistical machine translation.* Cambridge University Press.

Binh Minh Nguyen, Hoang Gia Ngo, and Nancy F Chen. 2016. Regulating orthography-phonology relationship for english to thai transliteration. In *Proceedings of the Sixth Named Entity Workshop*, pages 83–87.

Taraka Rama and Karthik Gali. 2009. Modeling machine transliteration as a phrase based statistical machine translation problem. In *Proceedings of the 2009 Named Entities Workshop: Shared Task on Transliteration*, pages 124–127. Association for Computational Linguistics.

Mihaela Rosca and Thomas Breuel. 2016. Sequence-to-sequence neural network models for transliteration. *arXiv preprint arXiv:1610.09565.*

Rico Sennrich, Barry Haddow, and Alexandra Birch. 2015. Neural machine translation of rare words with subword units. *arXiv preprint arXiv:1508.07909.*

Ilya Sutskever, Oriol Vinyals, and Quoc V Le. 2014. Sequence to sequence learning with neural networks. In *Advances in neural information processing systems*, pages 3104–3112.

Paola Virga and Sanjeev Khudanpur. 2003. Transliteration of proper names in cross-lingual information retrieval. In *Proceedings of the ACL 2003 workshop on Multilingual and mixed-language named entity recognition-Volume 15*, pages 57–64. Association for Computational Linguistics.

Shao Yan and Joakim Nivre. 2016. Applying neural networks to english-chinese named entity transliteration. In *Sixth Named Entity Workshop, joint with 54th ACL.*

Comparison of Assorted Models for Transliteration

Saeed Najafi, Bradley Hauer, Rashed Rubby Riyadh, Leyuan Yu, Grzegorz Kondrak
Department of Computing Science
University of Alberta, Edmonton, Canada
`{snajafi,bmhauer,riyadh,leyuan,gkondrak}@ualberta.ca`

Abstract

We report the results of our experiments in the context of the NEWS 2018 Shared Task on Transliteration. We focus on the comparison of several diverse systems, including three neural MT models. A combination of discriminative, generative, and neural models obtains the best results on the development sets. We also put forward ideas for improving the shared task.

1 Introduction

Transliteration is the conversion of names and words between distinct writing scripts. It is an interesting and well-defined task, which is suitable for testing sequence-to-sequence models. In this edition of the NEWS Shared Task on Machine Transliteration, we tested a number of different approaches on all provided languages and datasets. Because of the sheer number of tested models, only minimal tuning was conducted. The results demonstrate that, on average, the neural models perform better than other systems, and that a combination of neural and non-neural models further improves the results. However, no individual system is clearly superior on all datasets.

2 Systems

In this section, we briefly describe the principal systems that we tested.

2.1 DIRECTL+

DIRECTL+ is a publicly available discriminative string transduction tool[1], which was initially developed for grapheme-to-phoneme conversion (Jiampojamarn et al., 2008). Previous University of Alberta teams have successfully applied DIRECTL+ to transliteration in the previous editions

of the NEWS shared task (Jiampojamarn et al., 2009, 2010; Bhargava et al., 2011; Kondrak et al., 2012; Nicolai et al., 2015). We apply M2M-aligner (Jiampojamarn et al., 2007) to align the source-target pairs before training.

Because of time constraints and the number of other models that we tested, we made only minimal effort to tune the parameters of DIRECTL+ on distinct language sets. This explains why our DIRECTL+ results may be lower than the ones in the previous shared tasks. In particular, the default maximum alignment length setting of 2 on both sides is known to produce poor results on language pairs that dramatically differ in the average word length, such as English and Chinese. Other important parameters include the source context size and joint m-gram size.

2.2 SEQUITUR

SEQUITUR is a joint n-gram-based string transduction system[2] (Bisani and Ney, 2008), which directly trains a joint n-gram model from unaligned data. Higher-order n-gram models are trained iteratively from lower-order models. The final order of the model is a parameter tuned on the development set. We found that 6-gram models work best for most language pairs, with the following exceptions: 4-gram for HeEn, 3-gram for ArEn and EnVi, and 2-gram for T-EnPe.

One limitation of SEQUITUR is that both the source and target character sets are limited to a maximum of 255 symbols. This precluded the application of SEQUITUR to Chinese and Japanese Kanji. For the English-Korean (EnKo) language pair, our work-around was to convert Korean Hangul into Latin characters using a romanization module.[3]

---

[1] *https://code.google.com/archive/p/directl-p*

[2] *http://www-i6.informatik.rwth-aachen.de/web/Software*
[3] *https://metacpan.org/Lingua::KO::Romanize::Hangul*

Proceedings of the Seventh Named Entities Workshop, pages 84–88
Melbourne, Australia, July 20, 2018. ©2018 Association for Computational Linguistics

2.3 OpenNMT

We adopt the OpenNMT tool (Klein et al., 2017), specifically the PyTorch variant[4], as a baseline neural machine translation system. We apply the system "as-is" to all language pairs, with all parameters left at their default settings. Word boundaries are inserted between all characters in the input and output, resulting in translation models which view characters as words and words as sentences.

2.4 Base NMT

As our main neural system, we implement a character-level neural transducer (NMT) following the encoder-decoder architecture of Sutskever et al. (2014), which is widely applied to machine translation. The encoder is a bi-directional recurrent neural network (RNN) applied to randomly initialized character embeddings. We employ the soft attention mechanism of Luong et al. (2015) to learn an aligner within the model. The NMT is trained for a fixed random seed using the Adam optimizer with a learning rate of 0.0005, embeddings of 128 dimensions, and hidden units of size 256. We employ beam search using a beam size of 10 to generate the final predictions at test time.

2.5 RL-NMT

RL-NMT is our implementation of an alternative system that specializes the neural encoder-decoder architecture to the sequence-labelling task, and trains with a biased Actor-Critic reinforcement-learning objective (Najafi et al., 2018). The NMT model is always conditioned on gold-standard contexts during maximum-likelihood training, while at test time, it is conditioned on its own predictions, creating a train-test mismatch (Ranzato et al., 2015). In order to alleviate this mismatch, we apply the Actor-Critic algorithm to fine-tune the network (RL-NMT) (Sutton and Barto, 1998; Bahdanau et al., 2016) by giving intermediate rewards of +1 if the generated character is correct, and 0 otherwise. We then assign the temporal difference credits for each prediction (Sutton and Barto, 1998). The critic model is a non-linear feed-forward network for estimating these assigned credits. After pre-training the NMT model, we apply a vanilla gradient descent algorithm for RL training with a fixed learning rate of 0.1.

[4] https://github.com/OpenNMT/OpenNMT-py

2.6 Linear Combination

We also consider the linear combination of multiple systems. One motivation for the combination is the observation that the non-neural models often perform better on datasets with fewer training instances. We make each individual system generate the 10 best transliterations for each test input, and combine the lists via a linear combination of the confidence scores. Scores of each model are normalized as described in (Nicolai et al., 2015, Section 4.1). The linear coefficients are tuned separately for each language pair on the provided development sets, using grid search with a step of 0.1.

2.7 Non-Standard DTLM

DTLM is a new system that combines discriminative transduction with character and word language models derived from large unannotated corpora (Nicolai et al., 2018). DTLM is an extension of DIRECTL+, whose target language modeling is limited to a set of binary n-gram features. Target language modelling is particularly important in low-data scenarios, where the limited transduction models often produce many ill-formed output candidates. We avoid the error propagation problem that is inherent in pipeline approaches by incorporating the LM feature sets directly into the transducer, which are based exclusively on the forms in the parallel training data. The weights of the new features are learned jointly with the other features of DIRECTL+.

In addition, we bolster the quality of transduction by employing a novel alignment method, which we refer to as precision alignment. The idea is to allow null substrings on the source side during the alignment of the training data, and then apply a separate aggregation algorithm to merge them with adjoining non-empty substrings. This method yields precise many-to-many alignment links that result in substantially higher transduction accuracy.

Since transliteration is mostly used for named entities, our language model and unigram counts are obtained from a corpus of named entities. We query DBPedia for a list of proper names, discarding names that contain non English characters. The resulting list of 1M names is used as a word-list, and also used to train the character language model.

Set	Development						Test					
System	DTL	SEQ	NMT			LC	DTL	SEQ	NMT			LC
			Open	Base	RL				Open	Base	RL	
RunID	8	3	6	1	2	13	8	3	6	1	2	13
ChEn	19.3	N/A	23.9	31.2	31.3	**32.2**	11.6	N/A	19.2	20.8	20.9	**21.0**
EnCh	69.6	N/A	70.1	70.6	70.9	**73.2**	24.6	N/A	27.1	26.0	**28.2**	27.5
EnBa	45.4	46.0	41.6	42.3	42.5	**50.7**	35.8	37.8	32.7	33.5	34.0	**40.7**
EnHe	58.1	60.5	58.2	59.2	58.6	**63.2**	15.3	16.8	**17.0**	16.8	16.8	16.1
HeEn	20.8	25.5	23.0	25.8	26.7	**29.2**	6.4	6.4	**9.2**	7.8	7.8	8.8
EnHi	45.9	45.9	29.2	34.3	34.9	**49.0**	**32.3**	30.3	29.4	26.8	25.4	32.2
EnKa	32.9	36.3	25.8	33.0	34.5	**39.9**	25.1	28.3	23.4	23.7	22.0	**30.4**
EnTa	40.2	38.0	28.8	32.8	33.1	**42.9**	19.3	19.7	18.1	17.9	18.5	**21.3**
EnTh	37.2	37.7	36.3	39.7	41.8	**44.3**	14.8	14.0	15.5	16.0	**16.6**	16.1
ThEn	22.5	44.9	39.5	43.8	44.0	**48.9**	13.0	22.1	27.1	26.9	26.2	**27.3**
EnVi	37.0	42.8	1.0	41.6	41.2	**47.8**	34.0	43.6	0.0	39.6	39.6	**45.4**
EnJa	48.8	48.9	47.7	51.6	52.4	**55.1**	32.9	32.0	34.6	35.9	36.8	**39.0**
JnJk	42.0	N/A	36.2	50.6	50.5	**53.9**	38.5	N/A	46.6	56.5	56.9	**59.3**
ArEn	21.4	32.1	25.8	33.9	34.4	**36.3**	33.0	35.2	**39.4**	36.3	37.3	39.1
B-PeEn	16.5	31.2	28.2	26.7	26.7	**33.6**	N/A	N/A	N/A	N/A	N/A	N/A
T-EnPe	55.5	56.0	48.8	57.2	57.6	**59.6**	0.0	0.0	0.0	0.0	0.0	0.0
T-PeEn	39.0	62.7	47.0	62.8	62.5	**67.8**	39.3	64.5	50.7	63.8	64.4	**68.2**
B-EnPe	79.0	76.8	70.5	76.3	77.4	**81.2**	61.2	61.2	53.2	58.4	59.2	**62.4**
EnKo	37.4	38.7	0.6	39.9	40.8	**47.6**	26.8	24.5	0.0	27.8	27.9	**34.0**
Avg	40.4	38.1	35.9	44.9	45.4	**50.3**	24.4	23.0	23.3	28.1	28.3	**31.0**

Table 1: Transliteration word accuracy on the development and test sets of the shared task.

2.8 Other submissions

We also submitted several other systems for evaluation. The neural models included an NMT model with a conditional random field (CRF) instead of decoder RNNs (RunID 10), self-critical reinforcement learning over NMT (RunID 11), and self-critical RL with intermediate rewards (RunID 12). For the language pairs on which we tested DTLM, we also submitted a corresponding baseline DIRECTL+ model (RunID 7). The remaining three submissions correspond to different linear combinations: SEQUITUR with RL-NMT ((RunID 5), SEQUITUR/RL-NMT with DIRECTL+ ((RunID 9), and our primary linear combination of DIRECTL+, SEQUITUR, and RL-NMT ((RunID 13), which we report in Table 1.

3 Development Experiments

We divided the available data into three parts for training, validation, and development testing. We created the validation sets for each language pair by randomly selecting instances from the provided training sets. Our validation sets had the same size as the provided development sets: 1000 instances

for each language pair, except 500 for EnVi. We trained the models on the remaining instances in the training sets. We used the provided development sets for development testing, as well as for selecting the SEQUITUR model order, and tuning the linear combinations coefficients.

Table 1 shows the development results (on the left). The average word accuracy is computed across all 19 language pairs, using a result of 0% for runs which could not be completed (N/A). On average, our two neural systems outperform the other individual systems, with RL-NMT better than NMT in most cases. Surprisingly, one of the two non-neural systems is the most accurate on about half of the datasets, even though DIRECTL+ (DTL) was not properly tuned, and SEQUITUR (SEQ) could not be run on three datasets. On the other hand, the OpenNMT tool is well below the other systems, and completely fails on EnVi and EnKo. Arguably, the most interesting outcome is that the linear combination (LC) of three diverse systems, DIRECTL+, SEQUITUR and RL-NMT substantially improves over the best-performing individual system on all datasets.

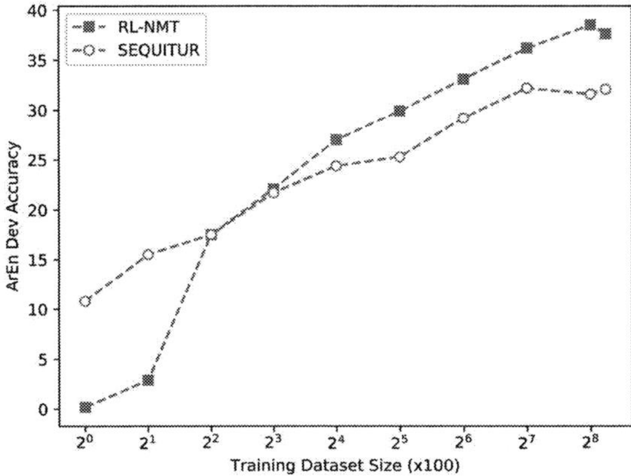

Figure 1: The effect of training size for RL-NMT and SEQUITUR on the ArEn development set.

We conjecture that traditional ML approaches perform better than neural networks on datasets with fewer training instances. The average training size for the sets on which the former surpass the latter is approximately 13 thousand vs. 20 thousand instances for the remaining sets. Further evidence is provided by Figure 1, which shows that SEQUITUR outperforms RL-NMT when the training set contains fewer than 400 instances.

4 Test Results

For the final testing, we kept the same training and validation splits as in the development experiments. In order to facilitate comparison between the development and test results, we decided not to augment the training data with the provided development sets, even though this would negatively affect our official results.

Table 1 shows the test results (on the right). The results in bold are the top-1 word accuracy on each dataset, which we designated as our primary runs for the leader-board of the shared task. Although, unlike in the development experiments, LC falls short of achieving the top result on each set, it is still the best on average. RL-NMT and NMT stand out among the individual systems, which confirms the development results. We observe a striking drop in accuracy across the board in comparison to the development results.

Table 2 shows the results of the non-standard DTLM system and the corresponding DIRECTL+ baseline on three datasets. The ability to leverage raw target corpora allows DTLM to substantially outperform all other models.

Set	Dev		Test	
System	DTL	DTLM	DTL	DTLM
RunID	7	4	7	4
ChEn	13.0	**37.7**	9.4	**30.0**
HeEn	21.9	**38.7**	6.8	**17.3**
ThEn	37.0	**48.0**	20.3	**31.2**

Table 2: The non-standard results of DTLM, and the corresponding standard baseline.

5 Problems

In this section, we describe a few issues which we hope will be resolved in the future NEWS tasks.

We found that the CodaLab environment did not facilitate the submission process. During the submission phase, we experienced multiple failures and delays due to the server being overloaded.

We could not obtain meaningful results on T-EnPe and B-PeEn, because the Persian characters in the train and test sets have incompatible encodings. Specifically, they seem to contain a mixture of visually similar characters from the Persian and Arabic scripts, which have distinct encodings.

We were not able to locate the progress test data described in the whitepaper (Chen et al., 2018).

After the results submission deadline, we became aware of the proposed baseline based on SEQUITUR. In our opinion, the official baseline results should have been made available at the time of the data release.

We believe that better publicity for the shared task (for example, on the ACL Portal) would help increase the number of participating teams. In addition, the requirement to pay for several datasets may be a deterrent to broader participation.

6 Conclusion

We described the details of the models that we tested in the shared task. In particular, we experimented with combining diverse ML systems, applying reinforcement learning to neural models, and leveraging target corpora for transliteration. Our results suggest that these techniques lead to improvements in accuracy with respect to the base systems. Finally, we recounted our experiences, and provided suggestions related to the management of the shared task. We hope that this report will serve as a useful reference for future experiments involving the datasets from NEWS 2018.

Acknowledgements

We thank Garrett Nicolai for the assistance with DTLM. We thank the shared task organizers for providing a review of our submission before the camera-ready deadline. This research was supported by the Natural Sciences and Engineering Research Council of Canada, Alberta Innovates, and Alberta Advanced Education.

References

Dzmitry Bahdanau, Philemon Brakel, Kelvin Xu, Anirudh Goyal, Ryan Lowe, Joelle Pineau, Aaron C. Courville, and Yoshua Bengio. 2016. An actor-critic algorithm for sequence prediction. *CoRR*, abs/1607.07086.

Aditya Bhargava, Bradley Hauer, and Grzegorz Kondrak. 2011. Leveraging transliterations from multiple languages. In *Proceedings of the 3rd Named Entities Workshop (NEWS 2011)*, pages 36–40.

Maximilian Bisani and Hermann Ney. 2008. Joint-sequence models for grapheme-to-phoneme conversion. *Speech Communication*, 50(5):434–451.

Nancy Chen, Xiangyu Duan, Min Zhang, Rafael E. Banchs, and Haizhou Li. 2018. Whitepaper on NEWS 2018 shared task on machine transliteration. In *Proceedings of the Seventh Named Entity Workshop*.

Sittichai Jiampojamarn, Aditya Bhargava, Qing Dou, Kenneth Dwyer, and Grzegorz Kondrak. 2009. Directl: a language-independent approach to transliteration. In *Proceedings of the 2009 Named Entities Workshop: Shared task on transliteration*, pages 28–31. Association for Computational Linguistics.

Sittichai Jiampojamarn, Colin Cherry, and Grzegorz Kondrak. 2008. Joint processing and discriminative training for letter-to-phoneme conversion. *Proceedings of ACL-08: HLT*, pages 905–913.

Sittichai Jiampojamarn, Kenneth Dwyer, Shane Bergsma, Aditya Bhargava, Qing Dou, Mi-Young Kim, and Grzegorz Kondrak. 2010. Transliteration generation and mining with limited training resources. In *Proceedings of the 2010 Named Entities Workshop*, pages 39–47. Association for Computational Linguistics.

Sittichai Jiampojamarn, Grzegorz Kondrak, and Tarek Sherif. 2007. Applying many-to-many alignments and hidden markov models to letter-to-phoneme conversion. In *Human Language Technologies 2007: The Conference of the North American Chapter of the Association for Computational Linguistics; Proceedings of the Main Conference*, pages 372–379.

Guillaume Klein, Yoon Kim, Yuntian Deng, Jean Senellart, and Alexander M. Rush. 2017. Opennmt: Open-source toolkit for neural machine translation. In *Proc. ACL*.

Grzegorz Kondrak, Xingkai Li, and Mohammad Salameh. 2012. Transliteration experiments on chinese and arabic. In *Proceedings of the 4th Named Entity Workshop*, pages 71–75. Association for Computational Linguistics.

Thang Luong, Hieu Pham, and Christopher D. Manning. 2015. Effective approaches to attention-based neural machine translation. In *Proceedings of the 2015 Conference on Empirical Methods in Natural Language Processing*, pages 1412–1421. Association for Computational Linguistics.

Saeed Najafi, Colin Cherry, and Grzegorz Kondrak. 2018. Sequence labeling and transduction with biased actor-critic training of RNNs. Submitted for publication.

Garrett Nicolai, Bradley Hauer, Mohammad Salameh, Adam St Arnaud, Ying Xu, Lei Yao, and Grzegorz Kondrak. 2015. Multiple system combination for transliteration. In *Proceedings of the Fifth Named Entity Workshop*, pages 72–77.

Garrett Nicolai, Saeed Najafi, and Grzegorz Kondrak. 2018. String transduction with target language models. Submitted for publication.

Marc'Aurelio Ranzato, Sumit Chopra, Michael Auli, and Wojciech Zaremba. 2015. Sequence level training with recurrent neural networks. *CoRR*, abs/1511.06732.

Ilya Sutskever, Oriol Vinyals, and Quoc V Le. 2014. Sequence to sequence learning with neural networks. In *Advances in Neural Information Processing Systems 27*, pages 3104–3112.

Richard S. Sutton and Andrew G. Barto. 1998. *Introduction to Reinforcement Learning*, 1st edition. MIT Press, Cambridge, MA, USA.

Neural Machine Translation Techniques for Named Entity Transliteration

Roman Grundkiewicz and **Kenneth Heafield**
University of Edinburgh
10 Crichton St, Edinburgh EH8 9AB, Scotland
{rgrundki,kheafiel}@inf.ed.ac.uk

Abstract

Transliterating named entities from one language into another can be approached as neural machine translation (NMT) problem, for which we use deep attentional RNN encoder-decoder models. To build a strong transliteration system, we apply well-established techniques from NMT, such as dropout regularization, model ensembling, rescoring with right-to-left models, and back-translation. Our submission to the NEWS 2018 Shared Task on Named Entity Transliteration ranked first in several tracks.

1 Introduction

Transliteration of Named Entities (NEs) is defined as the phonetic translation of names across languages (Knight and Graehl, 1998). It is an important part of a number of natural language processing tasks, and machine translation in particular (Durrani et al., 2014; Sennrich et al., 2016c).

Machine transliteration can be approached as a sequence-to-sequence modeling problem (Finch et al., 2016; Ameur et al., 2017). In this work, we explore the Neural Machine Translation (NMT) approach based on an attentional RNN encoder-decoder neural network architecture (Sutskever et al., 2014), motivated by its successful application to other sequence-to-sequence tasks, such as grammatical error correction (Yuan and Briscoe, 2016), automatic post-editing (Junczys-Dowmunt and Grundkiewicz, 2016), sentence summarization (Chopra et al., 2016), or paraphrasing (Mallinson et al., 2017). We apply well-established techniques from NMT to machine transliteration building a strong system that achieves state-of-the-art-results. The techniques we exploit include:

- Regularization with various dropouts preventing model overfitting;

- Ensembling strategies involving independently trained models and model checkpoints;

- Re-scoring of n-best list of candidate transliterations by right-to-left models;

- Using synthetic training data generated via back-translation.

The developed system constitutes our submission to the NEWS 2018 Shared Task[1] on Named Entity Transliteration ranked first in several tracks.

We describe the shared task in Section 2, including provided data sets and evaluation metrics. In Section 3, we present the model architecture and adopted NMT techniques. The experiment details are presented in Section 4, the results are reported in Section 5, and we conclude in Section 6.

2 Shared task on named entity transliteration

The NEWS 2018 shared task (Chen et al., 2018) continues the tradition from the previous tasks (Xiangyu Duan et al., 2016, 2015; Zhang et al., 2012) and focuses on transliteration of personal and place names from English or into English or in both directions.

2.1 Datasets

Five different datasets have been made available for use as the training and development data. The data for Thai (EnTh, ThEn) comes from the NECTEC transliteration dataset. The second dataset is the RMIT English-Persian dataset (Karimi et al., 2006, 2007) (EnPe, PeEn). Chinese (EnCh, ChEn) and Vietnamese (EnVi) data originates in Xinhua

---

[1] http://workshop.colips.org/news2018

89

Proceedings of the Seventh Named Entities Workshop, pages 89–94
Melbourne, Australia, July 20, 2018. ©2018 Association for Computational Linguistics

ID	Languages	Train	Dev	Test
EnTh	English-Thai	30,781	1000	1000
ThEn	Thai-English	27,273	1000	1000
EnPe	English-Persian	13,386	1000	1000
PeEn	Persian-English	15,677	1000	1000
EnCh	English-Chinese	41,318	1000	1000
ChEn	Chinese-English	32,002	1000	1000
EnVi	English-Vietnamese	3,256	500	500
EnHi	English-Hindi	12,937	1000	1000
EnTa	English-Tamil	10,957	1000	1000
EnKa	English-Kannada	10,955	1000	1000
EnBa	English-Bangla	13,623	1000	1000
EnHe	English-Hebrew	10,501	1000	1000
HeEn	Hebrew-English	9,447	1000	1000

Table 1: Official data sets in NEWS 2018 which we use in our experiments.

transliteration datasets (Haizhou et al., 2004), and the VNU-HCMUS dataset (Cao et al., 2010; Ngo et al., 2015), respectively. Hindi, Tamil, Kannada, Bangla (EnHi, EnTa, EnKa, EnBa), and Hebrew (EnHe, HeEn) are provided by Microsoft Research India[2]. We do not evaluate our models on the dataset from the CJK Dictionary Institute as the data is not freely available for research purposes.

We use 13 data sets for our experiments (Table 1). The data consists of genuine transliterations or back-translations or includes both.

No other parallel nor monolingual data are allowed for the constrained standard submissions that we participate in.

2.2 Evaluation

The quality of machine transliterations is evaluated with four automatic metrics in the shared task: word accuracy, mean F-score, mean reciprocal rank, and MAP_{ref} (Chen et al., 2018). As a main evaluation metric for our experiments we use word accuracy (Acc) on the top candidate:

$$Acc = \frac{1}{N} \sum_{i=1}^{N} \begin{cases} 1 & \text{if } c_{i,1} \text{matches any of } r_{i,j} \\ 0 & \text{otherwise} \end{cases}.$$

The closer the value to 1.0, the more top candidates $c_{i,1}$ are correct transliterations, i.e. they match one of the references $r_{i,j}$. N is the total number of entries in a test set.

3 Neural machine translation

Our machine transliteration system is based on a deep RNN-based attentional encoder-decoder

[2]http://research.microsoft.com/india

model that consists of a bidirectional multi-layer encoder and decoder, both using GRUs as their RNN variants (Sennrich et al., 2017b). It utilizes the BiDeep architecture proposed by Miceli Barone et al. (2017), which combines deep transitions with stacked RNNs. We employ the soft-attention mechanism (Bahdanau et al., 2014), and leave hard monotonic attention models (Aharoni and Goldberg, 2017) for future work. Layer normalization (Ba et al., 2016) is applied to all recurrent and feed-forward layers, except for layers followed by a softmax. We use weight tying between target and output embeddings (Press and Wolf, 2017).

The model operates on word level, and no special adaptation is made to the model architecture in order to support character-level transliteration, except data preprocessing (Section 4.1).

3.1 NMT techniques

Regularization Randomly dropping units from the neural network during training is an effective regularization method that prevents the model from overfitting (Srivastava et al., 2014).

For RNN networks, Gal and Ghahramani (2016) proposed variational dropout over RNN inputs and states, which we adopt in our experiments. Following Sennrich et al. (2016a), we also dropout entire source and target words (characters in our case) with a given probability.

Model ensembling Model ensembling leads to consistent improvements for NMT (Sutskever et al., 2014; Sennrich et al., 2016a; Denkowski and Neubig, 2017). An ensemble of independent models usually outperforms an ensemble of different model checkpoints from a single training run as it results in more diverse models in the ensemble (Sennrich et al., 2017a). As an alternative method for checkpoint ensembles, Junczys-Dowmunt et al. (2016) propose exponential smoothing of network parameters averaging them over the entire training.

We combine both methods and build ensembles of independently trained models with exponentially smoothed parameters.

Re-scoring with right-left models Re-scoring of an n-best list of candidate translations obtained from one system by another allows to incorporate additional features into the model or to combine multiple different systems that cannot be easily ensembled. Sennrich et al. (2016a, 2017a), for rescoring a NMT system, propose to use separate

ID	Original	+Synthetic	R
EnTh	59,131	154,232	×1
ThEn	58,872	153,973	×1
EnPe	32,321	127,314	×1
PeEn	32,616	127,609	×1
EnCh	81,252	176,367	×1
ChEn	80,818	175,933	×1
EnVi	2,756	139,175	×16
EnHi	12,607	145,507	×4
EnTa	10,702	137,887	×4
EnKa	10,662	137,727	×4
EnBa	13,389	148,635	×4
EnHe	18,558	132,070	×2
HeEn	18,388	131,730	×2

Table 2: Comparison of training data sets without and with synthetic examples. The original data are oversampled R times in synthetic data sets.

models trained on reversed target side that produce the target text from right-to-left.

We adopt the following re-ranking technique: we first ensemble four standard left-to-right models to produce n-best lists of 20 transliteration candidates and then re-score them with two right-to-left models and re-rank.

Back-translation Monolingual data can be back-translated by a system trained on the reversed language direction to generate synthetic parallel corpora (Sennrich et al., 2016b). Additional training data can significantly improve a NMT system.

As the task is organized under a constrained settings and no data other than that provided by organizers is allowed, we consider the English examples from all datasets as our monolingual data and use back-translations and "forward-translations" to enlarge the amount of parallel training data.

4 Experimental setting

We train all systems with Marian NMT toolkit[3,4] (Junczys-Dowmunt et al., 2018).

4.1 Data preprocessing

We uppercase[5] and tokenize all words into sequences of characters and treat them as words. Whitespaces are replaced by a special character to be able to reconstruct word boundaries after decoding.

---

[3] https://marian-nmt.github.io

[4] The training scripts are available at http://github.com/snukky/news-translit-nmt.

[5] The evaluation metric is case-insensitive.

We use the training data provided in the NEWS 2018 shared task to create our training and validation sets, and the official development set as an internal test set. Validation sets consists of randomly selected 500 examples that are subtracted from the training data. If a name entity has alternative translations, we add them to the training data as separate examples with identical source side. The number of training examples varies between ca. 2,756 and 81,252 (Table 2).

4.2 Model architecture

We use the BiDeep model architecture (Miceli Barone et al., 2017) for all systems. The model consists of 4 bidirectional alternating stacked encoders with 2-layer transition cells, and 4 stacked decoders with the transition depth of 4 in the base RNN of the stack and 2 in the higher RNNs. We augment it with layer normalization, skip connections, and parameter tying between all embeddings and output layer. The RNN hidden state size is set to 1024, embeddings size to 512. Source and target vocabularies are identical. The size of the vocabulary varies across language pair and is determined by the number of unique characters in the training data.

4.3 Training settings

We limit the maximum input length to 80 characters during training. Variational dropout on all RNN inputs and states is set to 0.2, source and target dropouts are 0.1. A factor for exponential smoothing is set to 0.0001.

Optimization is performed with Adam (Kingma and Ba, 2014) with a mini-batch size fitted into 3GB of GPU memory[6]. Models are validated and saved every 500 mini-batches. We stop training when the cross-entropy cost on the validation set fails to reach a new minimum for 5 consecutive validation steps. As a final model we choose the one that achieves the highest word accuracy on the validation set. We train with learning rate of 0.003 and decrease the value by 0.9 every time the validation score does not improve over the current best value. We do not change any training hyperparameters across languages.

Decoding is done by beam search with a beam size of 10. The scores for each candidate translation are normalized by sentence length.

---

[6] We train all systems on a single GPU.

System	EnTh	ThEn	EnPe	PeEn	EnCh	ChEn	EnVi	EnHi	EnTa	EnKa	EnBa	EnHe	HeEn
No dropouts	0.434	0.467	0.566	0.365	0.754	0.306	0.390	0.466	0.451	0.387	0.450	0.616	0.286
Baseline model	0.467	0.503	0.594	0.390	0.739	0.347	0.458	0.481	0.455	0.418	0.465	0.632	0.284
Right-left model	0.462	0.502	0.598	0.402	0.751	0.351	0.458	0.476	0.446	0.403	0.476	0.606	0.287
Ensemble $\times 4$	0.477	0.526	0.605	0.407	0.752	0.366	0.478	0.504	0.469	0.438	0.489	0.633	0.291
+ Re-ranking	0.475	0.534	0.606	0.436	**0.765**	0.365	0.494	0.515	**0.483**	0.441	**0.488**	**0.638**	0.294
+ Synthetic data	**0.484**	**0.728**	**0.610**	**0.585**	0.760	**0.759**	**0.496**	**0.519**	0.471	**0.455**	0.484	0.626	**0.615**
Test set	0.167	0.328	—	—	0.304	0.276	0.502	0.333	0.237	0.340	0.461	0.187	0.153

Table 3: Results (Acc) on the official NEWS 2018 development set. Bolded systems have been evaluated on the official test set (last row).

4.4 Synthetic parallel data

English texts from parallel training data from all datasets are used as monolingual data from which we generate synthetic examples[7]. We do not make a distinction between authentic examples or actual back-translations, and collect 95,179 unique English named entities in total.

We back-translate English examples using the systems trained on the original data and use them as additional training data for training the systems into English. For systems from English into another language, we translate English texts with analogous systems creating "forward-translations". To have a reasonable balance between synthetic and original examples, we oversample the original data several times (Table 2). The number of oversampling repetitions depends on the language pair, for instance, the Vietnamese original data are oversampled 16 times, while Chinese data are not oversampled at all.

5 Results on the development set

We evaluate our methods on the official development set from the NEWS 2018 shared task (Table 3). Results for systems that do not use ensembles are averaged scores from four models.

Regularization with dropouts improves the word accuracy for all language pairs except English-Chinese. As expected, model ensembling brings significant and consistent gains. Re-ranking with right-to-left models is also an effective method raising accuracy, even for languages for which a single right-to-left model itself is worse then a baseline left-to-right model, e.g. for EnHi, EnKa and EnHe systems.

The scale of the improvement for systems trained on additional synthetic data depends on the method that the synthetic examples are generated with: the systems into English benefit greatly from back-translations[8], while other systems that were supplied by forward-translations do not improve much or even slightly downgrade the accuracy.

6 Official results and conclusions

As final systems submitted to the NEWS 2018 shared task we chose ones that achieved the best performance on the development set (Table 3, last row). On the official test set, our systems are ranked first for most language pairs we experimented with[9].

The results show that the neural machine translation approach can be employed to build efficient machine transliteration systems achieving state-of-the-art results for multiple languages and providing strong baselines for future work.

Acknowledgments

This research is based upon work supported in part by the Office of the Director of National Intelligence (ODNI), Intelligence Advanced Research Projects Activity (IARPA), via contract #FA8650-17-C-9117. The views and conclusions contained herein are those of the authors and should not be interpreted as necessarily representing the official policies, either expressed or implied, of ODNI, IARPA, or the U.S. Government. The U.S. Government is authorized to reproduce and distribute reprints for governmental purposes notwithstanding any copyright annotation therein.

---

[7]More specifically, we use the source side of EnTh, EnPe, EnCh, EnVi, EnHi, EnTa, EnKa, EnBa, EnHe, and the target side of ThEn, PeEn, ChEn, HeEn data sets.

[8]The part of improvements might come from the fact that the ThEn, PeEn, ChEn and HeEn data sets have been created via back-translations and may include some of the examples from the development set.

[9]Due to issues with the test set, at the time of the camera-ready preparation, there were no official results for Persian.

References

Xinhua News Agency. 1992. Chinese transliteration of foreign personal names. *The Commercial Press.*

Roee Aharoni and Yoav Goldberg. 2017. Morphological inflection generation with hard monotonic attention. In *Proceedings of the 55th Annual Meeting of the Association for Computational Linguistics (Volume 1: Long Papers)*, volume 1, pages 2004–2015.

Hadj Ameur, Farid Meziane, Ahmed Guessoum, et al. 2017. Arabic machine transliteration using an attention-based encoder-decoder model. *Procedia Computer Science*, 117:287–297.

Jimmy Lei Ba, Jamie Ryan Kiros, and Geoffrey E Hinton. 2016. Layer normalization. *arXiv preprint arXiv:1607.06450.*

Dzmitry Bahdanau, Kyunghyun Cho, and Yoshua Bengio. 2014. Neural machine translation by jointly learning to align and translate. *arXiv preprint arXiv:1409.0473.*

Nam X. Cao, Nhut M. Pham, and Quan H. Vu. 2010. Comparative analysis of transliteration techniques based on statistical machine translation and joint-sequence model. In *Proceedings of the 2010 Symposium on Information and Communication Technology, SoICT 2010, Hanoi, Viet Nam, August 27-28, 2010*, pages 59–63.

Nancy Chen, Xiangyu Duan, Min Zhang, Rafael Banchs, and Haizhou Li. 2018. Whitepaper of NEWS 2018 shared task on machine transliteration. In *Proceedings of the Seventh Named Entity Workshop*. Association for Computational Linguistics.

Sumit Chopra, Michael Auli, and Alexander M Rush. 2016. Abstractive sentence summarization with attentive recurrent neural networks. In *Proceedings of the 2016 Conference of the North American Chapter of the Association for Computational Linguistics: Human Language Technologies*, pages 93–98.

Michael Denkowski and Graham Neubig. 2017. Stronger baselines for trustable results in neural machine translation. In *The First Workshop on Neural Machine Translation (NMT)*, Vancouver, Canada.

Nadir Durrani, Hassan Sajjad, Hieu Hoang, and Philipp Koehn. 2014. Integrating an unsupervised transliteration model into statistical machine translation. In *Proceedings of the 14th Conference of the European Chapter of the Association for Computational Linguistics, volume 2: Short Papers*, pages 148–153.

Andrew Finch, Lemao Liu, Xiaolin Wang, and Eiichiro Sumita. 2016. Target-bidirectional neural models for machine transliteration. In *Proceedings of the Sixth Named Entity Workshop*, pages 78–82. Association for Computational Linguistics.

Yarin Gal and Zoubin Ghahramani. 2016. A theoretically grounded application of dropout in recurrent neural networks. In *Advances in neural information processing systems*, pages 1019–1027.

Li Haizhou, Zhang Min, and Su Jian. 2004. A joint source-channel model for machine transliteration. In *Proceedings of the 42Nd Annual Meeting on Association for Computational Linguistics*, ACL '04, Stroudsburg, PA, USA. Association for Computational Linguistics.

Marcin Junczys-Dowmunt, Tomasz Dwojak, and Rico Sennrich. 2016. The AMU-UEDIN submission to the WMT16 news translation task: Attention-based nmt models as feature functions in phrase-based SMT. In *Proceedings of the First Conference on Machine Translation*, pages 319–325, Berlin, Germany. Association for Computational Linguistics.

Marcin Junczys-Dowmunt and Roman Grundkiewicz. 2016. Log-linear combinations of monolingual and bilingual neural machine translation models for automatic post-editing. In *Proceedings of the First Conference on Machine Translation: Volume 2, Shared Task Papers*, volume 2, pages 751–758.

Marcin Junczys-Dowmunt, Roman Grundkiewicz, Tomasz Dwojak, Hieu Hoang, Kenneth Heafield, Tom Neckermann, Frank Seide, Ulrich Germann, Alham Fikri Aji, Nikolay Bogoychev, André F. T. Martins, and Alexandra Birch. 2018. Marian: Fast neural machine translation in C++.

Sarvnaz Karimi, Andrew Turpin, and Falk Scholer. 2006. English to persian transliteration. In *String Processing and Information Retrieval, 13th International Conference, SPIRE 2006, Glasgow, UK, October 11-13, 2006, Proceedings*, pages 255–266.

Sarvnaz Karimi, Andrew Turpin, and Falk Scholer. 2007. Corpus effects on the evaluation of automated transliteration systems. In *ACL 2007, Proceedings of the 45th Annual Meeting of the Association for Computational Linguistics, June 23-30, 2007, Prague, Czech Republic*.

Diederik P Kingma and Jimmy Ba. 2014. Adam: A method for stochastic optimization. *arXiv preprint arXiv:1412.6980.*

Kevin Knight and Jonathan Graehl. 1998. Machine transliteration. *Computational Linguistics*, 24(4):599–612.

Jonathan Mallinson, Rico Sennrich, and Mirella Lapata. 2017. Paraphrasing revisited with neural machine translation. In *Proceedings of the 15th Conference of the European Chapter of the Association for Computational Linguistics: Volume 1, Long Papers*, volume 1, pages 881–893.

Antonio Valerio Miceli Barone, Jindřich Helcl, Rico Sennrich, Barry Haddow, and Alexandra Birch. 2017. Deep Architectures for Neural Machine Translation. In *Proceedings of the Second Conference on Machine Translation, Volume 1: Research Papers*, Copenhagen, Denmark. Association for Computational Linguistics.

Hoang Gia Ngo, Nancy F. Chen, Binh Minh Nguyen, Bin Ma, and Haizhou Li. 2015. Phonology-augmented statistical transliteration for low-resource languages. In *INTERSPEECH 2015, 16th Annual Conference of the International Speech Communication Association, Dresden, Germany, September 6-10, 2015*, pages 3670–3674.

Ofir Press and Lior Wolf. 2017. Using the output embedding to improve language models. In *Proceedings of the 15th Conference of the European Chapter of the Association for Computational Linguistics: Volume 2, Short Papers*, volume 2, pages 157–163.

Rico Sennrich, Alexandra Birch, Anna Currey, Ulrich Germann, Barry Haddow, Kenneth Heafield, Antonio Valerio Miceli Barone, and Philip Williams. 2017a. The University of Edinburgh's neural MT systems for WMT17. In *Proceedings of the Second Conference on Machine Translation, WMT 2017*, pages 389–399.

Rico Sennrich, Orhan Firat, Kyunghyun Cho, Alexandra Birch, Barry Haddow, Julian Hitschler, Marcin Junczys-Dowmunt, Samuel Läubli, Antonio Valerio Miceli Barone, Jozef Mokry, and Maria Nadejde. 2017b. Nematus: a toolkit for neural machine translation. In *Proceedings of the Software Demonstrations of the 15th Conference of the European Chapter of the Association for Computational Linguistics*, pages 65–68, Valencia, Spain. Association for Computational Linguistics.

Rico Sennrich, Barry Haddow, and Alexandra Birch. 2016a. Edinburgh neural machine translation systems for WMT16. In *Proceedings of the First Conference on Machine Translation*, pages 371–376, Berlin, Germany. Association for Computational Linguistics.

Rico Sennrich, Barry Haddow, and Alexandra Birch. 2016b. Improving neural machine translation models with monolingual data. In *Proceedings of the 54th Annual Meeting of the Association for Computational Linguistics (Volume 1: Long Papers)*, pages 86–96, Berlin, Germany. Association for Computational Linguistics.

Rico Sennrich, Barry Haddow, and Alexandra Birch. 2016c. Neural machine translation of rare words with subword units. In *Proceedings of the 54th Annual Meeting of the Association for Computational Linguistics (Volume 1: Long Papers)*, pages 1715–1725, Berlin, Germany. Association for Computational Linguistics.

Nitish Srivastava, Geoffrey Hinton, Alex Krizhevsky, Ilya Sutskever, and Ruslan Salakhutdinov. 2014. Dropout: A simple way to prevent neural networks from overfitting. *J. Mach. Learn. Res.*, 15(1):1929–1958.

Ilya Sutskever, Oriol Vinyals, and Quoc V. Le. 2014. Sequence to sequence learning with neural networks. In *Proceedings of the 27th International Conference on Neural Information Processing Systems - Volume 2*, NIPS'14, pages 3104–3112, Cambridge, MA, USA. MIT Press.

China Xiangyu Duan, Soochow University, Singapore Rafael E Banchs, Institute for Infocomm Research, China Min Zhang, Soochow University, Singapore Haizhou Li, Institute for Infocomm Research, and India A Kumaran, Microsoft Research, editors. 2015. *Proceedings of the Fifth Named Entity Workshop*. Association for Computational Linguistics, Beijing, China.

China Xiangyu Duan, Soochow University, Singapore Rafael E Banchs, Institute for Infocomm Research, China Min Zhang, Soochow University, Singapore Haizhou Li, Institute for Infocomm Research, and India A Kumaran, Microsoft Research, editors. 2016. *Proceedings of the Sixth Named Entity Workshop*. Association for Computational Linguistics, Berlin, Germany.

Zheng Yuan and Ted Briscoe. 2016. Grammatical error correction using neural machine translation. In *Proceedings of the 2016 Conference of the North American Chapter of the Association for Computational Linguistics: Human Language Technologies*, pages 380–386.

Min Zhang, Haizhou Li, and A Kumaran, editors. 2012. *Proceedings of the 4th Named Entity Workshop (NEWS) 2012*. Association for Computational Linguistics, Jeju, Korea.

Low-Resource Machine Transliteration Using Recurrent Neural Networks of Asian Languages

Ngoc Tan Le
Universite du Quebec a Montreal / Canada
le.ngoc_tan@uqam.ca

Fatiha Sadat
Universite du Quebec a Montreal / Canada
sadat.fatiha@uqam.ca

Abstract

Grapheme-to-phoneme models are key components in automatic speech recognition and text-to-speech systems. With low-resource language pairs that do not have available and well-developed pronunciation lexicons, grapheme-to-phoneme models are particularly useful. These models are based on initial alignments between grapheme source and phoneme target sequences. Inspired by sequence-to-sequence recurrent neural network-based translation methods, the current research presents an approach that applies an alignment representation for input sequences and pre-trained source and target embeddings to overcome the transliteration problem for a low-resource languages pair. We participated in the NEWS 2018 shared task for the English-Vietnamese transliteration task.

1 Introduction

Transliteration means the phonetic translation of the words in a source language (*e.g. English*) into equivalent words in a target language (*e.g. Vietnamese*). It entails transforming a word from one writing system (the *"source word"*) to a phonetically equivalent word in another writing system (the *"target word"*) (Knight and Graehl, 1998). This transformation requires a large set of rules defined by expert linguists to determine how the phonemes are aligned and to take into account the phonological system of the target language. Many language pairs have adopted various rules for transliteration over time, and most transliteration depends on the origin of a word (Waxmonsky and Reddy, 2012).

In recent work on sequence-to-sequence neural network-based machine translation, the input vocabulary is large. Moreover, statistics for many words must be sparsely estimated (Sutskever et al., 2014; Jean et al., 2014). To deal with this linguistics aspect, neural network-based approaches use continuous-space representations of words or word embeddings, in which words that occur in similar context tend to be close to each other in representational space. The benefits of using neural networks, particularly, recurrent neural networks, to deal with sparse problem are very clear.

We have observed that the state-of-the-art grapheme-to-phoneme methods were based on the use of grapheme-phoneme mappings (Oh et al., 2006; Bisani and Ney, 2008; Duan et al., 2016). However, recurrent neural networks approaches do not require any alignment information. In this study, we propose a novel method to build a low-resource machine transliteration system, using RNN-based models and alignment information for input sequences. Given a new word in the source language that does not exist in the bilingual pronunciation dictionary, this system automatically predicts the phonemic representation of a word in the target language. We are interested in solving out-of-vocabulary words for machine translation systems, such as proper nouns or technical terms, for a low-resource language pair, in this case English and Vietnamese.

The structure of the article is as follows: Section 2 presents the state of the art on machine transliteration. In section 3, we describe our proposed approach. Then, in section 4, we present our experiments, compare our system's performance with other systems. Finally, in section 5, we present our conclusions and perspectives for future research.

2 Related Work

Transliteration can be considered as a subtask of machine translation, when we need to translate source graphemes into target phonemes. In other words, an alignment model needs to be constructed first, and the translation model is built

Proceedings of the Seventh Named Entities Workshop, pages 95–100
Melbourne, Australia, July 20, 2018. ©2018 Association for Computational Linguistics

on the basis of the alignments. Transliterating a word from the language of its origin to a foreign language is called *Forward Transliteration*, while transliterating a loan-word written in a foreign language back to the language of its origin is called *Backward Transliteration* (Karimi et al., 2011).

Statistical techniques based on large parallel transliteration corpora work well for rich-resource languages but low-resource languages do not have the luxury of such resources. For such languages, rule-based transliteration is the only viable option.

From 2009 to 2018, various transliteration systems were proposed during the Named Entities Workshop evaluation campaigns[1] (Duan et al., 2016). These campaigns consist in transliterating from English into languages with a wide variety of writing systems, including Hindi, Tamil, Russian, Kannada, Chinese, Korean, Thai and Japanese. We can see that the romanization of non-Latin writing systems remains a complex computational task that depends crucially on which language is involved. Through this workshop, much progress has been made in methodologies for resolving the transliteration of proper nouns. We see the emergence of different approaches, such as grapheme-to-phoneme conversion (Finch and Sumita, 2010; Ngo et al., 2015), based on statistics like machine translation (Laurent et al., 2009; Nicolai et al., 2015) and neural networks (Finch et al., 2016; Shao and Nivre, 2016; Thu et al., 2016). Other work used attention-less sequence-to-sequence models for the transliteration task (Yao and Zweig, 2015). One study used a bidirectional Long Short-Term Memory (LSTM) models together with input delays for grapheme-to-phoneme conversion (Rao et al., 2015).

Another important challenge with the extraction of named entities and automatic transliteration is related to the vast variety of writing systems. All these difficulties are aggravated by the lack of bilingual pronunciation dictionaries for proper nouns, ambiguous transcriptions and orthographic variation in a given language. In addition to transliteration generation systems, there are also transliteration mining systems that try to obtain parallel transliteration pairs from comparable corpora (Klementiev and Roth, 2006; Kumaran et al., 2010; Sajjad et al., 2017; Tran et al., 2016; Udupa et al., 2009).

In our literature review, we found a few cases in which Vietnamese had been studied for the transliteration task. (Cao et al., 2010) applied the statistical-based approach as machine translation in the transliteration task for the English-Vietnamese low-resource language pair, with a performance of 63 BLEU points. (Ngo et al., 2015) proposed a statistical model for English and Vietnamese, with a phonological constraint on syllables. Their system performed better than the rule-based baseline system, with a 70% reduction in error rates. (Le and Sadat, 2017) explored RNN, particularly, LSTM, in the transliteration task for French and Vietnamese. Their results showed that the RNN-based system performed better than the baseline system, which was based on a statistical approach. In this research, we propose a new approach by using alignment representation for input sequences and pre-trained source/target embeddings in the input layer in order to build a neural network-based transliteration system to solve the problem of scattered data due to a low-resource language.

3 Methodology

Our proposed approach for an efficient transliteration consists of three main steps: *(1) pre-processing, (2) modification of the input sequences based on alignment representation and (3) creation of an RNN-based machine transliteration*. The whole pipeline is illustrated in Figure 1.

(1) Firstly, the learning data is pre-processed with normalization in lowercasing, removing the hyphens separating syllables and segmenting all syllables at the character level.

(2) Secondly, we extract the alignment output from the bilingual pronunciation dictionary and modify the input sequences based on the alignment results (Figure 1).

(3) Then we train an RNN-based machine transliteration (Figure 2).

4 Experiments

4.1 Configuration

To evaluate the efficiency of our proposed transliteration system in low resource settings, we used a bilingual pronunciation dictionary that has been provided by the NEWS 2018 shared task[2]. The

---

[1] `http://workshop.colips.org/news2016/`

[2] `http://workshop.colips.org/news2018/`
`documents/news2018whitepaper.pdf`

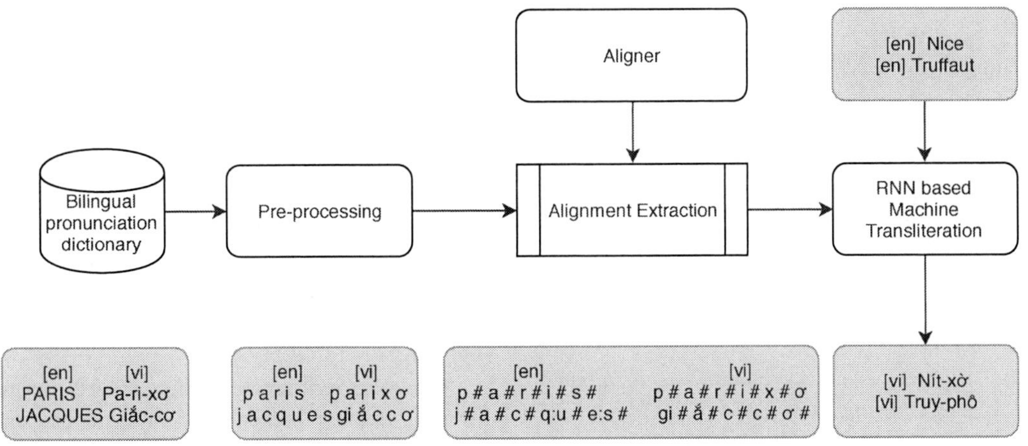

Figure 1: The architecture of machine transliteration for a low-resource language pair dealing with bilingual named entities.

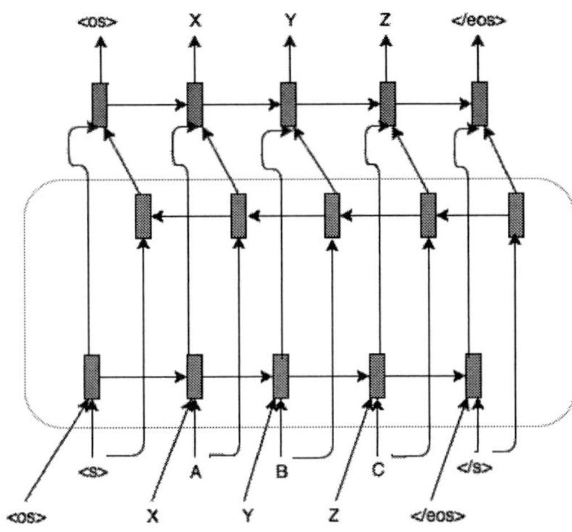

Figure 2: Our RNN-based model architecture with encoder-decoder bi-directional LSTM and alignment representation on input sequences. We use <s> and </s>, <os> and </eos> markers to pad the grapheme/phoneme sequences to a fixed length.

learning data comprise 3,256 pairs of bilingual English-Vietnamese named entities pairs, 500 pairs for the development set and 500 pairs for the testing set. We found that most of the named entities were persons, locations and organizations. To overcome the problem of the scattering of learning data, we performed the pre-processing step with segmentation of all syllables at the character level and presented the whole dataset in lowercase.

To deal with the alignment representation, we used the *m-2-m aligner*[3] toolkit (Jiampojamarn et al., 2007) to align the training data at the character level. We chose $m = 2$ (bigram-align) for all experiments; this means that a maximum of two graphemes on the source side will be aligned with a maximum of two phonemes on the target side. For the pre-trained source and target embeddings, we applied the word2vec[4] toolkit (Mikolov et al., 2013) with a dimension of 64, a continuous space window size of 5 and the 'skip-gram' option.

We applied the *nmt-keras*[5] toolkit to train our transliteration model for the English-Vietnamese language pair. In the transliteration system configuration, we used two-layer encoder-decoder bi-directional LSTM cells (Hochreiter and Schmidhuber, 1997) for the RNN model, with a 64-dimension projection layer to encode the input sequences and 128 nodes in each hidden layer. We used the *'Adam'* optimizer to learn the weights of the network with a default learning rate of 0.001. For decoding, the beam search was assigned the size of 6. All the RNN hyper-parameters were determined by tuning on the development set. This implementation is based on Python *Theano* (Al-Rfou et al., 2016), which allows for efficient training on both central processing units (CPU) and graphics processing units (GPU).

---

[3]https://github.com/letter-to-phoneme/m2m-aligner/

[4]https://code.google.com/archive/p/word2vec/

[5]https://github.com/lvapeab/nmt-keras/

4.2 Evaluation

In this work, we built a machine transliteration method which was inspired by neural machine translation. Hence, we applied different evaluation metrics such as *BiLingual Evaluation Understudy (BLEU)* (Papineni et al., 2002), *Translation Error Rate (TER)* (Snover et al., 2009), and *Phoneme Error Rate (PER)*.

To evaluate our proposed approach, we implemented five systems (Table 1):

(1) Baseline system A : *phrase-based statistical machine translation (pbSMT)*.
We implemented a *pbSMT* system with *Moses*[6] (Koehn et al., 2007). We used *mGIZA* (Gao and Vogel, 2008) to align the corpus at the character level, and *SRILM* (Stolcke et al., 2002) to create a character-based 5-gram language model for the target language.

(2) Baseline system B : *multi-joint sequence model for grapheme-to-phoneme convertion*.
We applied the *Sequitur-G2P*[7] toolkit to train a transliteration model.

(3) System 1 : *encoder-decoder bidirectional + attention mechanism*.

(4) System 2 : *encoder-decoder bidirectional + attention mechanism + alignment representation for input sequences*.

(5) System 3 : *encoder-decoder bidirectional + attention mechanism + alignment representation for input sequences + pre-trained source and target embeddings*.

The difference between the two baseline systems' performance is minor. Baseline system B seems slightly more efficient than baseline system A, with a gain of +4.40 BLEU points, as well as reduced translation errors (TER), at -3.58 points and phoneme errors (PER), at -6.20 points (Table 1).

By comparing the two baseline systems and systems 1, 2 and 3 (*our proposed approach*), we note significant results up to 68.60 points for BLEU, and reductions in TER and PER up to 15.92 and 30.03 points, respectively (Table 1).

In addition, system 3 performed better than systems A and B, with gains of +7.30 and +2.90

BLEU points, reductions of -8.16 and -4.58 TER points, -14.17 and -7.97 PER points, respectively (Table 1).

In general, the proposed approach performed the transliteration task very well, with significant gains, and reduced the phoneme error rate. We observed that the output quality of the proposed approach, based on recurrent neural networks, was more fluid, coherent and had fewer errors than other systems, that use statistical-based approaches (Table 2).

All the experimental results showed that using the alignment representation and the pre-trained source and target embeddings resulted in significant advances over other methods.

5 Conclusions and perspectives

In this paper, we presented a novel approach for machine transliteration in low research settings, that combines several techniques based on neural networks - encoder-decoder, attention mechanism, alignment representation for input sequences and pre-trained source and target embeddings - in machine transliteration systems.

In the future work, we intend to test our proposed approach with a larger bilingual pronunciation dictionary as well as to study other approaches such as semi-supervised or non-supervised.

Acknowledgements

We thank the anonymous reviewers for their insightful comments.

References

Rami Al-Rfou, Guillaume Alain, Amjad Almahairi, Christof Angermueller, Dzmitry Bahdanau, Nicolas Ballas, Frédéric Bastien, Justin Bayer, Anatoly Belikov, Alexander Belopolsky, et al. 2016. Theano: A Python framework for fast computation of mathematical expressions. *arXiv preprint arXiv:1605.02688* 472 (2016), 473.

Maximilian Bisani and Hermann Ney. 2008. Joint-sequence models for grapheme-to-phoneme conversion. *Speech communication* 50, 5 (2008), 434–451.

Nam X Cao, Nhut M Pham, and Quan H Vu. 2010. Comparative analysis of transliteration techniques based on statistical machine translation and joint-sequence model. In *Proceedings of the 2010 Symposium on Information and Communication Technology*. Association for Computing Machinery, 59–63.

---

[6]http://www.statmt.org/moses/
[7]https://www-i6.informatik.rwth-aachen.de/web/Software/g2p.html

Experiments	BLEU ↑	TER ↓	PER ↓
Baseline system A (pbSMT)	61.30	24.08	44.20
Baseline system B (Sequitur-G2P)	65.70	20.50	38.00
System 1 (encoder-decoder + attention mechanism)	66,68	16,70	31,50
System 2 (encoder-decoder + attention mechanism + alignment representation)	67,57	16,23	30,63
System 3 (encoder-decoder + attention mechanism + alignment representation + pre-trained source target embeddings)	**68,60**	**15,92**	**30,03**

Table 1: Evaluation of scoring for all systems : BLEU, TER and PER.

PARIS			MANHATTAN		
No	TOP-5	Probability	No	TOP-5	Probability
1	**p a r i x ɔ**	**0,633242**	1	m a n h á t t â n	0,321082
2	p a r í t	0,153536	2	**m a n h á t t a n**	**0,288677**
3	b a r i	0,065151	3	m â n h á t t â n	0,080221
4	b a r í t	0,037314	4	m â n h á t t a n	0,072125
5	b a r í t x ɔ	0,028526	5	m a h á t t â n	0,058193

Table 2: Illustration of the transliteration predictions of the named entities obtained by our proposed approach before the re-ranking of the list of k-best results, with the top-5 ($k = 5$) first best results for the named entities : *PARIS* and *MANHATTAN*

Xiangyu Duan, Rafael E Banchs, Min Zhang, Haizhou Li, and A Kumaran. 2016. Report of NEWS 2016 Machine Transliteration Shared Task. *ACL 2016* (2016), 58–72.

Andrew Finch, Lemao Liu, Xiaolin Wang, and Eiichiro Sumita. 2016. Target-Bidirectional Neural Models for Machine Transliteration. *ACL 2016* (2016), 78–82.

Andrew Finch and Eiichiro Sumita. 2010. Transliteration using a phrase-based statistical machine translation system to re-score the output of a joint multigram model. In *Proceedings of the 2010 Named Entities Workshop*. Association for Computational Linguistics, 48–52.

Qin Gao and Stephan Vogel. 2008. Parallel implementations of word alignment tool. In *Software Engineering, Testing, and Quality Assurance for Natural Language Processing*. Association for Computational Linguistics, 49–57.

Sepp Hochreiter and Jürgen Schmidhuber. 1997. Long Short-Term Memory. *Neural Comput.* 9, 8 (Nov. 1997), 1735–1780. https://doi.org/10. 1162/neco.1997.9.8.1735

Sebastien Jean, Kyunghyun Cho, Roland Memisevic, and Yoshua Bengio. 2014. On using very large target vocabulary for neural machine translation. *arXiv preprint arXiv:1412.2007* (2014).

Sittichai Jiampojamarn, Grzegorz Kondrak, and Tarek Sherif. 2007. Applying Many-to-Many Alignments and Hidden Markov Models to Letter-to-Phoneme Conversion. In *HLT-NAACL*, Vol. 7. 372–379.

Sarvnaz Karimi, Falk Scholer, and Andrew Turpin. 2011. Machine transliteration survey. *ACM Computing Surveys (CSUR)* 43, 3 (2011), 17.

Alexandre Klementiev and Dan Roth. 2006. Weakly supervised named entity transliteration and discovery from multilingual comparable corpora. In *Proceedings of the 21st International Conference on Computational Linguistics and the 44th annual meeting of the Association for Computational Linguistics*. Association for Computational Linguistics, 817–824.

Kevin Knight and Jonathan Graehl. 1998. Machine transliteration. *Computational Linguistics* 24, 4 (1998), 599–612.

Philipp Koehn, Hieu Hoang, Alexandra Birch, Chris Callison-Burch, Marcello Federico, Nicola Bertoldi, Brooke Cowan, Wade Shen, Christine Moran, Richard Zens, et al. 2007. Moses: Open source toolkit for statistical machine translation. In *Proceedings of the 45th annual meeting of the ACL on interactive poster and demonstration sessions*. Association for Computational Linguistics, 177–180.

A Kumaran, Mitesh M Khapra, and Haizhou Li. 2010. Report of NEWS 2010 transliteration mining shared task. In *Proceedings of the 2010 Named Entities Workshop*. Association for Computational Linguistics, 21–28.

Antoine Laurent, Paul Deléglise, Sylvain Meignier, and France Spécinov-Trélazé. 2009. Grapheme to phoneme conversion using an SMT system. In *Proceedings of INTERSPEECH, ISCA*. 708–711.

Ngoc Tan Le and Fatiha Sadat. 2017. A Neural Network Transliteration Model in Low Resource Settings. In *Proceedings of the 16th International Conference of Machine Translation Summit, September 18-22 2017, Nagoya, Japan, volume 1, Research Track*. 337–345.

Tomas Mikolov, Wen-tau Yih, and Geoffrey Zweig. 2013. Linguistic regularities in continuous space word representations.. In *hlt-Naacl*, Vol. 13. 746–751.

Hoang Gia Ngo, Nancy F Chen, Binh Minh Nguyen, Bin Ma, and Haizhou Li. 2015. Phonology-augmented statistical transliteration for low-resource languages.. In *Interspeech*. 3670–3674.

Garrett Nicolai, Bradley Hauer, Mohammad Salameh, Adam St Arnaud, Ying Xu, Lei Yao, and Grzegorz Kondrak. 2015. Multiple system combination for transliteration. In *Proceedings of NEWS 2015 The Fifth Named Entities Workshop*. 72–79.

Jong-Hoon Oh, Key-Sun Choi, and Hitoshi Isahara. 2006. A machine transliteration model based on correspondence between graphemes and phonemes. *ACM Transactions on Asian Language Information Processing (TALIP)* 5, 3 (2006), 185–208.

Kishore Papineni, Salim Roukos, Todd Ward, and Wei-Jing Zhu. 2002. BLEU: a method for automatic evaluation of machine translation. In *Proceedings of the 40th annual meeting on association for computational linguistics*. Association for Computational Linguistics, 311–318.

Kanishka Rao, Fuchun Peng, Haşim Sak, and Françoise Beaufays. 2015. Grapheme-to-phoneme conversion using long short-term memory recurrent neural networks. In *Acoustics, Speech and Signal Processing (ICASSP), 2015 IEEE International Conference on*. IEEE, 4225–4229.

Hassan Sajjad, Helmut Schmid, Alexander Fraser, and Hinrich Schütze. 2017. Statistical models for unsupervised, semi-supervised and supervised transliteration mining. *Computational Linguistics* (2017).

Yan Shao and Joakim Nivre. 2016. Applying Neural Networks to English-Chinese Named EntityTransliteration. In *Sixth Named Entity Workshop, joint with 54th ACL*.

Matthew G Snover, Nitin Madnani, Bonnie Dorr, and Richard Schwartz. 2009. TER-Plus: paraphrase, semantic, and alignment enhancements to Translation Edit Rate. *Machine Translation* 23, 2-3 (2009), 117–127.

Andreas Stolcke et al. 2002. SRILM-an extensible language modeling toolkit.. In *Interspeech*, Vol. 2002. 2002.

Ilya Sutskever, Oriol Vinyals, and Quoc V Le. 2014. Sequence to sequence learning with neural networks. In *Advances in neural information processing systems*. 3104–3112.

Ye Kyaw Thu, Win Pa Pa, Yoshinori Sagisaka, and Naoto Iwahashi. 2016. Comparison of Grapheme-to–Phoneme Conversion Methods on a Myanmar Pronunciation Dictionary. *Proceedings of the 6th Workshop on South and Southeast Asian Natural Language Processing 2016* (2016), 11–22.

Phuoc Tran, Dien Dinh, and Hien T Nguyen. 2016. A Character Level Based and Word Level Based Approach for Chinese-Vietnamese Machine Translation. *Computational intelligence and neuroscience* 2016 (2016).

Raghavendra Udupa, K Saravanan, A Kumaran, and Jagadeesh Jagarlamudi. 2009. Mint: A method for effective and scalable mining of named entity transliterations from large comparable corpora. In *Proceedings of the 12th Conference of the European Chapter of the Association for Computational Linguistics*. Association for Computational Linguistics, 799–807.

Sonjia Waxmonsky and Sravana Reddy. 2012. G2P conversion of proper names using word origin information. In *Proceedings of the 2012 Conference of the North American Chapter of the Association for Computational Linguistics: Human Language Technologies*. Association for Computational Linguistics, 367–371.

Kaisheng Yao and Geoffrey Zweig. 2015. Sequence-to-sequence neural net models for grapheme-to-phoneme conversion. *arXiv preprint arXiv:1506.00196* (2015).

Author Index